John Randolph Spears

The gold diggings of Cape Horn

A study of life in Tierra del Fuego and Patagonia

John Randolph Spears

The gold diggings of Cape Horn
A study of life in Tierra del Fuego and Patagonia

ISBN/EAN: 9783742891365

Manufactured in Europe, USA, Canada, Australia, Japa

Cover: Foto ©ninafisch / pixelio.de

Manufactured and distributed by brebook publishing software (www.brebook.com)

John Randolph Spears

The gold diggings of Cape Horn

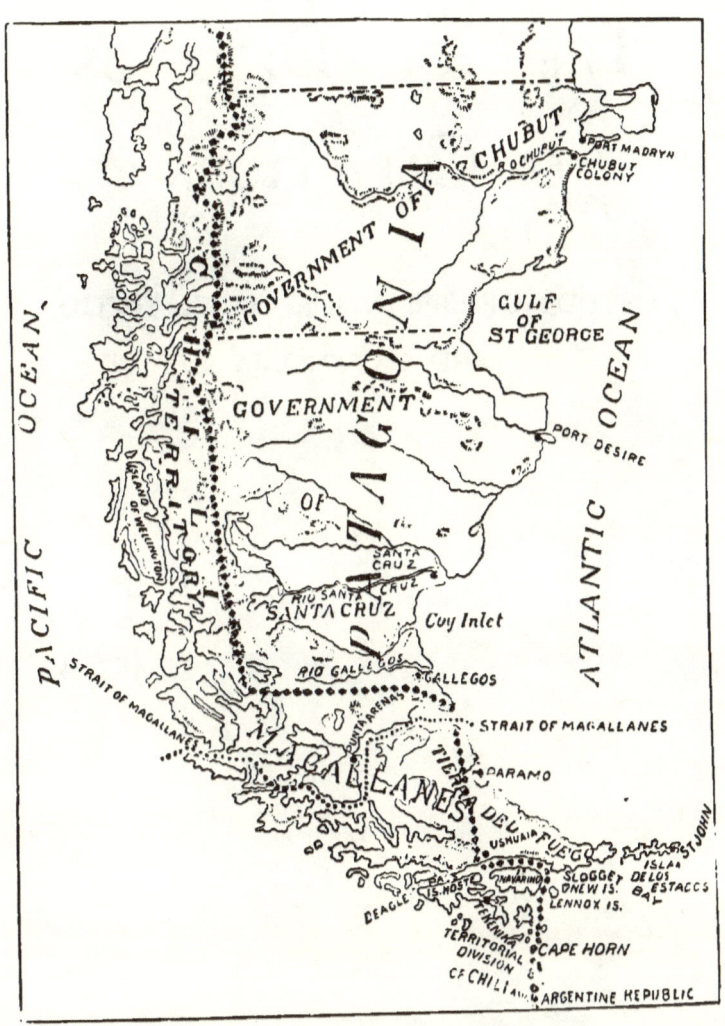

MAP OF THE CAPE HORN REGION.

The Gold Diggings of Cape Horn

A STUDY OF LIFE IN TIERRA DEL FUEGO AND PATAGONIA

BY

JOHN R. SPEARS

ILLUSTRATED

G. P. PUTNAM'S SONS
NEW YORK   LONDON
27 WEST TWENTY-THIRD STREET   24 BEDFORD STREET, STRAND
The Knickerbocker Press
1895

TO ALL WHO LOVE THE RED ABORIGINES OF THE AMERICAS
AS GOD MADE THEM.

PREFACE

I AM impelled to say, by way of preface, that the readers will find herein such a collection of facts about the coasts of Tierra del Fuego and Patagonia as an ordinary newspaper reporter might be expected to gather while on the wing, and write when the journey was ended. It was as a reporter of *The Sun*, of New York, that I visited the region described. And instead of giving these facts in the geographical sequence in which they were gathered, I have grouped them according to the subjects to which they relate. So it happens that the work is what may be properly called a collection of newspaper sketches rather than the conventional story of a traveller. I make this explanation the more freely for the reason that book-buyers as a rule, so book publishers have repeatedly told me, do not take kindly to newspaper sketches bound in book form. They resent as an attempted imposition, it is said, the masking of such writings in the garb that belongs to literature, just as they would resent the sale of cotton-seed oil under the name of lard. However this may be I am bound to avoid even the appearance of any such deceitful intent.

On the other hand there are people who depend almost entirely on the newspapers for their reading matter. They seem to prefer the style of the newspaper writers. Perhaps a book that is avowedly the work of a reporter will meet their approval. At any rate I should be particularly sorry to have any of them think, when the book is offered to them by the bookseller, that it is anything different from what it is.

Then there is the pleading of the baby act in literature —the offering of apologies for shortcomings and asking for the leniency of the reader. I do not think I ought to do it. It is as if a dairy farmer, while asking full price for his butter, should say : " I 've a realizin' sense that the smell haint just right. The dinged cows was eatin' leeks afore I know'd it, but I done my best at the churnin' an' I hope ye 'll make allowances." If a buyer is looking for a book with the odor of flowers and new-mown hay in it I do not think it is becoming to ask him to take one flavored with garlic instead. Save for the matter manifestly from books and records I obtained the facts herein by observation and interviews ; and I am willing to abide by the press law that a blunder is inexcusable. It is, of course, the honest intent of the news-gatherer to write his facts so that they will not be ignored or misunderstood or forgotten, but when he fails to reach that standard he loses his market, and he ought to lose it. And the man who essays the creation of something permanent ought not to ask that he be judged by a lower standard than that of the writers for "ephemeral publications."

I am under great obligations to many of the people whom I met in the course of the journey, for assistance in gathering facts, but of the whole number Mr. E. L. Baker, the American Consul at Buenos Ayres ; Herr Bruno Ansorge, of the Paramo Mining Company ; Mr.

Adolph Figue, a merchant at Ushuaia ; and Revs. John Lawrence and Thomas Bridges, missionaries, were at especial pains to help me. I should like to thank them again for what they did. And were I not prohibited from doing so I would include one other name—that of the runaway sailor boy from New York whom I found in the desolate harbor at the east end of La Isla de Los Estados.

Having said this much I can very cheerfully face the inevitable—the fact that the work will be judged by its merits. If it succeeds I shall be glad, of course ; if it fails I shall know better what to do next time.

J. R. S.

CONTENTS.

	PAGE
CHAPTER I.	
AFTER CAPE HORN GOLD	1
CHAPTER II.	
THE CAPE HORN METROPOLIS	27
CHAPTER III.	
CAPE HORN ABORIGINES	47
CHAPTER IV.	
A CAPE HORN MISSION	79
CHAPTER V.	
ALONG-SHORE IN TIERRA DEL FUEGO	107
CHAPTER VI.	
STATEN ISLAND OF THE FAR SOUTH	137
CHAPTER VII.	
THE NOMADS OF PATAGONIA	151
CHAPTER VIII.	
THE WELSH IN PATAGONIA	168
CHAPTER IX.	
BEASTS ODD AND WILD	183
CHAPTER X.	
BIRDS OF PATAGONIA	201

CONTENTS.

CHAPTER XI.
SHEEP IN PATAGONIA 215

CHAPTER XII.
THE GAUCHO AT HOME 228

CHAPTER XIII.
PATAGONIA'S TRAMPS 250

CHAPTER XIV.
THE JOURNEY ALONG-SHORE . . 260

LIST OF ILLUSTRATIONS.

	PAGE
MAP OF THE CAPE HORN REGION . .	*Frontispiece*
GOLD-WASHING MACHINES. PARAMO, TIERRA DEL FUEGO	14
PUNTA ARENAS, STRAIT OF MAGELLAN . . .	30
YAHGANS AT HOME [1]	48
THE MISSION STATION AT USHUAIA [1] . . .	92
USHUAIA, THE CAPITAL OF ARGENTINE TIERRA DEL FUEGO [1]	108
AN ONA FAMILY [1]	128
ALUCULOOF INDIANS [1]	134
GOVERNMENT STATION AT ST. JOHN. (FROM A SKETCH BY COMMANDER CHWAITES, A.N.) [1] .	138
A TEHUELCHE SQUAW [1]	158
TEHUELCHES IN CAMP [1]	166
GAUCHOS AT HOME	228
AMONG THE RUINS AT PORT DESIRE, PATAGONIA .	270
SANTA CRUZ, PATAGONIA [1]	276
THE GOVERNOR'S HOME AND A BUSINESS BLOCK IN GALLEGOS, THE CAPITAL OF PATAGONIA [1]	282

---

[1] Reproduced by permission of Charles Scribner's Sons, from an article, by the author of this book, in Scribner's Magazine, entitled "At the end of the Continent."

THE GOLD DIGGINGS OF CAPE HORN.

CHAPTER I.

AFTER CAPE HORN GOLD.

IF any of the readers of this book have an unrestrainable longing for wild adventure, with the possibility of suddenly acquiring riches thrown in as an incentive to endurance, let them pack their outfits and hasten away to the region lying between Cape Horn and the Straits of Magellan to dig for gold. Neither Australia nor California in their roughest days afforded the dangers, nor did they make the showings of gold —real placer gold for the poor man to dig—that have been, and are still to be found in Tierra del Fuego, and the adjoining islands. Nor is the gold in all cases too fine to be saved by ordinary rude sluices, for "nuggets as big as kernels of corn"—the ideal gold of the placer miner—have been found by the handful, and may still be had in one well-known locality if the miner is willing and able to endure the hardships and escape the dangers incident to the search.

But because of the hardships and dangers it is a veritable tantalus land. There are many more skeletons of dead miners than authentic records of wealth acquired in Tierra del Fuego, while those who have now and again struck it rich and gotten clean off with the dust usually have gone no further with it than Punta Arenas in the Straits of Magellan, for Punta Arenas is to this region what San Francisco was to California and Virginia City to the deserts of Nevada.

The story of the Cape Horn gold diggings is especially remarkable in this, that the gold there should have remained undiscovered during the centuries that passed after the first navigators landed in the region. Consider that Magellan first saw Patagonia and the strait that bears his name more than 350 years ago. Consider further the character of Magellan, and the host of explorers that followed him. They were all admirals, or bore other titles of high rank, and we call them famous, but they were almost to a man notion peddlers—men who started out with stocks of gewgaws and trifles which they were to swap for valuables. Magellan went out, not to make himself famous as a navigator, but to reach the Spice Islands by a shorter, and therefore more profitable, route than that by the Cape of Good Hope. He was out for fortune, and the fame of making discoveries was an incidental matter. And so for the rest. They were not very particular or nice as to how they got gold to ballast their ships. They plundered harmless people on the African coast and elsewhere; robbed ships found under other flags than their own; even sacrificed innocent human lives in their thirst for gold. Not one of these greedy sailors and pirates but would have gone almost wild with joy at the finding of a mine of gold.

And yet here, in the streams that empty into the Straits of Magellan, even in the streams near Port Famine, where Sarmiento's colony starved to death, and in the sands of the coast of Patagonia, were gold diggings— the genuine placer diggings, as said. These navigators sailed along with their eyes on the gold-bearing shores. They even filled their water casks in the gold-bearing streams. It is likely that the time came when scarcely a day in the year passed when some sailor's eye was not on land in the Cape Horn region where gold could be found, but not until the latter half of the nineteenth century was gold actually obtained there.

Then, when gold was found, comes another curious feature of the story. It probably took twenty years after the finding of the first dust—twenty years, during every one of which, some gold was found in the region—to create anything like a stir in the matter. I say probably twenty years because the actual dates are not known.

The story of the Cape Horn mining region begins on the mainland of Patagonia north of the Straits of Magellan, and it is at the beginning a very hazy story. I could not learn definitely either the name of the first man who found gold in the vicinity of the strait, or the exact locality in which it was found. I talked with miners and merchants of the region on the subject, but no one knew anything about it worth mention. An *Official Memoria General* on the subject of Mines, printed in Buenos Ayres in 1889, says that "several years before 1867 it was known that gold existed on the east coast of Patagonia, and also in the little streams that run from different points of the Andes. This fact has been confirmed in various places and at different times by Chilean miners and shipwrecked seamen." And that is the best information I could get on the subject.

Early in 1869 Commander George Chaworth Musters of the English navy, visited Punta Arenas, en route for a journey across Patagonia with the Tehuelche Indians. In one of the stores of the town, where he stopped for the purpose of "purchasing tobacco and other necessaries," he found some nuggets of gold. He speaks of them incidentally along with the Indian weapons, girdles, and other curios, that the store contained, but a Yankee sailor from the schooner *Rippling Wave*, who happened into the store while Musters was there, became enthusiastic over it and said :

"Ah, that's the stuff we used to grub up in a creek in Californy. I guess if the old boat lays her bones on these here shores, I'll stop and turn to digging again."

In 1877 and again in 1878, Don Ramon Lista, an Argentine explorer and writer, visited Punta Arenas, and on his return to Buenos Ayres he printed his experiences in a pamphlet. In that he says :

> The creek called Las Minas that bounds the settlement on the north abounds in grains of gold; and from 1866 until 1877 many natives of the island of Chiloé have lived well on the daily product of their labors in washing the gold-bearing sand.

In the year 1876, a small schooner engaged in the seal fishery, and commanded by a noted Argentine sailor, Don Gregorio Ibañez, was stranded near Cape Virgin, the extreme southeast corner of Patagonia. The crew, without exception, had the good fortune to escape to the land with some provisions and other valuables, including a shovel. The shovel may seem to be a novel tool for shipwrecked seamen to carry through the surf, but Don Gregorio knew what he was doing.

Patagonia is a desert region very much like certain parts of the United States. One may travel hundreds of miles without seeing a drop of sweet water, and yet with a shovel water a-plenty may be had by him who knows where to dig. Don Gregorio, having landed his provisions, put a man at work digging in the sand not very far from the surf in search of water. Whether he found water or not tradition does not tell. The story tellers all forget about the water as they relate how, when the digger had gotten down about three feet, he began to throw out a layer of black sand such as no one of the crew had seen before—a black sand that was dotted all over with little and big dull yellow particles. That was such an odd-looking sand that Don Gregorio and the digger and all hands had to take a proper look at it. And when they had taken this look, they almost went crazy with excitement, because those yellow particles were pure gold.

But, as I said, neither this discovery nor the gold that was dug from Las Minas creek at Punta Arenas, nor the stories of these doings which were carried to England and to California by ships passing that way, had any effect in creating a rush to the diggings near the straits.

In explanation of this indifference, it may be said that the diggings, even of Las Minas creek were, on the whole, rather lean. Instances of considerable finds are mentioned by the old timers of Punta Arenas. Men cleaned up the stuff by the ounce, in spots, but the run of what men got was "mere day wages." The find of Don Gregorio's sailors was not considered of any importance—the tiny nuggets were supposed to be a stray deposit, and not indicating any bed of gold-bearing sand. The stuff lay in the sand of the beach, and who had ever heard of such a thing as placer diggings in the sand along the shore?

In 1877 as many as 120 men worked the sands of Las Minas creek and made day wages at it. In the United States the fact that 120 men with hash bowls could wash out even " mere day wages " would create a rush to the region, while the finding of an occasional nugget "of the weight of 300 grammes," as occurred in Las Minas creek, would create a stampede, of course, but in the Spanish-American countries the conditions and the people are different.

However, a time came when even the people of Punta Arenas got excited. The steamship *Arctic* of one of the lines running through the strait was, in 1884, wrecked on Cape Virgin very near the place where Don Gregorio's sealing schooner went ashore. Like the inhabitants of the Bahama Islands, the people of Punta Arenas used " to thank God for a good wreck." The *Arctic* was a remarkably good wreck, for she was a well-found, handsomely fitted passenger ship. A motley crew of men hastened from Punta Arenas to the beach at Cape Virgin, some to get what they could from her lawfully, and some to get what they could in any way. It is said now that some one of the number was familiar with the story of what Don Gregorio's sailors found when digging for water, and so the old story of gold discoveries there was retold as the gang smoked and talked and sorted their plunder. Thereat some of them went digging "just for luck," and found something more exciting even than the silk fittings, chronometers, cordage, and anchors which they had taken from the *Arctic*—they found gold.

One Fred Otten cleaned up seventeen kilos (37.4 pounds) of gold in the course of two weeks, they say, and that sort of luck was enough to rouse even the phlegmatic wreckers of the Straits of Magellan.

Here, then, at the wreck of the steamship *Arctic*, is found the real beginning of the story of the Cape Horn gold diggings. In those days Punta Arenas was a supply depot for a fleet of sealing schooners that eventually destroyed the rookeries of the region to the south. The sealing sailors took a hand in with the gold washers. They did more than that. They had, as they would have said, a severe look at the ground round about as well as at the layer of sand in which the gold was found. The lofty banks—in fact, everything in sight from the beach—was what geology sharps would call an alluvial formation. The lofty precipices were composed of layers of clay, sand, pebbles, shells, the débris of prehistoric seas and floods. In one of these layers—a layer that cropped out under the tide waters—was gold galore. Jack couldn't explain it, and he didn't want to; but when he had helped to skin the gold-bearing layer from the clay as far as he could reach, he remembered that he had seen just such beaches with banks behind them elsewhere—on Tierra del Fuego, on New Island, on Lennox, on Navarin, on Wollaston, on Hermit, on Cape Horn itself. He had seen those lofty banks from the decks of sealing schooners, and he was game to go to them to see if there was gold in the sand along the shore there as there was at Cape Virgin. Why shouldn't there be? And there was.

Nor were the citizens of Punta Arenas the only ones excited by this find of gold dust in the sand at Cape Virgin. The Argentine Government sent an engineer to examine the region, and the opinion formed by the engineer was that "the gold-bearing sands of Patagonia are richer than those of California and Australia." So says an old public document. Further than that, "there was much agitation in Buenos Ayres among speculators in mines who had great hopes that grand fortunes might be obtained easily in Patagonia. A great number of persons solicited from the government concessions of mines of gold. But as the greater part of the solicitors had never been in Patagonia, and were obliged to gather their information from others as to the desirable points, it happened that much confusion arose."

"Much confusion" just describes what happened. Many concessions were not only issued on overlapping claims, but on the same claims, and there were many heart-burnings and feuds over patches of sand that were not worth anything.

One Don Gregorio Lezama, with a capital of $70,000, organized an expedition, and sent it out with sluices and wind-mill pumps to supply the sluices. They reached the diggings and set up both sluices and pumps. Then they found that when the wind did not blow the pumps could not supply the sluices with water, and when the wind did blow the men could not supply the sluices with gold-bearing sand, because that sand was found only where the waves would then prevent the work of the men.

So the wind-mill outfit was abandoned and another pumping arrangement to be worked by mules was sent out. The record contains this paragraph as to the subsequent doings :

The company continued its operations for more or less months, and obtained some pounds of gold ; but the general outlook was not very encouraging, the work was suspended, and the company liquidated itself.

So it happened, of course, to the majority of people

who went in the rush to Cape Virgin diggings. They eventually suspended operations and liquidated themselves. Nevertheless a number had "struck it rich," and that, as said, started the search for the precious metal along the stormy coasts and under the towering precipices of the islands away south to Cape Horn.

My first view of a Cape Horn mine camp was obtained on the east coast of Tierra del Fuego. I had taken passage on an Argentine naval transport that was bound on a voyage with supplies for the officials and troops at various stations which the Argentine Government has established in recent years throughout the region. To promote the development of its territories the government carries prospectors and their outfits at very moderate charges, considering the kind of navigation. Accordingly this transport had on board four men and about three tons of provisions and other supplies to be landed at El Paramo, the first mine camp established on the east coast of Tierra del Fuego.

Paramo is a Spanish word meaning desert. It is a very good name for the camp. When one has heard the story of this desert camp he will have gained some idea of the life of a prospector and miner in the Cape Horn region.

The founder of El Paramo was one Julius Popper, one of the pioneer prospectors of Tierra del Fuego. He was, in fact, the first prospector to make a journey across the island, though missionaries, of whom a curious story will be told at another time, had explored it on another quest. Popper was an engineer of rare attainments—a civil, mechanical, and mining engineer—good in all three branches: an astronomer; a linguist who spoke and wrote a dozen languages fluently. He could with equal grace and precision conduct a lady to dinner or knock all the fight out of a claim jumper. Unfortunately, when just beginning to realize on his investments in Tierra del Fuego, he died at the hands of murderers. He was poisoned in Buenos Ayres by men whom he had offended in the south.

In the year 1886 the Cape Virgin diggings were so far worked out that no more than day wages—a paltry $5 a day, as the miners call it—could be had. Only the plodders would remain there, and Julius Popper was never a plodder. So an exploring company of eighteen was gotten together, with pack horses and a mining outfit, together with arms, ammunition, and a permit from the Argentine Government to use them whenever necessary.

The landing was made at Future Bay, opposite Punta Arenas. It was in the month of September, the spring of the southern latitude. Snow lay so deep on the mountains that a track had to be cleared with shovels for miles. Then the brush was elsewhere so thick that axes had to be used to open a passage for miles, but after five days' labor they got to Santa Maria River, where they found eight men at work on a sluice taking out about 700 grains of gold a day. This was mere day wages, and they pushed on until they reached Useless Bay, and then took an easterly course which they held clear across the island, reaching the coast at the north of San Sebastian Bay.

Here, in a tongue of sand that encloses the northeast side of the bay, they found the gold they were looking for in a layer of black sand, exactly like the layer that had been found at Cape Virgin, although there was no bank of any kind behind the beach.

Having staked claims here they went away south, discovering and naming capes, rivers, and ranges of hills, with here and there more placer gold. It was an open prairie country, with a species of sagebrush on it such as is found in Patagonia, but instead of a desert they here found plenty of water everywhere, and sometimes too much in the shape of swamps ; but, unfortunately, the gold was usually found where there was not a running stream within miles. It was apparent that all sluices would have to be supplied by means of pumps.

Eventually they fell foul of the Indians. A shower of arrows came at them from the brush, but all fell short. The number of Indians was estimated at eighty, armed with bows. The eighteen white men turned loose Winchesters in reply, the Indians lying down while the fire lasted, and jumping up to discharge their arrows when it slackened. By the time the magazines of the rifles were empty the Indians abandoned the fight. One gets an idea of the quality of the white fighters from the fact that but two of the Indians were killed, and the further fact that when the fight was over Mr. Popper posed his men in the attitude of troops repelling a charge, took a position himself astride one of the dead Indians, and then had the outfit photographed for subsequent use, on the cover of a pamphlet in which he described the journey he had made.

To the camp called Paramo, that was established in consequence of Popper's expedition, came, as said, the Argentine naval transport, bringing four men and some tons of supplies, on the morning of May 12th.

Considering its age, the number of men employed— from thirty to forty—, and the fact that it is also a government station, having a prefect, a chief of police, a schoolmaster, a secretary to the prefect, and a squad of soldiers to maintain the dignity of the officials, it was a remarkable camp. There was just three buildings in sight—a boarding-house for the miners, a home for the mine bosses, and a combined stable and storehouse. The camp of the government was said to be located two leagues back in the country. The buildings were of wood, roofed with corrugated, galvanized iron. They were huddled together so that they looked from the ship as one building. They were on the usual mine-camp model of North America—one story high, box shaped, and with small windows and no superfluous doors. A barbed wire corral stood at one side of the buildings, which were located so near the beach that a high surf at spring tide was sure to send the foam quite to the foundations on which they stood. Indeed, one of them was protected from the surf by a sort of a wooden sea wall.

Beyond the houses stretched a low yellowish grassy plain that was very like a Nebraska prairie in appearance, and a league away to the north rose a low range of treeless hills.

The diggings lay right in the beach. When Popper first discovered the claim the black sand that contained the gold lay in a bed of from three to four inches thick, that was for the most part under a layer of coarse gravel two to three feet thick, though in some places the black sand was found free of any cover at low tide.

Of the richness of the diggings in the early days it may be said that the mine was discovered in September, 1886. Popper had to return to Buenos Ayres and organize a company to work the deposit as well as perfect his title to the claims according to Argentine law, and then ship a steam pumping plant with sluices and material for the camp to the locality. This all took time, and it was not until the end of the following antarctic winter that he got his plant in operation. He was then able to pass an average of fifty cubic yards of sand through his sluices per day. From this he cleaned up in the course of the first year, after the discovery, 154 pounds (weight avoirdupois) of pure gold.

As another indication of the richness of this territory, I can say that we took on a government official who had been at the station two leagues back considerably less than a year, but he had cleaned up enough gold to satisfy him. He was going home to Buenos Ayres, rich. He had worked diggings outside the Paramo claim, using common sluice boxes.

While this easily-obtained gold-bearing sand was being worked off, the miners observed that the supply was renewed somewhat by every storm that raged, and further, that when a storm happened to come at the time of the spring tides, a very much larger quantity of gold-bearing sand was washed up by the waves than in ordinary storms. This had happened, too, at Cape Virgin, but the renewal of the gold supply by the storms was not so notable there. However, it appears that eventually a time came when the miners at Paramo were able to work off all the black sand between storms. So it happened —so it happens in these days that the miners sit down and smoke their pipes till the storm comes and goes. After the surf of the storm is gone and the tide runs out, a fresh layer of black sand is found with gold in it. The miners say the sand is washed up from a streak that crops out somewhere below low tide. They think that this layer could be reached by sinking a shaft near the buildings, but they can't sink a shaft profitably on account of the water coming in. The black sand lies on clay, and all the layer, and the other layers above it, are, so to speak, afloat with water. So they work only after a heavy surf. The weather, on the average, keeps them busy about half the time.

The land is controlled by a German-Argentine corporation, of which Herr Carlos Backhausen and Herr Bruno Ansorge are superintendent and foreman. The men work the sand on shares, and do so well that, paradoxical as it may seem, there is difficulty in keeping a full gang of men at work. The trouble is, that, as soon as the men get a few ounces of dust to their credit, they must take it and go away to Punta Arenas and swap it for such joys as may be had in that tiny metropolis.

At Paramo, on the beach, they now use a combination of wooden sluices and a copper-plate machine with which all gold miners are familiar, but which could not be briefly described here. The riffles in the sluices save the coarser gold, while the mercury on the copper plates takes up the flour gold as it drifts away over the plates. Water for all the machines is pumped from the sea, and it is worth while telling that experiments there show that some pay streaks can be profitably worked with salt water when fresh water fails to save a satisfactory return.

Geologists find this gold-bearing layer of black sand (it is a magnetic iron sand) a most interesting study. They say the deposit at Paramo is a continuation of that found at Cape Virgin, and that deposit is found at intervals on the Patagonia coast to the Gallegos River. The geologists are even confident that it crops out at intervals for over a thousand miles along the Patagonia coast—always below the water line. Of course, this bed

GOLD-WASHING MACHINES. PARAMO, TIERRA DEL FUEGO

of sand was deposited where it is now found by the action of water, and it must have existed at one time in the form of a reef or vein a thousand miles long in some prehistoric range of mountains. What a lead that would have been for some lone prospector!

Returning north from Paramo on the east coast of Tierra del Fuego, the transport entered the Straits of Magellan and went to Punta Arenas. From Punta Arenas we went down through Cockburn Channel to the Antarctic Ocean, and then, turning east, cruised through Brecknock Pass, Desolation Bay, Whale Sound, Darwin Sound, and Beagle Channel via the Northwest arm. Thence we coasted along east and up through the Straits of Le Maire on the north side of Staten Island, which we followed to St. John Bay on the east end. These are positively the wildest, most dangerous waters in the world. As will be told, the hidden reefs and the whirling tornadoes formed combinations that made experienced travellers look serious, although in a steamer that was as good a seaboat as ever floated. And yet the prospectors of Punta Arenas have sailed all over that route, summer and winter, in twenty-five catboats, looking for gold.

At Ushuaia, the capital of Argentine Tierra del Fuego, a small village in Beagle Channel, I fell in with Harry Hansen, a Punta Arenas prospector, who for six months had been cruising about the islands to the south of the channel, and was on his way home very much disgusted with the life of a prospector. He, with a brother, had faced every kind of a storm known to the Cape Horn region. They had been obliged to live for weeks, as the Indians do, on limpets and clams only. Their only home had been the tiny cabin of a 25-foot sloop. As a result of the six months of hardship and work they had about twenty-five ounces of gold dust. So they sold their sloop and took passage with us for the Gallegos River. As we steamed along they told stories of gold hunting around Cape Horn.

Lennox Island is just now the centre of interest in that region. Lennox has high banks and sandy beaches, exactly like those of Cape Virgin, and the gold is found in a layer of black sand that crops out below sea level, and is washed up within reach by the waves. But, according to the Hansens, the best of the diggings there were worked out. There was no longer any fresh, unworked ground, with its layers of dust that could be scraped up with a table knife at the rate of three kilos a day, and so Lennox was not worth the attention of any enterprising prospector. The plodders who were willing to carry mercury to put in the sluices, and to sit down and wait for the storms to bring up fresh sand could make a couple of guineas a day easily enough, but the Hansens did not want any such wages as that.

Under the point of New Island, very appropriately called the Asses' Ears, a wide beach was pointed out as the location where an extraordinary find was made. A party from Punta Arenas had landed there, and had sunk a wide shaft several feet into the sand, looking for the gold-bearing layer, but without finding it, although the indications along shore were good. They abandoned the spot after a day or two and went away. Then another party came along some time later, and just for luck concluded to sink the well a little deeper. That was the luckiest conclusion they ever came to.

Within one foot they struck pay dirt, took out over 100 pounds weight (48 kilos) within a month, and sailed away content. Their story, when told at Punta Arenas, sent a host of eager fellows down there to get what was left, and, singular to relate, about every man who went there among the first three boat-loads did well. But when I was passing this point only the smoke of the camp-fire of one lone gold-digger could be seen faintly beneath the Asses' Ears. He was the last of the plodders, according to the Hansens, and was likely to become as rich and as mean as some folks they knew in Punta Arenas—men willing to get rich by saving and scrimping out of a paltry $10 a day.

And then there was the little bay on the Tierra del Fuego mainland, called Port Pantaloons. No man of any experience ever thought of landing there to look for gold. One glance was sufficient to show that no gold could be found there. So everybody supposed, at least. Instead of steep banks, showing the well-known layer formation of Cape Virgin, was a gentle, grassy slope, with a brook that came splashing down a woody ravine. It was a pretty enough place—in fact, the scenery was probably what made a party of seven greenhorns from Punta Arenas, out with a little schooner, put in there and land.

Did I believe in the old saying "A fool for luck"? Well, if I did n't I would after living in Punta Arenas a while. These seven greenhorns made a camp and went washing for gold at Port Pantaloons. At the end of five weeks to a day from the time they left Punta Arenas they were back again, and had exactly four kilos of gold (say nine pounds) each. And every man of them took the first steamer for Europe, intending to settle down and live on the interest of his money instead of having a good time in Punta Arenas, as he might have had.

Of course, there were a lot of people at Punta Arenas who made haste to go down to Port Pantaloons to clean up what these greenhorns had left ; but, remarkable to tell, when the experienced miners came to wash where the greenhorns had been, there was found nothing left to clean up. The greenhorns had found a pocket, and had cleaned it themselves.

And then there were the Cape Horn group and New Year's Island off the north coast of Staten Island. The Hansens had visited both localities and had found, as they said :

Plenty of the stuff, but it was too fine for our sluices without mercury. Besides, we did n't have a proper ship for these waters. She was only a ten-tonner. If you want the gold you can have it, but nobody from Punta Arenas will help you get it. It takes too much capital to set up copper-plate machines there, and those that have the capital have n't the pluck to face the sea in these waters. I suppose you could average fifteen grammes a day without mercury if that would satisfy you.

But of all spots in the Cape Horn region, Sloggett Bay, on the south coast of Tierra del Fuego, about forty miles west of the Strait of Le Maire, is the most tantalizing. More expeditions have been fitted out in Punta Arenas to go to Sloggett Bay than to any two gold diggings besides. Almost every expedition has gotten gold, and yet never did an expedition there pay the outfitters. Indeed, more lives have been lost trying for Sloggett Bay gold than at any two points besides. And that is saying a good deal.

There is a man now in Punta Arenas who went down to this bay in a well-built little schooner, which was manned by fourteen men all told. They had heard of the gold found there—gold " in nuggets as big as kernels of corn "—, and nothing should stop them in the work of getting it, they said. They moored their little craft with long cables and chains, and made everything as snug and safe as the most experienced sailors and sealers could suggest. Then they went to work, stripping off the six-foot layer of gravel that overlies the gold-bearing sand and carrying the latter up out of reach of the waves; for they had to work at low tide. The gold is all under water at high tide.

They were a hardy lot and enthusiastic. They worked all of every low tide, and ate and slept during high water. They got on well with their work, for a time, but they made a terrible mistake. They slept in their schooner and kept no lookout—trusted to their moorings to hold them fast. One night they went to sleep, as usual, well-tired from hard labor. Then came one of those fearsome gales that characterize the region. With a speed and power that are beyond description, it picked up the schooner on the crest of a wave and dashed it into kindling wood on the beach—dashed out the lives of thirteen of the men as well. One only was left alive, and, curiously enough, he was entirely uninjured.

"The first I knew that there was a storm," he said, "was when I woke up lying on the beach, with the wreckage around me."

This man did just what might be expected, they say, of any one of the Cape Horn miners. He camped on the beach, and worked away at the pay streak as best he could, until rescued by other prospectors; and he is still a gold seeker in the Cape Horn region.

Sloggett Bay is really no bay at all. It is a roadstead with sheltering walls on the northerly and westerly sides, and a very good bottom to hold an anchor. It is about as much of a harbor as a ship would find on the bar off Sandy Hook, save that there are mountains along shore instead of low, sandy beaches. For a northerly or westerly gale the shelter is as good as any one could wish, but the waves from the southeast drive in with appalling fury. Indeed, any southerly gale is dangerous, for the whirling squalls slew a small boat around until broadside to the combers, and then the end comes before the unfortunate gold hunter has time to think twice.

The gold of Slogget Bay is marvellous gold. It is, as said, nugget gold as distinguished from gold dust. The traditional " nuggets as big as kernels of corn " are to be had there. I have seen them myself, and when one has seen a handful of such stuff he does not wonder that prospectors keep trying again and again, in spite of the fair certainty of death.

The pay streak at Sloggett Bay lies under water, as it does elsewhere throughout the Cape Horn region, but it is harder to get, because it can hardly be said to crop out at all. One must strip off about six feet of sand and gravel at low tide, and then shovel out the pay streak, carry it up clear of high tide, and there wash out the gold. Of course, when the tide comes in again the space stripped of the covering sand is recovered, and stripping must be done over again at the next low tide. That is very discouraging work, but no form of coffer dam yet devised by the miners has saved it.

They all agree that there is only one way in which the Sloggett Bay field can be worked, and they think that that way would probably fail too. The ideal Sloggett Bay outfit would be a big steam dredge, fitted to scoop up sand, gravel, and pay streak all together, and after running the stuff over the sluices and copper plates, to discharge the débris in a lighter, that could be towed away and emptied in water too deep to work. If such an outfit could hold on for a week, they say it would pay for itself. If it could hold on for a month it would make its owners rich. That it might hold on for a week or two is reasonably probable, but the chances are that it would become a mass of wreckage even before it reached the bay. The prospectors say that no dredge ever built for harbor work could stand a southeast gale there for an hour, and yet the sailors among them say that a dredge built specially for the work on the lightship model, with proper ground tackle for mooring fore and aft, could stand the gales there as well as the storms on the Georges Bank of Massachusetts are weathered by the lightship.

Among the stories the miners tell of the luck they have had is one that, whether true or false, is interesting, for even if false it shows that the man who told it was an original liar; as a matter of fact, I have no reason for doubting the story. Mr. Theo Benfield, whom I met in Punta Arenas, said that during a journey from the strait up the coast he stopped one day under one of the vertical earth banks called barancas in that country to pick out a fossil that he saw protruding. The relic proved to be a part of a mastodon's lower jaw, having two teeth still in place. It was in bad condition, and he was about to throw it away, when he saw that in a split in the top and side of one tooth was a bit of some foreign substance to which he applied his knife. He found that it was gold, that had, as he believed, been deposited there in fine grains by the action of water, and that the grains had united as deposited. The gold, as he says, was in a split in the tooth evidently made there when the jaw was broken. He related the story in support of a theory in regard to the origin of nuggets which he held, thus : Gold, as it comes from the broken-down quartz veins is usually very fine, but as the grains are carried along by the water they fall into little cavities, where, by the action of chemicals in the water, they are united. The split in the old tooth had at some time been lying in a place where gold dust had silted into it until it was about full, and the particles uniting had formed a curious nugget. Unfortunately Mr. Benfield was more interested at that time in getting gold than in questions relating to the origin of nuggets, and so smashed the tooth to get the stuff. He got, he says, over eight grammes from the tooth. If his story be true, he might have obtained many times the value of that much gold for the relic intact, but he did not think of that at the time, and so we have only one man's word in relation to the matter.

It is a remarkable fact that, in spite of all the prospecting done, no gold-quartz veins have yet been found. Louis Figue, a merchant at Ushuaia, in the Beagle Channel, showed me a specimen of nickel ore that had yielded a remarkable per cent. on the first assay ; but the only bit of gold ore I saw or heard of was a small piece of free-milling stuff belonging to Bruno Ansorge of Paramo. It was rich, but where the vein was none could tell, for it was from a bit of drift rock called float by the miners, and had been picked up between Useless and San Sebastian Bays.

Very likely the placer gold found in all the streams of Tierra del Fuego (stream gold as distinguished from that in the beach), and that in the streams emptying into the Straits of Magellan, comes from veins yet to be found up in the mountains where the streams rise. Very likely systematic search would discover the veins. But the search would have to be made under circumstances that would make the fair-weather prospectors of Colorado and the grubstake eaters of the Mojave desert gasp. The mountains of the Cape Horn region are snow-topped the year round. The cold is not so intense as the early travellers would make one believe, but there is a strength and a twist to the gales—especially a twist—that is beyond description. And the gales come every day in summer and every week in winter. Expeditions have traversed Tierra del Fuego with horses, but the cheapest and the most comfortable way (in spite of the danger) to prospect the region is from a well-found boat. Moreover, every land expedition must contain enough men to keep up a military guard, because of the hostility of the Indians, while two well-armed, sober men, can defend a well-found boat from the savages, and if skilful and cool can usually escape the danger of storms.

But neither from boats nor from a land expedition has any one as yet been able to explore the higher parts of the mountain sides. Indeed, where nothing else prevents it, the tropical luxuriance of the evergreen beeches and magnolia brush heads off the hardy prospector. It is hard work climbing up rocky gulches and declivities under the most favorable circumstances, but when one must face fierce gales of wind and at the same time hew his way through a solid mass of brush covering the whole space to be explored, the task becomes too great even for a Yankee prospector. It never has been accomplished, and possibly it never will be accomplished; but, as they say very often down there, who knows?

There is not a mine camp in all the Cape Horn region south of the strait, though Paramo, with its three buildings, and say thirty men, is known as a camp. The placers, as found on almost every sandy beach of the region, are all soon worked over, and thereafter pay only day wages. So no camp or village springs up, as would happen were a rich true fissure vein to be found. But Ushuaia, in the Beagle Channel, the capital of Argentine Tierra del Fuego, has three stores and a small mixed population, besides the troops that maintain Argentine dignity, and, with its occasional Indian visitors, its happy-go-lucky architecture, and its heaps of empty bottles, is not unlike a North American mine town.

The headquarters of the Cape Horn miners will be found at Punta Arenas. The peculiarities which makes Punta Arenas at once one of the most interesting, and one of the most disappointing towns in the world, will be described in the next chapter but it may be said now that miners' supplies—picks, pans, clothing, and food—are cheaper here than at any other miners' supply town in the world. But while a man may get these things at a low price, he has to buy a boat instead of the burros he would buy in the States to carry his outfit. A couple of burros cost say $35 in Colorado, but here he must buy a sloop or a catboat, and he ought to buy a schooner fifty feet long instead. Now any kind of a boat fit to carry even the amphibious prospector of the Cape Horn region costs at least $100 in gold, and must be fitted out at a cost of from $25 to $100 more, not to mention the mining outfit proper.

The prospecting sloop of the Cape Horn region is usually of the model of the little oyster sloops to be found about the harbor of New York. The hold is stowed full of provisions, tools for mining, and lumber for sluices. Naturally these prospectors carry a much better supply of food than prospectors elsewhere do. The Rocky Mountain prospectors with their burros must needs be content with meal, beans, bacon, and, perhaps, coffee, but in the Cape Horn region they carry a great variety of stuff in tin cans and Chili claret by the half barrel. All this costs money, but it is none too good for that climate. And even the best-provided outfits are sometimes away from home so long that the supplies are exhausted.

They sail away south feeling quite certain that they will be back soon with their vessel ballasted with gold, but the shortest time spent away from port by any party I heard of was that of the seven who returned from Port Pantaloons in five weeks. The Hansens were away eleven months in 1892-93.

Every year some sail away, and the sail disappears beneath the white peak of Mt. Sarmiento, plainly seen from the water front of Punta Arenas. After three or four months the "White Wings outfit" or the "Mary G. outfit" is casually mentioned by the bar-room groups as one that should be heard from before long. Two or three months later the outfit is mentioned frequently and with ominous looks and shakings of the head, while an anxious-faced wife or mother is seen hurrying to the beach whenever a sail appears in the south, to learn if it be the one she thinks of as she lies awake every night listening to the Cape Horn gales. She goes down quickly, but she comes back slowly and with a dry throat as she learns that it is neither the *White Wings* nor the *Mary G.*

The region seems but a narrow space as one looks at the maps, but it is a wide one with labyrinthian channels and hidden bays, the ports of many a missing sloop and catboat of which never a trace will be found to tell the tale of disaster. It is a region where no man with a wife or other person depending on him should enter, but for the young and independent fellow, who can gain vigor and courage in facing the mad freaks of an Antarctic gale, there is no place better than that beyond the Straits of Magellan. He may not get rich—the chances are that he'll be glad to work his way north in the stoke hole of some steamer—but he will have had an experience that will make him contented to live thereafter in the milder region of Uncle Sam's domain, and will, moreover, fit him to make his way there better than he could have been prepared in any other way.

CHAPTER II.

THE CAPE HORN METROPOLIS.

THIS is the story of what may be called the Cape Horn metropolis, for it is the story of a town which, though a village in population, is the business centre of the region extending from Port Desire, on the Patagonia coast, to the little island whose southern angle is called Cape Horn, and from the Falkland Islands on the east to the limits of the islands on the west coast of the southern continent. Moreover, it is a town whose characteristics are absolutely astounding, even to an experienced traveller who visits it for the first time, and, curiously enough, the more he may have read and heard about it the more he is likely to be astonished when he at last sees it himself.

"La Colonia de Magallanes," as Punta Arenas is styled in the public documents of Chili, is more than fifty years old, and that, to the traveller looking at it from a ship's deck, is one of the most astonishing statements made about the town. On "the 21st of April, 1843, the Government of Chili planted the tri-color banner in the ancient port of Famine, thus taking possession, in the name of Chili, of the Straits of Magallanes," as the Chilian record says.

It is tolerably easy to guess that the Chili Government did this act more from a sentimental desire to hold possession of the territory that had been famous in history, than from any expectation that the region would be worth the expense of holding.

Besides the desire to hold ground with historical associations, the government wanted a penal colony that would be a very long way from the capital. A penal colony, it was argued, would not only hold troublesome convicts, but would serve as a place for employing members of the army suspected of plotting a revolt against the government.

This colony at Port Famine depended entirely on supplies of food from Valparaiso, and as navigation in those days was much more uncertain than now, the settlement sometimes well-nigh repeated the experience of Sacramento's colony, that in the sixteenth century starved to death there. Because of their sufferings, the convicts rose up one day and took possession of the settlement. The Governor was killed. Then a ship happened along and the mutineers boarded it and compelled the crew to sail on, but a Chilian man-o'-war overtook them, whereat the convicts were for the most part hanged to the yard-arms. It is said that a man was seen hanging from every yard-end on the warship, and she was a full-rigged ship—had twenty-four yard ends to hang men to.

The buildings at Port Famine having been burned by the convicts, the government decided to re-establish the colony just south of a long tongue of sand made by a mountain stream emptying into the strait some miles north of Port Famine. The new settlement was named from the old one—La Colonia de Megallanes—but because of that tongue of sand it was nicknamed Sandy

Point by English-speaking seamen and Punta Arenas (which means Sandy Point) by all others, and so the town is called by everybody in the region.

As said, this was a place far out of the way. The life which the unfortunates there had to endure may, perhaps, be imagined by those who understand human nature, but not fully realized. Here were men condemned to live shut off from all civilized associations because of crimes of which they had been convicted. They were put in charge of men suspected of trying to commit other crimes. In most cases keeper and prisoner were guilty as charged, but in many cases both were innocent. In all cases the keeper was an absolute monarch with the power, if not the right, to take the life of any convict under him ; and, for that matter, the officers could shoot the soldiers without very great risk of adequate punishment.

"It 's coolish like the year round," said an old sailor there who had known the town twenty-five years ago, " but when I saw the colony first it was n't a cable's length from hell."

That the colony did not remain a mere penal settlement with a mental atmosphere like that of sheol was primarily due to the enterprise of a Yankee from Newburyport, Mass., Mr. William Wheelwright, who founded the steamship line called the Pacific Steam Navigation Company. This company began running steamers through the Straits of Magellan in 1868, and they all stopped at the colony perforce, because it was a convenient place to take on coal from hulks that were kept there for the purpose. It was natural that a trade in fresh meats and vegetables should grow out of the coming of the steamers. And that trade was to Punta

Arenas what a long drink of Chili claret is to the wayfarer from the Patagonia desert. It brought a new life to the place. On the day the first steamer called the population was 195 souls. In 1872 it numbered 800.

Then other elements of growth appeared. There was the gold, for instance, as told in the last chapter. The gold did not bring a stampede, but it affected the population in a curious fashion.

"Men don't have to slave it for a boss in a gold camp. When they get out of grub they can take a pick and shovel and go dig some gold," said Mr. H. Grey, a Yankee merchant there. As the abundance of food affects the increase of wild animals, so the certainty of earning a living affects the growth of a human population.

But Punta Arenas grew from one cause that had nothing natural about it, save as some seafaring people seem to be naturally of a devilish disposition. One of the most prominent promoters of the growth of Punta Arenas was the hard-fisted Yankee skipper—he who commanded the sealer and whale ship fitted out in New London or New Bedford to skin the rookeries of Staten Island and others farther south. Not that the skipper deserved thanks or praise from the people of Punta Arenas or any other people in this matter. He did not do it intending to promote the prosperity of Punta Arenas or its people. The skipper who helped the growth of Punta Arenas was an infamous scoundrel, who got sailors to toil and drudge for him until they had filled his ship with skins and oil, and then by cruelty that is shocking to consider drove them ashore at Punta Arenas that he might rob them of their hard-earned wages. Some other sea captains than Yankees have driven sailors ashore there, too, but the Yankees have done the most of it.

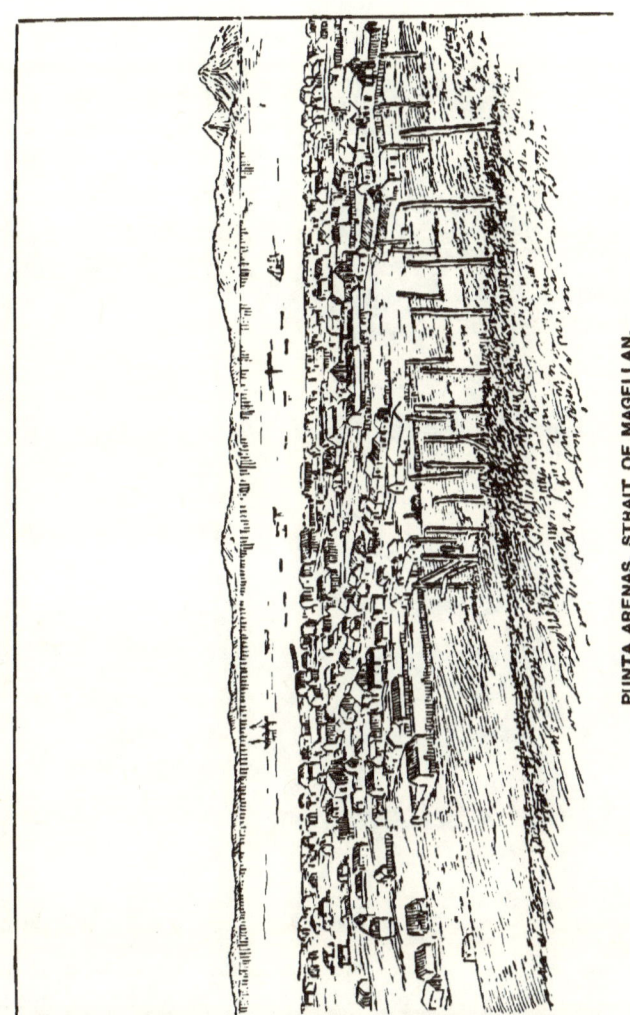
PUNTA ARENAS, STRAIT OF MAGELLAN.

Nine tenths of the population with whom I talked had been sailors. Not all had been hazed from ships, but the majority had.

Last of all came the one industry that was to make Punta Arenas the antarctic metropolis. Mr. H. L. Reynard, an Englishman living in Punta Arenas, rented Elizabeth Island early in the seventies, and brought some sheep there from the Falklands. The sheep took kindly to their new home, and increased so rapidly that Mr. Reynard soon had to move some of them to the mainland. They say he now owns over 100,000 sheep, besides horses and cattle galore, and enjoys—really enjoys—an income of not far from £400 per week.

The people of Punta Arenas did not wait until Mr. Reynard became rich before following his example. They began to invest in sheep as soon as they saw that sheep were profitable, and so far as I could learn every man there who had gone into the business and had given it ordinary care had made money. So the sheep spread far and wide over the region, and men came to care for them and Punta Arenas was the point to which all these men came for supplies. And, as has happened elsewhere, so here the rearing of cattle and horses goes along with the rearing of sheep.

It appears that during the early years the garrison in charge of the convicts numbered on the average sixty soldiers of the line. Besides these the government employed a lot of men to hunt the guanaco and the cattle that ran wild in the Cordilleras, in order to keep the garrison supplied with meat, and, incidentally, to help the soldiers hunt runaway convicts of whom not a few were found brave enough to face the terrors of the Patagonia desert for the sake of liberty. Such tales as may be gathered of the doings and sufferings of these runaways are almost beyond belief. To follow the beach to the Santa Cruz River, a journey of from two to three weeks, subsisting on the few raw fish that might be cast up by the sea, and passing two days at a stretch without water, were matters of common experience. To wander inland and perish miserably while striving to reach a mirage lake often happened.

However, it was not so much for the love of liberty that men fled from the Punta Arenas prison, as it was because they could not endure the sufferings peculiar to their situation. It was because officers as well as soldiers of the line and convicts were in exile, and because the worse instincts of the officers were brought out by the hardships they endured. In such a penal settlement as that was matters naturally went from bad to worse, and a second mutiny was inevitable.

On the night of November 10, 1877, the soldiers and convicts united to take the town, and succeeded. And for three days they held it. They caught the commander of the garrison and revenged the cruelties of which he had been guilty by cutting off his nose, cutting out his tongue, putting out his eyes, hacking off his limbs, and last of all severing his head from his body, and setting it upon a pole at the prison gate. With equal animosity they sought the Governor and the chaplain, but both had fled in time, the former deserting his wife and children that he might save his own skin whole. Then the mutineers sacked the town and lived riotously until a Chilian man-o'-war appeared in the offing, when they gathered their plunder together and started away, according to one account, 180 in number, and, according to another, in a mob numbering 120. Incredible as it may seem, these mutineers, although they had

forty horses in all, took not one scrap of food with
them. Instead of food they loaded themselves and the
animals with clothing, bales of dry goods, fancy cutlery,
bric-a-brac—almost anything and everything the town
afforded that would be of no benefit in the journey that
was before them.

The Chilian authorities made no pursuit worth mention, though a handful of men well armed and mounted could have rounded up the whole company. Unmolested they marched away. The first night they killed three horses for food. The next night and the next and the next they continued to kill horses. They kept at it till all were gone. Other horses were captured from incoming Gauchos, but these did not suffice. Many mutineers were killed in murderous quarrels, but more died because of the hardships of the route. They found freedom on the desert pampas, but hunger and thirst overtook them, and crawling beneath the scant shelter of the thorny bushes growing there, they died, and the foxes and vultures ate them.

At the end of three months a company of forty reached the Welsh settlement on the Chubut River, and these were carried to Buenos Ayres by the Argentine Government, and were there eventually turned loose.

With the burning of the prison an incubus that had weighed upon Punta Arenas vanished. The town was free to rise and flourish as the exuberant fancy of its people might dictate, for the prison was never rebuilt.

I first saw Punta Arenas on the 15th of May, 1894. I was on the deck of the Argentine naval transport *Ushuaia*, and the reader should remember that May there corresponds to November in the North, while the latitude of the Magellan region is precisely that of the coast of Labrador. With these geographical facts in mind, the appearance of things about Punta Arenas was astonishing, for it was a waterside settlement, backed by grassy, rolling hills, above which rose mountains green with verdure that never fades. Indeed, but for the snow-capped peaks away back in the Cordilleras, one would have had hard work bringing himself to realize that this was the Magellan of which the early navigators drew such bleak pictures. And yet Port Famine, where Sarmiento's colony starved to death, was but a few miles away to the south,—in sight, in fact, from the masthead. The general aspect of the scenery beyond the settlement was very much like that to be found in the Adirondacks after an early snow has whitened the higher peaks, leaving the foothills showing darker and greener by contrast.

But the similarity to an Adirondack picture ended at the village limits. There is nothing in the New York wilderness, nor yet in the camps that are found in the Rocky Mountains, that may be compared to Punta Arenas as it appeared from the water. Four streets ran from the beach up over the gentle slope—streets yellow with sand, then black with mud and glistening bright with pools of stagnant water. A stirring population kicked up sand and mud and splashed through the water. Between these streets and facing them were massed, of course, the houses—wall after wall and roof after roof, almost every wall of wood and every roof of corrugated iron, the exceptional walls being made of iron, like that in the roofs. But more singular still was the fact that every building appeared new—a shining mass of pine boards and zinc-white iron, save in those cases where paint had been used, and these houses looked more conspicuous even than the rest, for the prevailing color of paint was a brilliant pink.

The harbor, which is simply an open roadstead, was by no means uninteresting. A great line steamship, as trim looking as a man-o'-war, was at anchor discharging and taking in cargo from big lighters alongside. A great German bark lay beside a big hulk, into which it was discharging coal brought from Cardiff. A handsome little man-o'-war of the cruiser type floated the tricolor flag of Chili above her quarter deck. And besides these a whole fleet—a score or more of schooners, sloops, and catboats, the trading and prospecting fleet of the region —bobbed about and tugged at their cables under the impulse of a smart wind from westward, while lighters and small boats were passing to and fro among the vessels at anchor.

One of the small boats came alongside with a grocery salesman seeking orders, and when it went away I went along. It was a clean-lined yawl, with able seamen at the oars, but it could not travel fast enough to please me.

I had seen mine camps in the Rockies, and in the deserts of California—Creede and Death Valley; I had camped with cowboys and shepherds in Jackson's Hole beyond the Teton Mountains, on the plains of No Man's Land, and in the forks of the Red River of the South; I was acquainted with the life of lumbermen in the Adirondacks and the wilds of Nova Scotia; and I had sailed from the Arsuk fiord in Greenland to Chicago. But here was a town with pink roofs that sheltered at once the miner, the prospector, the cowboy, the lumberman, and happy-go-lucky Jack. What might not one expect in the way of wild life in such a town as this?

A long wood-and-iron pier furnished a landing for passengers, and at the head of this stood a new wood and iron hotel, two stories high, and having a bar-room in the corner next to the pier. I registered there under the eye of the clerk, who also served as bartender. My observations of this man were encouraging. He was talking French to one customer and Spanish to another as I entered. He addressed me in English when I came in, and then a moment later opened a door behind the bar and called for hot water in German. Judging from what I saw later still, when a pretty girl passed, I should say he was not unfamiliar with the sign language. He also knew how to mix hot whiskeys. After a little talk about the variety of people in the population of the town, I determined to take a look at the gambling-houses of the place by daylight, so I said :

"How many sporting houses in town ?"

The barkeeper smiled blandly.

"A plenty," he said ; "you'll find the best looking girls in the second house beyond the postoffice right up this street."

"I meant gambling-houses," said I, "but since you've mentioned sporting women, how many dance-houses does this place support ? "

"One. It's the house I mentioned. Both the girls like to dance, but of course one of them has to furnish the music. They've got one of these—how do you call them—pianos that turn with a crank, eh? It's a fine instrument, I tell you. Of course, if you want to take a chum along you can get a boy to turn the crank."

"Wait," said I. "What was the number of the biggest gang of cowboys you ever saw come to town ? "

"I suppose as many as twenty."

" Did they have any money ? "
" You bet they did."
" And did they spend it ? "
" As quick as the Lord would let 'm."
" How many men have you seen coming from the diggings with dust ? "
" Half a dozen, maybe. Why ? "
" Did they blow in the dust ? "
" Well, rather."
" And yet there is only one dance-house in town and that has but two women in it ? "
" That 's just the size of it."
" Let us return to the subject of gambling-houses. How many have you ? "
" One."
" Do they have big play there ? "
" That 's what they do—sometimes."
" Where is it ? I 'd like to see it."
" Um—"

The barkeeper hesitated a moment, and then went to the door and looked up and down.

" I don't see a member anywhere," he said, " but some of them will be in at dinner, and I 'll introduce you."
" Does one need an introduction to get in ? "
" Certainly."
" What ! Police watch it in a town like this ? "
" Police ? No. It 's a private club, gentlemen, eh ? They would admit you on your card, I dare say, but it pleases the army and navy members to observe the usual formalities. Did you think it was run like a saloon ? "

As was said, Punta Arenas is a town whose characteristics are absolutely astounding, even to an experienced traveller. Cowboys, shepherds, lumbermen, miners, and sailors gather there to waste their substance in riotous living, and do so waste it, but there is not one public gambling-house in town, and the one lone dance-house there has but two girls in it and a hand-organ for music.

"How long have you been in this town?" said I to the drink mixer.

"About twelve years."

"Professional gamblers ever come to town?"

"I think so—one came. He was a Yankee, they say."

"What made you think that?"

"Well, we were up in Bray's billiard saloon. Bray is the boss billiard player of this town, and he was showing us some fancy shots, when a stranger dropped in and had a drink, and then we sat around and chatted. But Bray wanted to play billiards, and so pretty soon he asked the stranger to take a cue. The stranger said he liked to play billiards, but it was not worth while to play against the boss player of the town.

"'Never mind that,' said Bray. 'We'll play for the drinks and see how we match.'

"So they began. The stranger was a pretty fair player, and pretty soon Bray had to do his best, though by doing his best he managed to beat the stranger. I think it was thirty-two or thirty-three points. The stranger showed interest in the game, but was going to put down the cue, when Bray said:

"'I'll just give you thirty points and beat you for ten dollars.'

"The stranger showed eagerness at once, and putting up the cash went at it. That was a right pretty game, let me tell you, for both men played well, but at the last Bray ran out, although the stranger had but one point to make. The stranger looked excited when Bray ran out, and taking out a wad said :

"'I'll bet you one hundred, or two hundred, or three hundred you can't do that again.'

"'I'll go you for three hundred,' said Bray. It was just what Bray had been aching for.

"It was Bray's first shot, and he made a string of nine. Thereat the stranger took his cue, chalked it, winked at the crowd, and ran out his string without a break. Then he picked up the cash, stuffed it in his pocket, and started out, whistling *Yankee Doodle*. We judged by that circumstance that he was a Yankee."

I was in Punta Arenas four days, and talked with a variety of people, but that was the only gambling story worth telling that I heard. I asked if fights and bloodshed were known to the town since the convict mutiny. They replied that fights were not unknown, but were rare.

"Do the fighters never kill each other?"

"I fancy not," said the barkeeper.

"Ever had cold-blooded murders for money?"

"Not in my day, anyhow."

"Then you've never lynched anybody here."

The barkeeper laughed.

"That's just like a Yankee," he said. "The only lynchings I ever heard of took place in the States. The government keeps soldiers here, and everybody is afraid of them."

This last statement explained why the town was peculiar. The government is monarchial in fact, though nominally republican. Chili is ruled, as all Latin-American countries are, by the army. Punta Arenas is ruled by an army officer sent from Santiago.

The town ordinances are backed by bayonets. The Texas town marshal in all his glory could not keep the peace as soldiers can. The government has decreed that there shall be no gambling-houses in Punta Arenas of the style found in United States mine camps. Neither shall there be dance-houses. Instead of these, drinking saloons are permitted in unlimited numbers, and one or two young women can get a license for a saloon as readily as a man can.

There are almost one hundred licensed bars in Punta Arenas. They are found scattered everywhere about town. The young women who own saloons commonly sit in the doorway knitting or sewing in the daytime. One who saw them said their trade would probably be larger if they remained behind the bar or wore veils. A more wretched-looking lot of women was never seen in the saloon business. It is in little wooden shanties, with corrugated iron roofs — utterly barren, squalid shanties—that the riotous living of Punta Arenas is found, and there is not one bright or picturesque feature about it to give excuse for its existence.

After leaving the bartender at the hotel, I started out to see so much of the town as could be observed in walking the streets. It is a town laid out on the checker-board plan, and like all Spanish-American towns has a plaza or public square. The streets are unpaved. This means that near the beach, where there is sand, the wheeling is pretty fair, save in the driest weather, and elsewhere is pretty bad when fair on the beach, and good when it is bad on the beach. But one can find much deeper mud even in the outskirts of New York city than is found in the streets of Punta Arenas.

The sidewalks are peculiar. Under a village ordinance every such walk is edged with a six-inch square timber. Between this timber and the front wall of the house could be found, in a few places stone, in fewer tile brick, in some well-packed beds of sand, but in the majority of cases little narrow lakes of water securely held in place by the timber sea-wall. The plaza showed a rich black loam and nothing else.

Facing the plaza was the old official residence of the Governor. It was one of the few buildings remaining from the early days. It was a wooden structure that had originally had a shingle roof over all, but the moss-grown shingles had rotted away in patches, and had been replaced with odds and ends of board, tin, and sheet-iron. The contrast between the Governor in his gorgeous uniform and his official house was something stunning. The home was the only real shabby building in town.

The traveller who lands in Punta Arenas and fails to climb the hills behind the town makes a mistake, because the picture is wonderfully beautiful and striking as well. The yellowish hills of Tierra del Fuego rise up in the east beyond the broad waters of the strait. The snow-capped peaks of Mt. Sarmiento and its neighbors appear above the horizon at the south, while in the west the evergreen mountains rise boldly up from the water's edge. And then, right at the foot of these dark-green mountains lies the zinc and pink town, the most absurd foreground to a magnificent landscape that ever was imagined.

The lower hills to the northwest of the town have been chopped over in part and are covered with dead trunks of trees, giving the landscape the appearance of what the early settlers in the forest districts of the

United States called a deadening. The trees seemed to have been killed by some kind of an epidemic. They say in the town that the trees were killed by lightning, but I did not see any marks of lightning on the trunks. However they died, the landscape there is wild enough to please an insane artist.

The only manufacturing industries of the place are the saw-mills and a brick-yard. The saw-mills are located some distance from the village, and are not novel, but the brick-yard is right at hand. I examined the brick, and found a product that I had not seen equalled since I saw the courthouse in Greer County, Tex., which had crumbled under a summer squall. Even the hardest burned brick in this kiln could be broken with the naked hands.

A worse industry than brick-making, however, was started some years ago in the town. What they called a vein of coal was discovered some five miles from the beach, and, after some talk, a company was formed to exploit it. A pier was built at the beach, a railroad laid thence to the mine, and rolling stock brought out from England. This done, they found that they had a lignite instead of a coal mine. The pier has gone to pieces, and the old locomotive could be seen partly buried in the sand not far from the head of the ruined pier. This is the coal of which all the writers who have visited the strait speak enthusiastically.

However, the town is going to have more industries, and there is to be still more business done by the traders. The increase in the number of sheep will soon compel the traders to establish a freezing establishment there in order that their surplus sheep may be shipped to market. Just now they sell their surplus to men wishing to establish ranches up country, but there will soon be no more room for new ranches up country.

Then Punta Arenas may yet manufacture goods from its wool, and it could very profitably tan its products of hides and skins. The region produces a bark so rich in tannin that it could be profitably exported to the States, but still more profitably used on the ground. The Chili Government will make liberal concessions to any man who knows the tannery business and has the capital to establish it there. But one must have the knack to get along comfortably with odd people if he would succeed in any business there.

The sales of merchandise in the town are naturally large in certain lines, and they are particularly satisfactory to the merchants, for the reason that many original packages are called for. It is a wholesale trade to a remarkable degree. Moreover, the merchants deliver goods to customers by means of sailboats instead of by wagons, as New York merchants do. But, one scarcely need add, there is no free delivery by boats. The navigation of the straits region is hazardous, and therefore expensive. Only the hardiest sailors will undertake the handling of a 25-foot catboat where, to quote Capt. Samuel Wallis, one of the early navigators, " even in midsummer the climate was cloudy, cold, and tempestuous."

The business feature of the town that interests travellers most is that of the dealer in Indian-made goods and curiosities. Indians from the pampas and from the southern islands come to Punta Arenas to sell skins, furs, feathers, baskets, arrow-heads—what not. The dealers find sale for more stuff, in fact, than the Indians bring, so they have some goods made to order in the town. The goods are all sold as genuine Indian-made things, and in a way so they are. There are squaws in town who make a living doing work of this kind. I saw one of them deliver an armful of rugs made of guanaco skins to one of the dealers. She was dressed in a tailor-made suit of good material; she had gold jewelry a plenty, and her hair was banged across her forehead. The dealer said she was a half-breed Tehuelche, and I did not doubt it, but when one buys Indian-made relics he does not suppose that the Indian wore a tailor-made suit and bangs. I asked Luis Zanibelli, who was formerly a Maiden Lane jeweller in New York, and is now in the relic business there, how to tell goods made in the wilds from those made by half-breed squaws with bangs.

"That's easy," he replied. "Smell of the goods. The genuine Indian goods from the pampas or the islands always smell bad."

The club of which the barkeeper had spoken as a gambling resort is an oddity in name, if in no other way. It is called the "Cuerpo de Bomberos," and that translated into English means the body or society of firemen. There is a neat little red club-house, built somewhat on the model of ancient colonial mansions in the States—that is, with pillars in front. There is a yard full of flower-beds in front of that, and there are flowers there in May, at least, if not later. The house is furnished as club-houses are elsewhere, except that it has no kitchen. The annual dues amount to less than a dollar a month gold, and for this the members have a remarkably pleasant resort. The barkeeper thought the play was heavy; this is interesting as showing what is considered heavy play at Punta Arenas. The heaviest loss of which I heard was 400 paper dollars—a trifle over $100 gold. The favorite game is baccarat, but the seductive influences of draw poker are not unknown. The list of members includes the merchants, sheep-owners, and officials living in the vicinity or stationed there by government, and in Punta Arenas the word vicinity covers a territory a hundred leagues away from the centre.

Speaking of the flowers in front of this club-house reminds me that Punta Arenas is the greatest town for flowers I ever saw. Every house has window gardens, and many houses have bays and rooms set apart for great masses of potted flowers and shrubs. It has many more flowers in proportion to the population even than the tropical cities like Rio. Flowers grow wild there in great profusion, too, among which the wild fuschias make the most profuse display, while the ferns and lichens are something to delight the eye of even the least observant.

For the rest, Punta Arenas claims a population of 3500. It is not unlike some United States towns in the matter of a local census, but after making due allowances for local pride and enthusiasm, it still is found a live and growing village. Lots in the business part of the town now sell for pounds sterling where paper dollars would have sufficed ten years ago. Indeed, a lot was sold while I was there for £500 that changed hands in 1886 for $400 national currency. The old settler goes about the street bewailing the fact that he did n't buy when he first came, and saying it is too late now. But those who buy now point to the growing traffic through the straits, and refer to the line of huge steam tugs now building in England that will tow sailing ships through the narrow waters and against the winds that vexed and baffled the early navigators ; they speak confidently of the spread of sheep ranches on Tierra Del Fuego, and the apparently unfailing discoveries of new gold-fields among the islands to the south ; they talk of the increased demand for the wood of the straits. They balance against the frosts and cold rains of midsummer the many Indian summer days of winter, and tell stories of invalids regaining health that would make both Denver and Los Angeles green with envy. They find, in fact, no end of signs of future prosperity for their austral metropolis, and if somebody does not dig a canal from the Caribbean Sea to the Pacific they are very certain to find these signs well founded. Even if such a canal is made, only one element of the prosperity of the place will be injured—the traffic through the straits—and that probably will not be wholly destroyed, while the other elements can scarcely fail to improve continually.

Mr. Julius Popper wrote in 1888 of Punta Arenas, that it was "a town that opened its doors at 11 A.M., and was more concerned about picnics and dances than business." Mr. Frank Vincent said in 1889, that it was a community scarce one of whom "would be willing to stay if he could get away." The people there say these remarks were libellous when written. I am bound to say that in 1894, if a man wanted to get to windward of a Punta Arenas man in the matter of business, it was necessary to get up in the morning before crow peep. And as for the people wishing to get away, one would have hard work to find a citizen there who could be driven away with a shotgun.

In spite of its climate and its government, it is a blooming and booming community, and because of the enterprise of its citizens it deserves all the prosperity the free pastures of the pampas and the waves of the sea are bringing to it.

CHAPTER III.

CAPE HORN ABORIGINES.

THIS is the story in part of one of the most interesting and most unfortunate tribes of Indians known in the history of American aborigines—interesting because of their remarkable qualities of mind and body, and unfortunate because they have been almost exterminated by changes in their habits, wrought by Christian missionaries. It begins with what was said of them and their country by the early explorers, and it ends where the missionaries began what was intended to be the work of civilizing them. It tells of the race as God made it. What the white man did for it will be told later.

The Cape Horn Archipelago, as the islands south of the Straits of Magellan may be called, contained when discovered, and still maintains, three distinct tribes of Indians. One tribe occupied the island of Tierra del Fuego to the north and east of the coast range of mountains, of which Mts. Darwin and Sarmiento are the chief peaks. It was a land tribe; that is, they rarely if ever built canoes, and they subsisted almost entirely on such products as the land afforded. Another race occupied the islands to the west of Cockburn Channel. They were always, so to speak, a race of sailors; they built canoes, cruised about their region as fancy or the prevalence of food dictated, and were very little dependent on land beasts for food.

Last of all, we come to the tribe that lived and now exists among the islands lying south of Tierra del Fuego and along the very narrow south beach of that great island itself—a tribe that might well be called the Antarctic Highlanders, since they live further south than any other known people—and the land they occupy is but a succession of mountain peaks. These people are known as the Yahgans.

The known history of the Yahgans begins in the stories told by the early navigators of the region—a brief matter—merely the record of what the early navigators saw of them—but it is worth printing in part here because it is interesting, and because the reading of the mistakes made by the early travellers will help to impress on the memory the peculiarities of this remarkable tribe.

Darwin, the naturalist, under date of December 25, 1832, wrote of the Yahgans:

> While going one day on shore near Wollaston Island, we pulled alongside a canoe with six Fuegians. These were the most abject and miserable creatures I anywhere beheld. On the east coast the natives, as we have seen, have guanaco cloaks, and on the west they possess sealskins. Among these central tribes the men generally have an otter skin, or some small scrap, about as large as a pocket handkerchief, which is barely sufficient to cover their backs as low down as their loins. It is laced across the breast by strings, and according as the wind blows it is shifted from side to side. But these Fuegians in the canoe were quite naked, and even one full-grown woman was absolutely so. It was raining heavily, and the fresh water together with the spray trickled down her body. In another harbor not far distant, a woman who was suckling a recently born child came one day

YAHGANS AT HOME.

alongside the vessel and remained there out of mere curiosity while
the sleet fell and thawed on her naked bosom and on the skin of her
naked baby! These poor wretches were stunted in their growth, their
hideous faces bedaubed with white paint, their skins filthy and greasy,
their hair entangled, their voices discordant, and their gestures violent.
At night five or six human beings, naked and scarcely protected from
the wind and rain of this tempestuous climate, sleep on the wet
ground coiled up like animals. Viewing such men one can hardly
make oneself believe that they are fellow-creatures and inhabitants of
the same world. . . . There is no reason to believe that the
Fuegians decrease in number.

Quotations might be multiplied but two or three brief
ones relating to the land in which the Yahgans lived will
suffice : King says that " the vegetation is magnificent
in some places, and under the shelter of the great forests
some plants are found that would be considered delicate in England." Captain Cook agrees with this, and
describes the wild celery as among the delicate vegetable
productions, but he concludes that " it is the most
savage country I have seen. There is no place in the
world which offers such desolate landscapes." To this
may be added the testimony of Admiral Anson, who
said emphatically that it was " the most horrible country
which it was possible to conceive."

On the whole, it appears from reading the stories of
these early navigators that the land of the Yahgans,
while lacking the eternal ice of the Eskimo land, was
bad enough, and in the matter of storms it was worse
even than the region of Baffin's Bay. As for the difference in the people, it is apparent that the Yahgans were
believed to be far more wretched than the people of the
North, because the Eskimos were clothed in the warm-
est of furs and lived in huts, which, if made of ice and
snow, were still perfect shelters from the furies of the

storms, while the Yahgans went naked and often slept unsheltered from the snow and the freezing sleet that fell in every month of the year.

The islands on which are found the homes of the Yahgan Indians are almost without exception mountains that rise from the depths of the Southern Sea. As one sails among them the idea that here is a mountain chain that at some time long past was suddenly submerged in the sea is irresistible. For miles and leagues one may coast along without finding a beach wide enough to furnish a foothold, not to mention a place for hauling up a yawl. That the mountain is as precipitous below the water as it is above is easily proved, for soundings with the deep-sea lead line often give 60 to 100 fathoms within 100 feet of the shore line.

Rising to the height of 1500 to 2000 feet, these precipitous mountain peaks are lacking in nothing to make them grand and impressive. That they seemed desolate to the early navigators none need doubt, however, for the old-time sailors had a ship wretchedly unfit for such stormy seas, and he was ill-clad, half-fed, and homesick. No mountains seen through riffs in storm clouds and between marching columns of freezing rain could seem pleasant to them.

But wherever there is shelter from the prevailing gales a narrow beach is found commonly. Above this grows a forest of trees, of which the greater number are the antarctic beech, and nearly all the rest are species of magnolia. Some grow to a diameter of two feet and a height of fifty. Nearly all of the trees are green the year round, and the magnolias are of a particularly bright and beautiful green.

As one climbs the mountains the trees are seen to be

of smaller and smaller sizes until at from 1000 to 1500 feet above the sea mosses take the place of trees. Above the mosses come barren rocks and eternal snows. In many parts of Beagle Channel, and especially at the east end, there are fairly level spaces bordering the water, with foothills that are rolling instead of craggy. Even at the foot of Mount Misery, on the east end of Navarin Island, a mountain that got its name from the severity of the gales that come from its gulches, the scenery is anything but desolate and horrible. Indeed, natural grassy meadows and green groves so alternate with park-like beauty over the undulating ground, that one scarcely can resist the idea that all those open spaces in the woodland are the work of man. The eye involuntarily seeks for farm-house and barn, while the sight of the red-haired guanaco makes the scene all the more pastoral, for the wild beasts seem in that picture very like domestic animals.

My own view of the picture was under peculiarly favorable circumstances, for, although in the month of May, which corresponds to the November of the North, the sun was bright and warm, the water sparkled, and a breeze sweet and gentle just stirred the grass on the lawns and lifted the green-leaved boughs of the trees. Seen on another day, when whirling snow-laden squalls came down from the mountain to rip open the sea and hurl its foam five hundred feet into the air, the picture would have had a different aspect, but no landscape which contains green meadows and green trees the year round can be called "desolate."

As to the meteorological condition among the islands the experience of the missionaries there during twenty odd years has cleared away many myths. Some of Captain Cook's men nearly froze to death in the land of the

Yahgans, but it is a fact that even the confined waters (salt) do not freeze over often or remain frozen for any long time, while a prolonged storm, during which the thermometer ranged from 10° to 15° Fahrenheit, is mentioned in the missionary records as an unusually cold spell. At the worst, the thermometer at Ushuaia has not gone lower than 12° below zero, Fahrenheit, and Ushuaia is about the coldest spot in the region, because it stands under lofty, glazier-covered mountains that shut out the rays of the sun for nineteen hours out of the twenty-four during the short days of winter.

One white man at Ushuaia told me that it was a climate in which winter and summer alternated every week, and that describes the matter fairly well. That it is better than people elsewhere suppose may be inferred by the fact that the white men now there, while admitting the frequent recurrence of boisterous storms, invariably said it was "the healthiest climate in the world," and a few said they liked it better than any other.

Having considered the Yahgans' country and its climate, we now come to their homes and home life. Of the Yahgans as architects and as tailors, I am bound to say that they have been well described by the old-time explorers. The hut was a structure made of poles and a thatch of brush and grass that was of about the shape of a Yankee haycock, and only a little larger. It was open on the lee side, the thatching, such as it was, covering two thirds of the circumference to windward.

The fire was built just within the door or opening, and the inhabitants sat on grass or moss that partly covered the earth floor. It was sometimes customary, where the Indians expected to live for some time in one place, to scoop out the earth of the bottom of the wigwam and heap it up against the brush wall, thus making a saucer-shaped cavity for the floor, the brim of which rose high enough to serve somewhat as a wind break. Moreover, the limpet and other shells gathered by the squaws were commonly piled to windward of the hut. But even then, if judged by any white man's standard, the Yahgan house was as bad as any in the world.

So, too, of his dress. He wore a single guanaco or sealskin across his shoulders, holding it in place by thongs that crossed his breast. This was the best he wore. They were often stark naked, save for a breach clout, and the children were always so. The traveller who visits Hermite Island, in the immediate vicinity of Cape Horn, will find them so at this day. Living thus, "shelterless and naked in a land of fierce and freezing storms," one need not wonder that even scientific observers believed the Yahgan "the most miserable specimen of humanity to be found on earth."

And yet all who thought him either physically or mentally uncomfortable when in his natural state were entirely wrong. On the contrary, he was about the healthiest and happiest savage that ever smashed the head of an egotistical, meddlesome white man.

The Yahgan was built for the climate where he was found. He was in one respect like the whale that lived in the waters about him. He had a coat of fat under his skin that was very much better for him than the best of flannels and blankets. Besides, he had a custom that at once protected him from the cold and rendered him offensive to his white discoverers. He greased himself all over frequently with any oil at his command, and that is a custom worth remembering by people who may be cast away or lost in cold climates. Had the early explorers imitated instead of despised the Yahgan, they would have had fewer tales of suffering to tell. In these later years, sporting men of the United States have learned that when about to enter long-distance swimming matches they can endure the cooling effects of a race through the water much better if they coat themselves thickly with some such grease as vaseline. The Yahgan used whale oil as we use vaseline. The explorers spoke of his "filthy greasy skin," but the scientific sporting man of New York now imitates the Yahgan, even though vaseline gathers during a swim any flotsam that comes handy by. The Yahgan was "shelterless and naked in a land of fierce and freezing storms," but he did not freeze; he did not even shiver in ordinary Cape Horn weather.

However, one can understand why the explorers did not perceive the real condition of the Yahgan. They were cold in spite of thick flannels, and it was but natural that they should judge others by themselves.

But one cannot so easily understand how the explorers fell into such errors as they did about the ingenuity and the mechanical skill of the native. The results of Yahgan handicraft were everywhere visible. He could not make either a good house or a broadcloth suit. In his hands a white man's coat was ripped to pieces and the strips used for decorations. But there were his canoes and his weapons—especially his canoes. The Yahgan boats are mentioned slightingly, if at all, by nearly every traveller who has visited the region.

"The boats are unwieldy and logy, and the Indians seem to have no knack of propelling them at any sort of speed," says a latter-day writer, who saw a canoe of the kind in the Straits of Magellan. This was the writer's judgment in the matter. But along with his judgment he gave the dimensions of the boat. It was "about twenty-five feet long, four feet wide, and three feet deep, with comparatively sharp ends." The facts as I saw them are so, save that the ends seemed to me to be extremely sharp.

Now let any civilized canoe expert imagine a boat of those proportions with lines in an exact arc of a circle, and then let him say whether he knows of any superior model among either civilized or savage nations—a model better adapted for combined speed, safety, and capacity than this. My own experience with Indian canoes includes the kayaks and oomiaks of the Eskimos in Greenland, the dugouts of old Providence Island in the Caribbean Sea, and the bongos of the Bay of Panama, but I am bound to say that the most graceful canoe, as well as the strongest, I ever saw was made by the Yahgan.

However, one fact about these canoes will convince any one who knows what Cape Horn storms are that the Yahgan canoe is of a remarkable model. The Yahgans used them in navigating the waters of the Cape Horn Archipelago. Further than that, both the Rev. Thomas Bridges and the Rev. John Lawrence, who for twenty years have been familiar with the Yahgans, told me that they never heard of a Yahgan being upset in his canoe until in these later years, when the possession of axes and the teachings of the missionaries led the Indians to substitute dugouts of an entirely different model for the canoes they had made in the old days.

Judged only by his house and his clothing, the Yahgan was of a lower grade of intelligence, or at least was worse off, than many brutes. Judged by his canoe, he was a naval architect who produced a model to which the designers of yachts in the United States and England are in these days of "spoon" bows approaching, but have not yet equalled.

When the Yahgan would build a canoe he stripped wide pieces of bark from the tallest and smoothest tree trunks he could find, using shell axes, in the old days, to cut the trees. The bark was stripped from the trunk with a wooden tool, something like a chisel, and of the very shape found most advantageous by the white men who, in Pennsylvania and the Adirondacks, supply hemlock bark to the tanneries. Having his bark off the tree, the Yahgan cut the strips into such shape that when sewed together they would form a canoe with a midship section, say four feet wide by three deep, that was almost the arc of a circle. From this section the model tapered away almost on the arc of another circle. It had a sheer at once pleasing to the eye and well adapted to ride the most tempestuous seas in the world.

To brace this bark sheathing the Yahgan made ribs of split saplings that looked like hickory barrel hoops—ribs at once strong and light—while the rails and beams were made of round wood. The bark strips were sewed together with whalebone taken from whales stranded on the beach. The ribs, rails, and beams were lashed in place by sinew, usually guanaco sinew, for that curious animal is found on several islands of the Yahgan region.

Into the bottom of this canoe the Yahgan put an inverted sod perhaps two by three feet large, and on this his squaw built a small fire for warmth. Forward and aft of the fire were put little layers of brush and grass. The man squatted on the grass forward of the fire, and his favorite squaw, if he had more than one, was just aft of it, the terms forward and aft being used to indicate only the direction in which the canoe travelled, for both ends were alike. The other squaws and the children were distributed further from the fire. A squaw with an infant would keep it in her lap. The squaws paddled, the men used the weapons.

But one may doubt whether the Yahgan canoe shows greater ingenuity than Yahgan weapons and implements for obtaining food do. Mention has been made of the shell axe. It was made of a five-inch clam shell, or one larger. A rounded stone was lashed with sinew to the hinge side of the shell to give weight and make a good hand hold. Then the opposite side was ground to a cutting edge by rubbing away the softer inner or convex surface on a smooth rock. Yahgan chips made with this tool were small, but to see the rapidity with which an old Yahgan makes the blows, or better still, to see the wavy surface of a strip of wood dressed with a shell axe—a paddle, for instance—is a matter of interest almost worth a journey to the region. With this tool the Yaghan felled trees, or fashioned his harpoon, or stripped the blubber from a stranded whale, or trimmed his o'er long bangs, as occasion required.

When compared with the stone axes used by aborigines who knew not iron, this shell axe is a striking illustration of noteworthy differences between the Yahgan and the other tribes. The shell axe was frail, but keen-edged. It required a quick but delicate hand to manipulate it. The stone axe was blunt and heavy. Impelled by a rude hand, it smashed its way through whatever opposed its progress. With the shell axe in hand, we begin to perceive somewhat of the mental habits and character of the Yahgan Indian—to see, at least, that he preferred to accomplish certain ends by delicate means rather than by sheer brute strength.

Then there were his harpoons. I have one of which the head, made from a whale rib, is twenty-five and one quarter inches long. To make a diagram of it let the reader place a dot on a sheet of paper to represent the point, and then draw from this dot two straight lines that shall diverge from each other only one inch and three quarters when twenty-one inches long. That will give an idea of the beautiful taper of the weapon. It has a single barb, at once deep and strong. It is secured to the shaft in such a way that when a seal was struck the harpoon head dropped from its place in the shaft, or handle, after which the handle was towed broadside on through the water by the wounded beast. Of course, towing the harpoon shaft in this fashion impeded the animal's flight more than towing it end on would do.

Another harpoon that I have is twenty-one inches long, and but one inch wide and a half inch thick at the base, but instead of one heavy barb near the base it has a series of twenty-six small ones along one side. These barbs hook back like shark's teeth, and are about as keen-pointed. Nothing of better shape to hold fast could be devised by a fish-hook maker. Indeed, the turtle hunters of the West Indies, who have a steel harpoon of a similar shape, do not make as well-formed barbs. The harpoon of one barb is for seals, otters, and small whales (large whales were never attacked unless stranded), while the other form was for the various kinds of birds found in the region.

For fish spears the Yahgan lashed two or three of the bird harpoon heads to a shaft in such a manner that the points were spread out; the harpoon heads formed a V or a tripod, as the case might be, and the barbs were all on the inside. The fish were speared at night by the light of a torch. By having two or more of the harpoon heads on the shaft the chances of hitting the dimly seen fish were of course increased, and, moreover, a fish caught between two of the harpoon heads and impaled by a third, was held no matter how it struggled or what its strength.

Nor were the spear and harpoon handles merely saplings cut in the forest. The Yahgan used a perfectly round handle for one harpoon and a six-square handle for the other, and both were worked from solid wood with his wonderful shell axe. I speak now, of course, of the original native weapon, and not of what the modern Yahgan buys of white traders.

If any reader owns one of the old specimens of Indian workmanship let him keep it with great care, for the workmen who could make them are dead and their art is lost forever.

Less showy but equally remarkable were the peculiar wooden chisels with which the squaws stripped limpets from rocks six feet under water and brought them to the surface, although they were as heavy and as ready to sink as stones.

For gathering shell-fish the squaws made baskets of rushes. These baskets were of the shape of the plain earthen cooking jars found in the old ruins and cave dwellings of New Mexico and Arizona.

For a long-range weapon the Yahgan used the sling. He saw the Ona Indians with their bows and arrows. The Onas also used the bolas, which are the favorite weapons of the Patagonian Indians. With the Ona Indians the bow and the bolas were used with great success in killing the fleet-footed guanaco. Now the Yahgan, as said, found the guanaco in his own proper country as well as when he went visiting the Onas on the borderland, and he must have fully appreciated all that the Onas could do with their bolas and bows. Some of the Yahgans even learned to use these Ona weapons, but they never adopted them. The reason is not far to seek. The Yahgan sling had a much greater range. The missionaries tell about Yahgans killing birds afloat at a distance of two hundred yards. To hit any wild fowl at that distance with a rifle would be called right good shooting. The guanaco was knocked down and stunned by heavy round pebbles at ranges up to one hundred yards.

Why, then, did not the Ona adopt the sling? The answer is an interesting one for the student of anthropology. The home of the Ona was on the prairies of Tierra del Fuego, where round pebbles are not to be found, but material for bows and arrows is abundant. The Ona could not burden himself with pebbles for a sling when journeying across these prairies. On the other hand, the Yahgan lived on the beaches, where rounded pebbles were forever at hand, and when he travelled it was not afoot, as the Ona did, but in a first-class canoe, where he could carry as many pebbles as he wanted.

The Yahgan sling was made of a piece of raw hide, to which were attached strings of braided sinew that always ended in fancifully wrought knots.

The Yahgans did not fish with hooks, because they could catch more fish without. The squaws caught the fish. They paddled to the fishing ground in the morning and at night, when for an hour each time, the light

CAPE HORN ABORIGINES. 61

being just right, the fish would bite. The line was a strand of seaweed, which may be had there, slender and strong, of any length up to a hundred fathoms, perhaps. Bait—meat—was tied to one end of the line, which was loaded with a sinker of stone rounded to a shape to sink swiftly. The fish swallowed the bait and the squaw drew it gently but quickly to the surface. Then she snatched the fish into the boat and the bait from its gullet with a motion that Georges Bank codfishermen understand, and then let her bait run quickly down again. Some fish, too large to land thus, were speared when they came in sight. The time for fishing was so short that the squaws had to improve it to the utmost advantage, especially as there were many days when the storms prevented all fishing. They had no time to waste in removing hooks from the gullets of fish. It is a fact that when hooks were given them by seamen they never used the things for fishing. The Yahgan squaws did not know the joys of taking four-pound trout with a seven-ounce rod, but they had just as much fun as do the New Yorkers who go out to the fishing banks every summer day, and they caught more fish, too.

The Yahgan household utensils were few in number and of the simplest character. He made neither pots, nor kettles, nor cups, nor basins, nor any sort of receptacle for liquids. He never boiled his food, and when the missionaries came to the Yahgan land the Indians found the spectacle of a pot full of boiling meat a most entertaining one. And yet the Yahgans tried out the oil from whale blubber and other fats, and stored it away for future use. The fat was impaled on a stick that was then thrust into the ground close to a bed of coals. The oil was tried out thus, and it dripped down into the shoulder blade of a guanaco kept for the purpose. When the hollow of this bone was full, the oil was poured into a bladder or into the bladder-like leaf of a seaweed that can be found everywhere in the region. Moreover, there were large clam and other sea shells on every beach. These served every need of the Yahgan in the way of cups and basins. What he needed to make he made with unusual neatness and skill, but he knew when he had enough and worked for nothing whatever beyond.

If, now, it has been demonstrated that the early explorers looked at the Yahgan products through prejudiced eyes, the reader will pass with increasing pleasure to a consideration of the habits of thought and mental capacity of this Antarctic highlander. I quote Darwin in this matter, because he was the most eminent of all who have seen the Yahgans, and should have been less liable than others to make errors.

Darwin had on his ship a Yahgan called Jemmy Button, who had been carried to England and taught some of the English language. Of this Yahgan Darwin said: " I should think there was scarcely another human being with so small a stock of language."

The Rev. Thomas Bridges, who now lives opposite Gable Island, in the Beagle Channel, has for nearly forty years made a study of the Yahgans and their language. He has made out of this study a complete grammar of their language, and has written what is practically a complete Yahgan-English lexicon. Fully to appreciate the facts that appear in these two manuscript books, one must not only be something of a linguist, but must have knowledge of other aboriginal tribes. For instance, it is helpful to know that Ensign Roger Wells, Jr., U. S. Navy, working in Alaska, prepared an Anglo-Eskimo Vocabulary of 2263 words, and an Eskimo-English Vocabulary of 2418 words. To quote from a pamphlet issued by the Alaskan Bureau of Education in 1890, *Circular of Information No. 2*, the most important contribution to a knowledge of the Eskimo language is in process of preparation by L. M. Turner, in his observations made in 1882-84, at Point Barrow. "It will contain a vocabulary of the Koksoagmyut of over 7000 words."

Cruden's *Concordance of the Bible* gives 7200 words exclusive of proper names; Cleveland's *Concordance to the Poems of Milton* gives Milton's Vocabulary as 17,377 words, while Shakespeare himself had a vocabulary of about 24,000.

But the Yahgans, despised by many as "savages of the lowest grade," pitied by a few as "most abject and miserable creatures"—these Yahgans had a language from which has been compiled a vocabulary of over 40,000 words.

As I have said, this is a story in part of one of the most interesting American tribes. How small is the proportion of the story that I can give may be inferred from what has just been said about their language. Where did they get or develop all those words? Are those 40,000 words the remains of a language which, under other circumstances, was greater, or is the vocabulary now at its greatest state of perfection? How does it happen that such a remarkable mental development was found in a people that lived as these Yahgans did? Questions multiply, but no answers are found.

Anthropologists suppose that the peoples living at the ends of the earth under adverse circumstances are "conquered races, exiles, or criminals." It is guessed by some who have read of the Yahgan that he comes from some ancient Peruvian or Brazilian civilized tribe, and fled in war time to Cape Horn. But the Yahgan language is not that of Peru or of Brazil, or even that of the lost tribes of Israel. There is in it nothing to connect it with any of the other great languages of the world. Why, then, should we think incredible the possibility of the Yahgans having originated where they are? In the alluvial beds of Patagonia and of Tierra del Fuego are found the petrified remains of the opossum, the kangaroo, and the monkey. The ostrich and a modified camel (the guanaco), now live on the desert plains of Patagonia. Who, then, shall say positively that the Yahgan race has not lived through the cataclysms that destroyed the opossum and the monkey and left the ostrich and the camel?

Some years ago the Chili Government sent an expedition to explore the Yahgan country. The report made by the commander on his return refers to the Yahgan language as "nasal and harsh; it sounds like the barking of a dog," but all who speak the language agree that it is as soft and sweet to the ear as a love-song in French.

To make a study of the construction of this language here would be impossible for lack of space, even if I knew the facts, but something of the way the Yahgans talked to one another will be interesting, because it gives an insight into their character. Let it be remembered that this was a tribe of so-called savages, and that among savages the squaw is supposed to be a wretched slave. To the casual observer the Yahgan squaw was a slave. She paddled the canoe "while the man sat in the bow holding his weapons." But the Yahgan squaw's life was certainly not without its amenities, if one may judge by the language.

Thus the Yahgan man never spoke to his squaw of any property in the family as "mine." He said "ours" instead. He even said "our harpoon." He never gave orders directly to either squaw or child. If he wanted something done he would use an expression that meant "Tell to do"; it was as if he said to his squaw, "Have some one do so and so." More remarkable still, there was no such word in the language as "obey." They said instead, "Oblige me by," "Make me the favor of," "Would you be pleased or be so kind as to do this or that?" Even when the Yahgan was angry and wished to drive away an offensive person he used a polite sentence.

As among civilized people certain terms and names may be used between man and wife, or when talking to a physician or between two men talking alone, without incurring an accusation of using indecent language, so among the Yahgans there were certain forms of expression for use in private and others for society. In short, it was a modest race; in this respect it was, perhaps, the most remarkable of all the American Indian nations.

They had poets and novelists and historians. They knew, for instance, how to tell in the most delicate fashion those sly stories in which the point was found in the thought of the listeners, and not in the words of the speaker—where the speaker's words suggested but did not say the thought. No people in the world enjoyed well-told stories of the kind more than they, but only the skilful—the literati—were permitted to tell them. A gross expression was never permitted in company. It is a lasting pity that none of these tales has been preserved for study. The missionary taught the Yahgans that their soul's salvation was imperilled by such thoughts, and the remnant of the race has become so degraded in every way that the best of this wonderful oral literature has been lost.

They had songs, but no music as civilized people understand that word. Their songs were what travellers call "monotonous chants." However, they danced to some songs, and their words were poetic if the song did lack jingle and varied intonations.

"Food was abundant in the old days," said the Rev. Thomas Bridges, "and life was easy with them." Hence the Yahgans had abundant leisure to sit about the hut fire and talk to one another. Their conversation is best described by the word bright. They were as quick-witted—as quick and brilliant at repartee as the Irish or French. They also made many puns. They were what may be called a "clubable race," to borrow a Johnsonian expression. The missionaries say that within their limits of knowledge they were ready and logical thinkers. Sarcastic remarks and cynical observations abounded in their fireside conversations, as well as flashes of kindly humor.

In politics and religion they were almost equally interesting. They had no form of government—neither chief nor legislative council—but public opinion ruled with an iron hand. Theirs was the simplest form of a republic. When men violated social usages, as sometimes happened, the guilty were ostracized, and such was the habit of thought among them that this ostracism drove the guilty one away to live by himself. Occasionally several families were thus driven into exile together, but I did not learn of the existence of any such colonies of outlaws as that found below St. Lawrence Bay on the Siberian coast or the Kevalinyes, whose home is back of Point Hope in Alaska.

Crimes against property were rare. As to the property of white men they were called thieves and robbers. Fitzroy is particularly severe on them in describing their lax notions about property. It seems to me, however, that the Yahgans and all aboriginal tribes, for that matter, have been unjustly condemned in this matter. That they took things that seemed of infinite value to them, which did not belong to them, is not denied. But this act was not morally what the same act on the part of a civilized man would have been. Among the aborigines —especially among the Yahgans—there was much property held in common. It was no harm among them to take of a neighbor's fuel ; his paints were freely divided ; his wood for use in making paddles or spear-shafts was practically common property. All food taken was equally divided, and when chance threw a prize, say a wrecked ship, in their way, all shared the valuables found. So when they saw among white men a superabundance of good things, the taking of what they saw did not seem the evil thing that it would have been to the conscience of a white thief. They were, in short, socialists rather than thieves.

Crimes against the person were avenged by the injured one or his relatives, so that feuds and vendettas led families to hunting each other, hither and yon, across stormy seas and into wild and secluded nooks and inlets. But the Yahgan did not delight in open warfare or bloodshed. Warfare with neighboring tribes was almost unknown. The nearest approach to it was when some Yahgan family went hunting some family of a neighboring tribe to avenge an injury suffered by some member of the aggressive family. On rare occasions other families in both tribes took up the quarrel.

The Yahgan could work himself into a foaming passion—he literally frothed at the mouth in his rage—but he preferred to make even murder a fine art. He would plan and scheme for months in order that he might revenge himself without making an open attack. It is said that even the strong and influential in a clan would work in this fashion when seeking revenge on the weaker ones, who might have been crushed by a blow at any moment.

A favorite way of killing an enemy was found in the practice of gathering the eggs of the sea fowl. In the Cape Horn region the sea fowl make their nests on the faces of precipices that literally overhang the stormy seas. There is but one way to reach the nests. The egg gatherer must be lowered by a rope from the brow of the cliff. The Yahgans had an excellent rope in the long stalks of seaweed common in the region, and the egg harvest was for most of them a time of rejoicing. It was also the time for bloody revenges. The one who sought revenge would ask his enemy to go seeking eggs, and that was an invitation not to be declined. Even when the invited one suspected a sinister motive in the cordiality of the request he must needs accept, because a refusal would be construed by his neighbors into an acknowledgment that the other had cause for seeking revenge. And such an acknowledgment would justify the other in more open means of revenge, and would stamp the refuser as a coward also.

So the invited one would smilingly accept the invitation. With his heart sinking within him, he would follow the leader to the crest of the awful precipice, look down five hundred feet to the crags at its foot, and then without a word suffer himself to be lowered over the brow at the end of a rope that he knew would soon be chafed until his weight would break it.

These Yahgans had no knowledge of God or of a life to come. That they should have faced certain death in a frightful form thus calmly when they were young, and life was still sweet, and a loved wife and children would be left to other hands, is one of their most interesting characteristics.

Although about all the crimes known to Yahgans grew out of the relations of the sexes—although there was almost invariably a woman in every case—it is a fact that the grossest crimes of passion known to civilized races (such as incest) were unknown among Yahgans.

Marriage was a matter of purchase and sale; wives were sold, sometimes, by husbands, and daughters were invariably sold by fathers. The marriage ceremony consisted in painting the girl in a certain fashion for several days before she was delivered to her husband. A new canoe was very often the price of a girl. It is a curious fact, illustrative of Yahgan society, that a father sometimes sold his girls to men whom he did not really like. A man of influence could have any girl he wished; her father would rather let the transfer be made than offend the man of influence, and that, too, when the influential fellow already had a wife or two. But there were forms and methods in the marriage negotiations that were dear to the Yahgan heart. The dicker for a wife as conducted amounted to what would be among civilized people at once an intrigue and the negotiating of a treaty. It was because of this delicacy of feeling among the

Yahgans that the brutal white whalers and seal hunters that came to the region were unable to do any serious damage to this race previous to the year 1870. The Yahgan would not tolerate the rude lasciviousness of the white seamen, and until taught that it was wicked, stood up, man fashion, and fought in defence of his wives and daughters.

In religion the Yahgans were oddities, though not unique. They knew nothing of God, and had no word expressive of such an idea. To the great grief of the missionaries, there was nothing in the Yahgan language by which the idea of an everlasting, all-powerful God who must be obeyed could be adequately conveyed to Yahgan listeners, nor had they any word for or thought of a future life.

But the Yahgan's mind was not wholly material. He believed in spirits or supernatural and invisible beings, but these were invariably terrible. There was a spirit of the forest, and another of the water, and another of the kelp. Crouching over his tiny fire by night, the Yahgan heard weird voices among the waving trees on the mountain side above him, he felt the breath that scattered the embers of his hearth, he saw the deluge that drowned out even his brightest flames, and all these were manifestations of a power that was ill-defined in his mind, but nevertheless real. The Yahgan mother in this fearsome presence clasped her babe more closely to her bosom, not that it was cold, but to save it from some grasping hand that was always expected, but never came.

In the eddying waters of the tide rip was a boisterous devil that strove at one moment to throw the canoe into the air, and the next to suck it down to the unknown region below, while in the beds of kelp lurked a silent spirit that with soft and slimy touch grasped the bottom of the canoe, and held it fast until at times the frantic occupants leaped overboard and disappeared.

In their thoughts of death the Yahgans were perhaps unique. They had a word which meant dead. When a seal had been harpooned, or a tree cut down, or a fish beheaded, they said that death ensued. The thing killed was dead. They had another word which meant lost. If a tool were mislaid so that it could not be found, or if a dog were left somewhere on the coast so that he could not find his way to his master's hut, the tool or the dog was lost.

In times of sickness or of wounds, the Yahgans gathered about an afflicted one and with rude incantations strove to save the ebbing life until the spirit had gone forever. Then they quickly took up the body, and, carrying it out of the wigwam, buried it where it could be most easily put out of sight. This done, they returned and painted their faces in such fashion that all other Yahgans who beheld them could tell how closely the dead one had been related to the living, and the cause of the death—whether by disease, by accident, or by murder. This was their only way of showing they were in mourning. They rarely spoke of the one who had passed away, and when they did so speak they never said he was dead. They said he was lost.

This also was a matter of grief to the missionaries. When they would have spoken to the Yahgan of his dead relatives they could not without offending him seriously; at least that was the condition of affairs when the missionaries first came.

They had a folk-lore that is now for the most part forgotten, but one of their traditions was at the foundation of a cruel custom. Long ago, they said, a Yahgan woman chose a great rock instead of a husband, and, in consequence, bore a child that was at once a human being and a stone. When this hybrid grew to man's estate it turned against the tribe, because, perhaps, of indignities suffered by its mother, who was ostracized. No Yahgan man could stand against it, though numbers could temporarily overpower it. They, therefore, combined and thrust harpoons through it; they chopped it to pieces; they weighted it with rocks and cast it into a lake; but after each apparent death it appeared again in another part of the coast as healthy as and rather more malicious than before. The monster was rapidly becoming an invincible terror, when, by chance, it stepped on a thorn, which pierced its heel and the monster was unable to extract it. Its heel was the one part of its body where a mortal wound could be inflicted. From the effects of this thorn it became gradually weakened, and they were eventually able to destroy it altogether. The memory of the deeds done by this being was so terrifying, that the tribe determined that no such thing should ever come again to wreck their peace.

To prevent such a coming they invariably destroyed at birth any infant that came into the world not perfectly formed. The Yahgan's stature was not such as to meet the approval of the British explorers from whom Americans have obtained their ideas of Yahgan forms, but there never was a natural-born cripple to be seen among them.

What the Yahgans' claims to physical beauty were may still be learned by one who sees them at the Hermite group of islands, but in the Beagle Channel they have been so altered by new clothing and habits of life that scarcely a trace of their old-time form remains. The description of the old-time navigator is not attractive :

> These poor wretches were stunted in their growth, their hideous faces bedaubed with paint, their skins filthy and greasy, their hair entangled.

They are elsewhere spoken of as having dark, copper-colored skins, or skins of the color of iron rust, while Captain Fitzroy pictures them as almost black.

One may admit that these old explorers had good eyes, that they generally described with accuracy what they saw, and yet may prove that the Yahgans were not hideous.

To begin the argument, it must be said that the missionaries, who had no interest in making the untutored Yahgan appear in a better light than that in which he was found, say that he was a polite and affectionate husband and father, faithful in the care of widows and orphans, a generous neighbor, and an ardent lover. Food was abundant, and hard labor rarely necessary. He delighted in what civilized people call the higher pleasures, the joys of good stories, witty sayings, quick repartee, and he had almost unlimited opportunity for cultivating the faculties which gave him greatest pleasure. How could such a man be hideous?

The answer to the allegation made by the explorers who called the Yahgan so is not far to seek. They never saw the Yahgan. They only saw the coating of paint and whale oil that covered him, and because this was offensive to them they called him hideous. The Yahgan when washed clean, did not look like the Yahgan clothed in whale oil, smoke from the ever-present fire, ashes, powdered iron ore, pipe clay—what not. When washed he was not black ; he was not even copper colored. He was as white as the quarter bloods one sees in the Cherokee nation and as well featured. The young women were very like those of mixed blood who grace the halls of the female seminary at Tahlequa, the Cherokee capitol. The modern tourist camera proves it. Yahgans had straight black hair, great dark eyes, full red lips, breasts like a Greek Venus, rounded limbs, and small hands and feet. Better yet, they had a merry, hearty laugh that was irresistibly infectious. They flushed with pleasure, and blushed and drooped as if from a blow when shamed.

If ever the moans of outraged Indian maidenhood were charged up by the Recording Angel against the brutality of the civilized man, it was when the sufficient arm that protected the Yahgan girl was withdrawn through a misapplication of the gospel of peace.

Just how the Yahgan maiden lost that protecting arm —just how it happened that the forecastle brutes came to be free to go and come as they pleased among the Yahgan homes—will be told in the next chapter, but what that arm was is found in the tales of seamen cast on these shores in the old days, or caught napping there when seeking fuel or water for their ships.

When a band of Yahgans saw a crew of white men ashore in former times, their course of action was governed entirely by the numbers of the whites, or, rather, by the comparative strength of the two parties. If the whites were stronger, the Indians were peaceable ; when it was safe to do so, the Indians set out to exterminate all the whites but one. Leaping into their canoes some of the Indians would paddle out to cut off retreat toward the sea, and when they were in place, the rest would rush down on the seamen, and if possible save all alive for the time being. Then all the clan gathered about the captives and selected one of the whites—saved him alive, but forced him to witness the dying struggles of the rest. Very often those doomed to death were made to stand in a row facing the one that was saved, that he might the better witness their despairing faces and see the blood gush from their wounds. Eventually the one who was saved was taken to the Straits of Magellan, and there placed on board the first ship that appeared. It was perfectly plain that a man from each crew was thus sent back to the whites that he might tell other whites of the fate that befell all foreigners who landed in Yahgan land. They wanted the whites to keep away from them, and they took a most effectual means to keep them away. With certain death staring in the face, any crew that was outnumbered by the natives, even the sealers, took care to avoid going among the Yahgans. The Yahgan's deliberate ferocity—ferocity that was exercised with a purpose—was the sufficient protection of the Yahgan maidens.

As has been said, the Yahgans had an abundance of food in the old days. The cold waters about Cape Horn swarmed with whales. So numerous were the fur seals that one sealing schooner got a "first knock down" on one island of 11,000 head. The hair seal, the otter, and the sea lion were found by the thousand. Swans, geese, ducks, penguins, gulls, beat the air and ploughed the waters in uncounted hosts. There were fish in the sea and guanacos on the land. For a vegetable food there was "a bright yellow fungus," "elastic and turgid," that had "a mucillaginous, slightly sweet taste, with a faint smell like that of a mushroom." There were wild currants and strawberries that tasted more like a raspberry than like its northern namesake. There was a berry that grew on a thorny bush (berberis). But the mainstay of the Yahgan was the shell-fish. Mussels and clams covered every rock under water, and these were alone sufficient in number and in food qualities to preserve life for long periods.

The explorers say the Yahgans ate guanaco meat raw. The Rev. Thomas Bridges denies this. He says, in a lecture on the Yahgans, prepared for delivery before white folks :

> They toasted whale or seal blubber on pointed sticks stuck in the ground, and caught the oil in large mussel shells placed underneath. As these filled they poured the oil into bladders for future use. They tried out fish fat by putting it in large shells and placing heated stones or shells on it. They cooked large birds whole by burying them in the coals with hot stones placed inside. They baked eggs by placing them, after a small hole had been made in each shell, on end close to the embers and turning them from time to time. They uniformly ate the blood of animals, but always cooked it in shells first. I have never seen or heard of the Yahgans eating any kind of meat or fish raw except certain kinds of limpets. I have occasionally heard of their heating water by dropping hot stones into it, but they did not cook their vegetable food. In winter, however, they warmed the frozen fungi that formed a part of their diet.

A thousand other interesting facts and characteristics of this long-despised tribe remain untold here.

There was their habit of carrying dry bird's down to catch the spark when they struck fire with the iron ore they found on one island only.

They had a tradition that in by-gone years a great

flood raised the waters to the level of certain lines on the mountains, to which they point the traveller.

They were sensitive about growing old, and it was because their beard grew late in life and so indicated advancing years that the men plucked it out.

They were a long-lived race, and some probably lived to be a hundred in the old days.

They were not cannibals, but held human life as sacred as civilized people do. It is admitted that in times of dire distress, through prolonged storms, they sacrificed one (an old woman) to save the rest, but if that made them cannibals then an American army officer held in high esteem is a cannibal.

When food was scarce those who got it divided all they had with those less fortunate, and while hunting away from the huts the men subsisted on the inferior parts, that they might carry the parts most esteemed to the women and children.

They did not beat their wives, nor did they punish their children.

To sum the matter up, this was a race, more than three thousand in number, called the most abject and wretched people in the world, and yet, " in their circumstances and with their materials, their work was perfect." They were called savages, and yet neither governor nor judge was needed to preserve the prosperity of the nation. They were called heathen, because they knew not God; and yet, prompted by an inner light, they took no thought for the morrow, they visited the widow and the orphan in their affliction; neither was there any among them that lacked. Clear-eyed and strong-limbed, they were able, twenty years ago, to face the white destroyer as they faced the howling gales that swept their rugged coasts.

To-day the traveller can find, though he search diligently, rather less than three hundred, but to one who knew them in the old days those seen anywhere now, save on Hermite Island, would not be recognizable. The Rev. John Lawrence told me that they were civilized, but to one who can understand and appreciate the aborigines as God made them, this change, instead of being a matter of congratulation, is one that should make every white man connected with it hide his head in shame, and every other one who sees it shed tears of pity.

CHAPTER IV.

A CAPE HORN MISSION.

THE reader who has at hand a good modern map of South America will find, on looking along the narrow channel that bounds the south side of Tierra del Fuego, a tiny settlement named Ushuaia. On some maps the settlement is located on Navarin Island, south of the channel, but the proper place for it is on a small bay that indents Tierra del Fuego, just east of the line between Chili and Argentine territory. The settlement is, in fact, an Argentine capital, the seat of the Government of the Argentine belongings lying south of the Straits of Magellan. Ushuaia, as a white man's capital, will be described at another time. In its earliest days the settlement was a missionary station, containing only a single log hut, the home of the first Christian who succeeded in gaining a foothold among the Indians of the Cape Horn region, and it is my purpose here to tell, as briefly as possible, the true story of this Cape Horn mission.

Something has already been told about the characteristics of the remarkable people, the Yahgans, who were indigenous to the region—of their apparent squalid wretchedness when, in fact, they were actually comfortable and living in the enjoyment of some of the highest pleasures known to civilized peoples. It is, therefore, necessary for the reader to shut out from his mind about all the real facts concerning them, and think only of what they seemed to be if he would fully appreciate the spirit and intent of the founders of the mission to the Yahgans. It must be remembered that the region was supposed to be bleak and desolate, that frightful storms followed each other in swift succession, that the cold was often intense in midsummer, and that in the midst of these terrors of nature lived a tribe of savages so low in the human scale that they did not know enough to build houses to shelter them, or even to sew skins together into a decent blanket for a covering.

People who had read the journals of the explorers of the region shuddered at the thought of the life of misery which the natives there were said to endure. Indeed, so dark was the picture of human life there, that, although men had been found to brave death at the stake in the valley of the Mohawk, none so much as suggested in the early days a mission to the Yahgans, save only as Sarmiento's ill-fated colony hoped to convert the heathen as well as hold the Straits of Magellan for the crown of Spain. Nevertheless, a time came when the very terrors of nature and the apparent degradation of the people there were the magnets to draw one man to them. This man came from a race and a profession "to whom an appeal for volunteers for a forlorn hope was never made in vain." The first missionary to the Fuegian Indians came from the British Navy.

Captain Allen Francis Gardiner, R.N., was born on June 28, 1794, at Basilden, Berks, England. He entered

A CAPE HORN MISSION.

the Royal Navy in June, 1810, and was rapidly promoted until he attained the rank of captain. He was from his youth an ardent Christian—so ardent, indeed, that he determined to devote his life to mission work, and only remained in the navy because he wished to learn what people of the earth was most neglected and forlorn—most in need of the Christian religion. Having caught a few glimpses of the Yahgans and their people, and having read the stories about them which Captain Fitzroy and Naturalist Darwin, with many others, wrote, Captain Gardiner naturally concluded that the Cape Horn archipelago was his field. Accordingly, he began work by organizing, in 1814, a mission society, after which he made an attempt to live in his chosen field.

"He and several devoted companions were landed on one of the small islands with a tent, materials for a wooden house, and stores and provisions to last six months," says the record. "But in a very few days the conduct of the natives showed the missionaries that to remain on land was impossible. Mercifully the vessel which had brought them was still within hail," and they were taken off and borne to England.

The trouble with the Indians, it appears, was that they looked with covetous eyes on the outfit of the missionaries. The record says they were robbers, but it now appears that this term is much too harsh. They did, indeed, strive to take valuables from the missionaries without making any return whatever for them, but it must not be forgotten that the Yahgans held practically all property in common. They naturally resented what seemed to them to be the selfishness of these white intruders just as they ostracized one of their own tribe who did anything contrary to Yahgan custom.

Finding, as he supposed, his life in danger when he tried to make a home among the Yahgans, Captain Gardiner returned home to try to raise money for a ship in which he could live in a Yahgan harbor. He believed he could repel any Yahgan boarders that might attack him, and eventually make friends with the repulsed. But he failed to get the money, because the English were skeptical as to the success of even a mission ship.

Thereat the determined captain bought instead two launches twenty-six feet long and decked them over. The sum of £1000 was deemed necessary for this enterprise, of which "a generous Christian lady of Cheltenham gave £700." Gardiner himself gave £300.

"Captain Gardiner, with three Cornish sailors, Christian men accustomed to stormy seas," "the ship carpenter who had gone with Captain Gardiner before," "two men as catechists, Mr. Maidment, and Mr. Richard Williams, the latter a surgeon in good practice,"—these seven sailed from Liverpool on September 7, 1850, in the ship *Ocean Queen*, which was bound to the booming town of San Francisco, but agreed to land them and their outfit in Tierra del Fuego. They carried stores for six months, and arranged for more to come before these should be exhausted. On December 5th their ship anchored in a bay called Banner Cove, in the west end of Picton Island. The missionaries landed, and then natives came. Fearing violence the missionaries took refuge on the *Ocean Queen* for a few days, and then, on December 18th, landed again, built a wigwam near the beach, moored their boats handy by, and let the big ship sail away.

Then came what the record calls "a terrible discovery." In taking their outfit from the *Ocean Queen* the missionaries had left on board about all the powder and lead with which to kill the Indians. "They were now alike without the means of self-defence and of obtaining food," is the way the story of Captain Gardiner's life puts it, but the plain English of the matter is that they had come relying on guns to protect them. They meant to shoot the Indians under certain circumstances. Their motto was, so to speak : " Trust in God, but keep your powder dry." Now, however, they had no powder and "they were left almost wholly dependent on meal, rice, and such things."

Thereafter they "went beating about among the islands, alarmed by every indication of the people for whose sake all this misery was encountered." In a diary, written by one of the party, one may read that " I applied the golden key to heaven's treasury, and with it opened the storehouse of God's exceeding great and precious promises. What I saw and felt of Christ's love no tongue can tell," but their faith in Divine protection was not strong enough to make them risk a visit to the Indians, and so, at last, they actually died of starvation, although the region produced and produces a prodigious supply of mussels and limpets, wild celery and other edible vegetables, not to mention fish and mammals easily snared by one not afraid to venture away from his boat.

" It does seem remarkable that Gardiner should have apparently erred from timidity and over-caution," says the writer of the life of that missionary, and then he piously adds : " We must look to the will of God in the whole affair."

The death of Gardiner through his own cowardice, to put the matter bluntly, is only one—the first of a long list of doings that " seem remarkable " in this story.

The Gardiner party sailed from Liverpool on September 7, 1850. The last entry in the diary of Captain Gardiner is dated September 5, 1851, while a letter was found dated the day following. Gardiner, who was the last survivor, probably died one year from the time he sailed. In October came the relief ship to the port in Picton Island. An inscription on a rock which the traveller can still see there was found. It was as follows:

>
Dig Below.
Go to Spaniard
Harbour
March
1851

Spaniard Harbor is now called Aguirre Bay. A gale of wind prevented the relief ship going there, but Her Majesty's ship *Dido* was sent out, and she recovered the papers of the dead missionaries and buried the human bones. Her colors were lowered and three volleys were fired by the marines after the funeral, because Gardiner had been a naval captain; and all this, having been well told, together with the stories found in the diaries, made a sensation in England.

To one who knows the region, the appeals thereafter made by the missionary society to the English-speaking world seem very remarkable. Though I do not doubt the honest intentions of the society people, some of their words would seem to be deliberate attempts to deceive, if coming from any other kind of society. Thus in *A Memoir of Richard Williams*, by James Hamilton, D.D., is an appeal for funds for the society, which (p. 255) says:

This agency may soon stud with gardens and farms and industrious villages these inhospitable shores. The mariner may run his battered ship into Lennox Harbour and leave her to the care of Fuegian caulkers and carpenters; and after rambling through the streets of a thriving seaport town, he may turn aside to read the papers in the Gardiner Institution, or may step into the week-evening service in the Richard Williams chapel.

Following the advice contained in papers which Captain Gardner left, and taking advantage of the emotions raised among church people by the story of the Captain's death, the society raised funds with which they built and manned a schooner fit for the stormiest sea, and sent it out to establish a station for the conversion of the Yahgans. She was commanded by Captain W. Parker Snow, and she carried Mr. Garland Phillips, as catechist, to Keppel Island, one of the Falklands then uninhabited. They arrived out on January 28, 1855, and found the island about eight miles long and four wide, with three fresh water lakes. It was "a barren, desolate place," Phillips thought, and according to the record he and his associates lived there for more than two years before they got a single Yahgan to come to live with them.

Eventually "a strong party" was sent out from England to re-enforce Phillips and "push the work vigorously." This party included "Tom Bridges, a good-looking, affectionate boy of fourteen, who loved everybody, and whom everybody loved," and this is the earliest mention of one who has since made himself the most noted of all who have worked in the mission. Thereafter matters went on better, because the "strong party" made a right good sheep ranch of Keppel Island, and in 1857 got the Yahgan named Button, his wife, and his children to go to Keppel.

With Button as interpreter, Phillips and some others went over to Navarin Island in November, 1858, and built a log-house there, in which they remained a month with the natives about them, returning the first of 1859 with nine natives, whom they proposed instructing on the ranch at Keppel Island. These instructions continued until the following October, when Phillips took them back in his schooner, which was manned by a captain, a mate, four seamen, a carpenter, and a cook, all "decidedly good men." On the way over (it was a voyage of six days), Phillips missed some valuables, and after accusing the Yahgans of stealing, searched their bundles. Of course the Yahgans were highly offended, but their anger was apparently appeased later, and a landing was affected on Navarin Island in peace.

But on the following Sunday, when all hands except the cook went ashore to hold church services, the Yahgans arose and killed the entire party that came to them. The cook escaped to the brush when the natives came after him, and there remained until hunger drove him out. The natives then bound him, stripped off his clothes, but gave him their own favorite article of clothing instead—a coat of whale oil, and with no other dress than whale oil this cook lived in perfect health, until he was rescued some three months later by a ship that came from the Falklands in search of the schooner.

This deadly assault on the missionaries is frequently referred to in the missionary publications to show how fierce and degraded the Yahgans were before the missionaries got a foothold among them.

During the three years that followed only two Yahgans, a man and his wife, lived on Keppel Island, but the young English boy spoken of—Tom Bridges—proved a natural linguist, and so rapidly learned their language from the Yahgans, that at the end of three years he could talk freely with them.

Then came a new man into the field, the Rev. W. H. Stirling, who now lives in Buenos Ayres, and is the Bishop of the Church of England for South America. On the arrival of Stirling " the interrupted work was resumed with vigor," and " forty or fifty Fuegians were brought at intervals " to Keppel.

Of the life led by the Yahgans and the missionaries on Keppel Island, the records speak freely, and it is worth while considering what that life was, because Keppel was the preparatory school of the mission.

It appears by direct statement that the missionaries believed "our hope for the material improvement of these natives lies in their adopting and following farming and agricultural pursuits with fishing." We must believe that the first object that the missionaries had in view in taking the Yahgans to Keppel was to teach them the Christian religion, because the missionaries say so; but it is apparent that "material" matters were never lost sight of. The records give the length of time devoted to these "material" matters every day, as well as that given to mental and spiritual pursuits. Up to 1879 the natives had two hours per day for instructions, but in October of that year the school hours were increased to three per day. The rest of the day was devoted to work on the sheep ranch and to the garden where the missionaries raised vegetables. But not all of the Yahgans there received even two hours' instruction per day, for a missionary who sent two to Keppel from Wollaston Island wrote regarding them, that they "will, I have no doubt, make very good men on the farm, but I do not think they will do anything at school." And the farmer reports : " I could send more lads to the day-school, but they are not the material Mr. Grubb requires." Mr. Grubb was the school teacher.

This teacher, W. Balbrooke Grubb, sums up his work in these words : " Moral training and example and the expounding of the Gospel, all who knew these natives will admit, has [sic] worked a great change upon them. Glorious conversions or wordy confessions I have not to report."

That Yahgan life was not all work and study on Keppel, however, appears from the report of the celebration of the birthday of one of Farmer Bartlett's children. " After tea we had several games, among which was the avenging the death of a murdered man by the Indians, and an Indian dance, which is a strange affair." Imagine the vendetta as an entertainment in the course of a revival in the United States!

But the worst is yet to be told about the treatment of these Yahgan boys on the Keppel Island farm, and lest some one think I am exaggerating, I give the words of the report of one of the missionaries :

"As I observed much carelessness and untidiness in the dress of the boys, I set aside a portion of one day in the week in which, under my supervision, they were encouraged to mend and repair their clothing." To this Mr. R. Whaits, the mission carpenter, adds that 'they are badly clothed ; boots they have none, nor blankets to cover them."

The unfortunate natives were not only made to toil at unaccustomed work the whole day through, but they had to do it unrewarded. They did not get even decent clothing in return.

I have given a good deal of space to this school, but it is because I suppose there are other mission schools in the world conducted in the same fashion, and the people who contribute money to missionary societies ought to know about these matters.

Having described the school in which sundry Yahgans were civilized, and "Tom Bridges, a good-looking, affectionate boy," was prepared for the missionary service, we come to the establishing of the missionary station in the Yahgan territory and the results of that work.

Until 1869 nothing was done beyond instructing the natives who could be induced to go to Keppel and learning from them their language. But in January of that year Mr. Stirling determined to take up his residence among the Yahgans. His reasons for this are important, and are as follows:

> My motive for living ashore is to exercise a direct and constant influence over the natives; to show my confidence in them; to encourage *a more general and regular disposition in them to adopt our ways* and to listen to our instructions, and to get the children within the zone of Christian example and teaching.

Accordingly, he built on the shores of what is now called Ushuaia Bay, near the present capital of Argentine Tierra del Fuego, a log-hut that was 20 x 10 feet large and had walls seven feet high. Here he lived for seven months. One of four boys who had been in England, and was subsequently continued in his educational career by being enlisted as cabin-boy of the mission schooner *Allen Gardiner*, became the housekeeper of the log-house, and was assisted in the work by another Yahgan boy. How the days were passed and the natives instructed is told clearly in the missionary's diary:

Wednesday, 27th (January)—Our *days* are devoted *to work*. In the morning, before breakfast, prayer and catechising. In the evening, ditto ; and what with putting the house and its surroundings in order, making and fencing gardens, superintending wood-cutting and charcoal-burning, I have passed a curious busy kind of time.

After seven months of the life thus briefly, but fully described, Mr. Stirling was called home to England for ordination as " Bishop of the Falkland Islands."

That he had lived unharmed among a tribe who ten years before had murdered a missionary, is counted among the marvels of the story of this mission ; and it is quoted to show that the sort of training the Yahgan boys had received at Keppel had tended to civilize them so much that, on their return to their native haunts, they had in turn civilized their fellows.

Meantime the boy Tom Bridges had grown to be a man of twenty-five years, and had prepared himself, with the aid of those who had had charge at Keppel, to become a missionary himself. With Mr. Stirling's approval he went to England while Stirling was founding Ushuaia, and before Stirling reached England Bridges had been ordained a catechist, had married, and had sailed for Keppel Island. With the departure of the Rev. Mr. Stirling for ordination as Bishop, Ushuaia was left unoccupied temporarily, but the vacancy was filled in 1870 by Mr. Bridges and his wife, who have ever since made their home on the shores of Beagle Channel, and have until recently taken the lead in the mission work done there.

Ushuaia Bay is a rounded hollow on the north side of the narrow Beagle Channel. Lofty, glacier-covered mountains wall off the sun on the north, and on every other side the ranges are not very far away. To the west, however, there is an open table land level enough for farm purposes, and to this came the young missionary and his wife to make a home.

They were apparently displeased with the location afterward, for we read that "at Ushuaia our position is exposed, and being about ninety feet above the sea is not favorable for procuring the best results. Many spots might be chosen where, shelter and greater heat being secured, the fruits of tillage would be both larger and more certain. But it is vain for us now to regret our situation."

The log-hut erected by Stirling remained intact, and that was at first their home; and straightway the work bringing the Yahgan Indians to Mr. Bridges's standard of civilization and righteousness was begun.

What this standard was has been put in writing, together with a plain statement of the means employed in raising the standard of righteousness. He says:

"Our hopes for the material improvement of these natives lie in their adopting and following farming and agricultural pursuits together with fishing." And again: "Our daily endeavor is to bind them with the bonds of Christ's love. To this end we have been of late showing them the authority of Christ as far greater than that of Moses."

A tribe of Indians that lived naked in a climate where snow-storms raged in every month of the year—lived happily and comfortably, too—even in perfect health on the spontaneous productions of the region, was to be transformed into a community of farmers there and then. A people who had in all their wonderful language of 40,000 words no term or idea of either God or a future existence; who never gave an order, and who had no such word or idea as to obey, were to be converted to

Christianity by sermons "showing them the authority of Christ as far greater than that of Moses!"

That the missionaries entered upon this tremendous task with a calm assurance that they could not be in error as to what the Indians needed, is perfectly plain to all who peruse the record ; and in that assurance they never faltered. They were as earnestly determined to create civilized villages and farming communities—that is to say on an English model—as they were to tell the story of the Christ.

The first "material improvement" work done was, naturally enough, the making of a comfortable home, with outbuildings and a big garden attached, for the use of the missionaries. Mr. Bridges reasoned that an object lesson in home comforts would impress on these wild people the advantages of civilization more forcibly than words could do ; and the work to which Mr. Bridges devoted the most time was that of impressing on them the advantages of civilization—*i.e.*, making them like white men. He had little faith in the notions of those missionaries who at various times have believed they could best reach the heathen heart by living with the heathen, suffering their hardships, learning to understand their joys, and so on. Mr. Bridges would not do that. Besides, in making gardens, building fences and houses, and caring for cattle and sheep, Mr. Bridges, by employing the Indians, was enabled to teach them the white man's arts and to encourage what he called "habits of industry."

He assumed that when employed as laborers raising turnips on a Tierra del Fuego farm, or in the saw-pit splitting logs into boards with a hand-saw, they would be very much happier than they had ever been while roam-

THE MISSION STATION AT USHUAIA.

ing at will about those seas and inlets in search of seals, birds, and fish, or when sitting beside a roaring campfire inventing and telling stories. It was, therefore, with a merry heart that Mr. Bridges, and those, too, who were sent to aid him, saw the Indians take up the axe to chop, the spade to dig in the garden, the saw to split the logs for lumber.

But just how the natives were handled and the kind of life they led about the station can be most convincingly told by a few extracts from the record, which are in all cases verbatim, save that I have italicized many words in order, as the missionaries might say, to bring home the lesson of the hour more forcibly.

In a letter describing to the people of England the work at Ushuaia after it was well under way (five years after the station was founded), we get not only Mr. Bridges's ideas about handling workmen, but also his way of composing a delicate family difficulty and a definite statement of the price he paid one laborer for two weeks' work. He says:

We need in no way be ashamed of the earthly parts of our duties here, and I hesitate not to set it plainly before you. *The society* has now *three and a half acres* of garden land in crop, chiefly with turnips (Swedish), most of which will be used by the natives in meat stews, thickened with flour, beans, or other farinaceous food. Besides, much work has been done to the road in carrying down the embankment, and we hope to have it available for our cart in a few weeks by diligent labor. A large quantity of wood has also been cut and brought down to the beach ready for shipment. Mr. Whaits has commenced sawing out boards from native wood with great success. We have had for weeks over thirty men employed. *The natives* have also considerably added to their own lands under crop this year, and have *four acres* in crop.

Peace, with a few and unimportant breaks, has reigned. I must relate a few instances of its interruption : Some nine or ten men were at work on the road. Stephen Lucia was in charge, and a few were vexed that he was not silent when they were idle. Angry, vengeful words were spoken, and Stephen, in great turmoil of spirit, came to me and asked to be employed elsewhere, saying that he could no longer work with the men with the cart. I set him to other work, and I went down to the men and reproved the guilty ones for violent language and threatening intimidations. Stephen, knowing that I would speak to them, came down, and some angry altercation took place. Yet, after some talking over the matter, peace was restored, and those who were angry shook hands at my suggestion, and real good-will has existed among them since.

Another occasion was in connection with a young Eastern called Hidugalahgoon. He came here with a wife that had been the wife of a man who had been very violent to her. The young fellow seemed very fond of her and she of him. He had friends here whom he was diligent to move in his favor by descanting on the cruelties of the other man. He was for several weeks employed, and regularly came to our meetings for worship and instruction. As payment he received a sufficiency of food and a shirt.

As to the row that the real or original husband of the woman raised when he came on and found that she would stay with her lover, Mr. Bridges says :

Being consulted by Hidugalahgoon, I advised that he should, under the circumstances, give what he could to restore peace. No doubt he has been a very guilty party in the matter, and I told him to give up his shirt ; he might soon earn another.

That is, instead of denouncing Hidugalahgoon as an adulterer, this missionary advised him to buy off the outraged husband. The effect of such teaching as this will appear further on.

We are not left wholly in darkness as to the kind and quantity of food served, for, in speaking of the day's routine, the record says :

The daily breakfast is a pound of navy bread per man. The dinner is cooked in our yard under the charge of Mr. Lawrence, who has one or two boys under him, and tea likewise. A break is made between the morning and afternoon working time, a space of four and three and a half hours, respectively, by a distribution of a refreshing drink of milk and water, slightly thickened with flour and sweetened.

Although not so stated here, the dinner was usually a meat stew with hard-tack. It was served in a quantity sufficient for the workmen only, as one may readily infer from a description written elsewhere of the milk-and-water "refreshing drink."

To encourage the men to work, besides the three meals daily, Mr. Lawrence used to bring us some milk and water, slightly sweetened, and a biscuit at 11 A. M. and 4 P. M. Then we would all throw ourselves down and enjoy ten or fifteen minutes' rest while we took this refreshment. The little children soon learned the course of things, and used generally to come for a bit from their fathers or brothers. They (the fathers or brothers) would have been *glad* to have eaten all, but invariably they shared.

Let the reader get this matter well in hand. The Yahgans were employed on road-making, chopping, pit-sawing and other work of the hardest kind. The white man had sufficient influence over them to keep a good many so employed. In return he gave to the laborers what he calls "a sufficiency of food," but he here distinctly admits that they "would have been glad to have eaten all"; in other words, it was a bare sufficiency. In addition, for "a few weeks' work," he gave a common shirt such as the farm laborers of England wear.

The rule to feed and clothe only those employed at labor was not rigorously enforced at all times. We read at Christmas time of a "distribution made to-day of the half-yearly gift of clothing *to the employed* and such natives as are more particularly under our charge, and to children supported by friends at home ; also *general* distribution of old but most acceptable clothing sent by kind friends in Stanley which was very much needed." Then, " after the morning service, we all had a happy time with the natives, who were abundantly supplied with good stew and pudding." In a letter we read that "the half-yearly distribution of clothing to the baptized natives took place on the 28th of June." Of course, this favoring of the baptized natives could have but one effect. If clothing could be had by professing this new religion the hypocrites among the tribe were pretty sure to see the point and make the profession. As will appear further on, however, there were not very many hypocrites among the three thousand Yahgans.

But that the system of paying a " sufficiency of food " and a shirt, such as laborers wear, for two weeks of labor did not prove entirely satisfactory to the Indians, save in time of famine, may be inferred from what is written in the same record :

The men, when left much to themselves, become very idle, and rest a great deal more than they should. They say they are tired and sore, and you have to be constantly at them to do a fair day's work. The natives have been culpably idle at this and all other work they do, and yet they clamor for more pay, and even speak of ceasing to work unless their pay is increased.

In fact, the missionary was quite incensed when he found that the heathen were not willing to do the work of English farm laborers in return for a "sufficiency of food " and a "semi-annual distribution of clothing."

If Mr. Bridges had trouble in teaching the tribe habits of industry as farm laborers, he was also worried somewhat in his efforts to impress on them the advantage of the kindred virtue of thrift. As wandering mussel-eaters they had no need of thrift, because mussels were almost everywhere abundant, and they were lacking in food only when storms prevented their journeying from a place which had been eaten bare to one which had not been visited for a time. As farmers, if they were to be farmers, they would need to be thrifty, especially so in such a climate. But here is the record, which gives at some length not only a picture of life at the station, but also the missionary's argument for overcoming their ancient heathen habit of holding all things in common:

> The natives, very much driven by hunger, were very importunate in coming to him (the Rev. Mr. Lawrence) in order to get something to eat. They brought logs of fuel by ones and twos, they brought baskets, spear heads, and spear shafts, others offered to work to earn some food, others came expressing their sad circumstances and sought to excite pity in order to get something to eat. Only three men were regularly employed, but four or five women were much employed in making shirts, so that these were envied by the rest, and certainly were much better off. During this time a party of natives arrived and brought a good supply of sprats. As the three above mentioned very properly kept their food supplies for themselves and families, to the great grievance of their neighbors, so now these sprat owners would not part with any of their sprats to them.
>
> One of the three expressed himself thus about this matter: "We hungry folks now: all other people plenty fish, only we poor." In reply to these remarks he was answered, "You ought not to be sorry, but glad that these poor people have plenty. Besides, you ought not to be hungry, because you get food for your work every day, and your wife also gets food for her sewing, and your son can gather mussels."

I have quoted the record verbatim because it seems important that people in the United States should know just how the heathen were treated at this typical mission, and have the missionary's statement of the case. It is a fact, incredible as it may seem, that the missionary gave to the heathen, in return for a day's hard work, only so much food as that heathen himself needed. To the squaw only as much as she needed was given. Under that system of pay an able-bodied man and an able-bodied woman could not together earn even enough food above their own wants to supply one child. "Your son can gather mussels," said the missionary when they complained to him that, having divided with their son, they were hungry. It is worth while to compare the attitude of the missionary in this matter with that of the heathen father and mother, who were willing to go hungry in order that they might divide their stinted allowance of food with their child. But to continue the quotation :

> I have striven very much to move the people against the prevalent habit of begging and giving, but as yet with but little seeming success. When a canoe arrives many make visits to the new-comers to get a share of any food they may have brought. They do not ask, but wait till they have received some. Each woman looks upon what supplies she gathers as her own. She gives to whom she will, so that to the same person a portion would be given by each of a man's two or three wives from their separate possessions. This habit is very hurtful.

Although it is aside from the object of this story, one cannot help noting here that among the Yahgans "they do not ask but wait," and that "each woman looks upon what supplies she gathers as her own." As a picture of savage customs that is interesting.

It would be instructive and interesting, though not to say pleasant, to follow these extracts further. They picture accurately the life led by both missionary and Indian at this station—a life encouraged and promoted by a society in England that had an income of from

$50,000 to $60,000 a year, and complained because it did not get more. Enough, however, has been quoted to convey an accurate idea of what was done there in "material" matters, and something will now be told to portray the "spiritual" teachings and the results thereof. The record is full of such things as these:

Subject of this morning's teaching, "Justification by faith in Jesus."
Subjects of instruction: Faith in God and its proper fruits, obedience to His will, love and gratitude for all His goodness, and confidence and joy for all His perfections.
We endeavored to rouse the attention and lively interest in the free treasures of the boundless love of God, of their God, their Lord, their Saviour, their Judge, their heaven, their hell, their own offered mercy and good.
Experienced the helping grace of God in speaking to and reasoning with the people of the truth of God, especially of Jesus, our representative before God, who in our stead has borne our sins, and pleads His—now by faith our—merits, on account of which we can alone be loved by the Father. Spoke also of the necessity of denying self and sin, of the works of the flesh, and the blessed fruits of the Spirit.

These extracts accurately illustrate the character of the preaching. The following from the same pages of the record will, with equal accuracy, show what the results were:

We vary as far as we can in illustration by anecdote and application, and *great effort is necessary to keep their attention.*
We long to see earnest love, to hear the people inquiring for Christ. When asked whether they love and wish to serve Jesus, they answer affirmatively, but *they never volunteer any remark or questions concerning spiritual things.*
Visited Mecugaz twice. Spoke to him earnestly as to a dying man who as yet shows no real faith or special interest in Jesus Christ as his Saviour and Lord. The conduct of Jemmy Button, Admiral

Fitzroy's protegé, *is ever being reacted here*. He would not tell the people what he had seen, but made capital of their ignorance and his knowledge by keeping it to himself. *He only became the greater impostor*, and assumed a pompous conduct toward his fellows, and did not a whit of good.

A paragraph will serve for one other matter. There came a time when the missionaries wanted a steamer to replace their old sailing vessel, and an appeal for the money needed for a steamer was made on the ground that the new vessel would enable the missionaries to extend their teachings to the other tribes of the region. They got their steamer, but when it came their zeal to preach to the Ona and to the Alaculoof had disappeared. Instead of using their steamer to carry the gospel to these tribes, they used it to carry their cattle between the farm on Keppel Island and the station in Beagle Channel.

However, in spite of the fact that the bay produced no food supply worth mentioning for the natives, in spite of a sterile soil and wretched location for farming, in spite of every drawback, the settlement grew in numbers, until, after eleven years, in 1881, such progress had been made that they had a "Christian village, with cottages instead of wigwams, and an extemporized church in the midst," six frame cottages which the Indians had made for themselves out of whip-sawed lumber. These cottages were of the ordinary packing-case model. They were divided within into one large "living-room" in the middle with two smaller rooms on each side of it. Two families occupied each house, using the middle room in common.

Cattle and goats had been introduced, and the Indians had purchased some with labor. More than ten acres of ground were cultivated. An orphanage had been erected, and "twenty-five children are here clothed, fed, and educated at the expense of friends in England."

Meantime, every Yahgan at the settlement, and many of them elsewhere, had learned to dress in "civilized garments," which they had obtained in exchange for labor, or for the furs they caught when hunting, and a very large proportion of them had learned to "prefer bread food" to any other. Meantime the baptismal register had attained to a length of 137 names, including infants.

But the one point of success attained, on which the missionaries laid greatest stress, was the change wrought in the treatment wrecked seamen received at the hands of the Yahgans.

"The natives had formerly been set against white men by the cruel treatment which they had met with from sealing vessels. When vessels were seen the women and children were sent to the woods for safety," says the missionary record. In return the Yahgans had slaughtered every wrecked crew of seamen that fell into their power, saving one man in each crew, however, whom they compelled to witness the slaughter of the rest, and whom they then took to some steamer in the Strait of Magellan, that he might go home and warn his countrymen to keep away from that region.

"It was only by degrees that a better state of things was brought about," says the record but in eleven years it was done.

Naturally, this apparent success of the mission attracted the attention of the Argentine Government. Ushuaia, "the Christian settlement," stood in Argentine territory, but it was very close, indeed, to the Chili line.

Being jealous of Chilian encroachment, the Argentines decided to establish a station down on the south coast of Tierra del Fuego to defend their landed rights. They naturally chose this "Christian settlement" as the site for the station. That was a great event in the history of the mission, and the missionaries were all "greatly pleased" with the sub-prefect and his staff, and troops, and sailors, and especially with the fact that thereafter at least monthly communications would be had with the civilized world.

But a marvellous change had been developing even for years without the knowledge of those who had brought it about. Something was found to be wrong with the Fuegian converts. The record begins to show such entries as these :

> In the orphanage we have one case of fatal disease. Excessive languor, without suffering, is his symptom. He is rapidly wasting away.
>
> We had heard of two families who had been suffering very much and asked to see me. At the first house we found eleven people sick, and one old woman who had recovered. They told us three had died, and pointed out several others whom they said would die, among them a little boy, who held his arms out to me and said: "No, no, I am not going to die, Mr. Whaits."
>
> At the next place we found three women, a little boy, and a man trying to get to a canoe to come to Ushuaia. The man told us he had buried four, but was so weak he could not bury the others who were in the house. We found one dear little fellow on his back, not quite dead. He asked me for water which I gave him. He died a few minutes after. In the same house we found a man who had been dead two days, and in his arms a poor little boy not dead. When I took him away he cried to go back to his father. We took him to Ushuaia, but he died on the way.
>
> We have now lost forty-three persons in three weeks at Ushuaia. How far it has spread I cannot say.

> *It has been a pleasure to go among them, for in almost every house we have heard the voice of prayer and praise in the midst of all their sufferings* [*sic*].

It is useless to continue these quotations or to tell in detail the pitiful stories of wretchedness, uncomplaining suffering, and death that had taken place in this settlement, when the missionaries once got the tribe well in hand. Let it, instead, be summed up:

The race had been "hardy and vigorous." They had actually increased in numbers while living naked and smeared with grease from head to foot. But when put to work as farm laborers, and washed and clothed like white folks, they complained of being "tired" and "sore," and had to be nagged into working steadily. They had slept naked in the freezing rain, but now, if they sat down in their shirt sleeves while at work, they caught a cold that developed into a fatal disease. Consumption and pneumonia appeared, and assumed frightful aspects. Little children that had been round-limbed and bright-eyed when naked in a canoe were wasting rapidly away in "excessive languor," though dressed in woolens and living in a warm house.

They continued to waste away until every one of the twenty-five children, "clothed, fed, and educated at the expense of friends in England," died, and so did every other child in that "Christian village," and from that day to this not one child in dozens born has survived its first year.

The frequent communications with the civilized world had been of advantage to the missionaries, but measles, grip, diphtheria—what not?—came on the steamers.

But that is not all, nor, for the tribe, the worst result

of the establishing of this mission in the region. Keep in mind that "the very ferocity of the natives of Tierra del Fuego protected them." Those are the words of one of the members of the missionary society, and they were true words. The ferocity of the Yahgans in their native state protected them from the devilish evils left in the wake of sailors who visit aborigines in any part of the world. The sailors, even the sealing sailors, kept well clear of the Yahgans so long as this ferocity lasted.

But the missionaries fully, if "only by degrees," overcame this ferocity and made boast of it, saying it was of "the greatest advantage to commerce." They taught the Yahgans not to kill white men. It would have been better for the Yahgans had a man-o'-war been sent there to kill the half of them rather than that they should have learned that lesson. For, alas, the missionaries made very little, if any, progress in overcoming the Yahgan notion that women might be bought and sold. Indeed, as in the case of Hidugalahgoon already mentioned, where one man had carried off another's squaw, the offender was advised to settle the trouble by paying for the woman.

The forecastle brutes from the Yankee sealers or any other vessels were at last free to go among any Yahgans save the insignificant few at Ushuaia, and to trade liquor and tobacco for women.

To stem the tide of disaster a new station was established at Tekenika Bay, some fifty miles south. It was in charge of the Rev. Mr. Burleigh and his wife until he was overturned in a boat in the bay and drowned, when two of the grown children of the Rev. John Lawrence of Ushuaia, brother and sister, took hold. They have a small cottage, in a wretched climate, and sacrifice almost every comfort to do what they believe to be good for the Yahgans.

But because Yahgan bodies were fitted by nature for nakedness in a bleak desert, and because Yahgan stomachs digest mussels and whale's blubber better than turnip soup or mixed milk and water slightly sweetened, the sacrifices of these young people can only hasten the decay that has fastened on the tribe.

As was said, here was a tribe, 3000 strong, healthy, hearty, and happy in spite of apparent adverse circumstances. They for twenty years were under the lead of a most adroit teacher. They listened to and said they accepted his spiritual teachings; they reluctantly took up his farming and mechanic arts; they eagerly sought his kinds of food and clothing. The missionaries declare the result has been that the whole tribe is civilized. I saw a score of Yahgans, and all to whom I spoke told me they were Christians and that other Yahgans were Christians.

But the truth is that of that tribe of three thousand untrammelled souls less than three hundred can now be found. Their civilization—or the evidences of their civilization, rather—consists in the use of wretched and dangerous dugouts in place of graceful and safe bark canoes; the ragged cast off clothing of prospectors and seamen; wretched little shanties like those in the New York goat district, and a partial knowledge of English and Spanish.

Worse yet, in place of what the explorers were pleased to call the hideous markings of paint, are the really hideous evidences of diseases that have come since Yahgan "ferocity" ceased to be a "protection" to Yahgan women.

Where the blame lies let the reader judge for himself, but none can dispute that the naked savage, who in the old days stood erect man fashion, and with furious anger fought in defence of wife and daughter or even for plunder, was a nobler being in the sight of God and man than the ragged, cringing hypocrite that he has come to be in these last days.

CHAPTER V.

ALONG SHORE IN TIERRA DEL FUEGO.

ALTHOUGH a considerable part of the story of Tierra del Fuego has been related already in the chapters on the Yahgans, their mission, and the Cape Horn gold diggings, there are yet a number of objects of human interest there which remain to be considered. According to the old-time explorers, a voyage around the coast of this great island was one of the dreariest as well as the most dangerous in the world. Dangerous it was and still is, but in a well-found steamer the traveller may find a sufficient variety in the island and its products and peoples to more than repay him for all the risk and discomfort.

Of the Tierra del Fuego matters not yet more than touched upon there is the settlement called Ushuaia, wherein is found the seat of Government of Argentine's part of the island. Ushuaia is a remarkable capital. It stands nearer the south pole than any other civilized village in the world, for one thing. For another, it probably has fewer inhabitants than any other capital town in the world.

Of the landing of the first white man on the present

site of Ushuaia, enough was told in the last chapter. That was the beginning of the settlement as a missionary station. The town, as an Argentine settlement, was founded in September, 1884, and the Argentine flag was for the first time unfurled over the first building erected for the use of the officials on October 12 of the same year. Ushuaia, however, was then made only a sub-prefectura—the residence of a naval Lieutenant, who had the powers of an American Mayor rather than those of the Governor of a Territory. The Argentine Government was at that time very busy planting colonies along the coast of Patagonia and at other points south, because the dispute which it had had with Chili over the light of possession had been settled but recently. These settlements were made to take actual possession of the land acknowledged to be Argentine territory, and one was necessary somewhere on the south coast of Tierra del Fuego, because Argentine had secured a large slice of that island.

Very few people knew anything about Tierra del Fuego in those days. The few hardy prospectors who had ventured across the Strait of Magellan from Punta Arenas in a search for gold nuggets had not been lucky enough to make them speak well of it. A few sheep ranchmen had gotten hold of some pasture land on the north coast, but they had had to keep their shepherds armed with Winchesters because of the predatory habits of the Ona Indians who lived on the prairies of that part of the island. There was one spot, however, where the Indians were known to be harmless, because white men had been living among them for a long time there, and that was the mission station on Ushuaia Bay, in the Beagle Channel. Moreover, Ushuaia Bay was known to

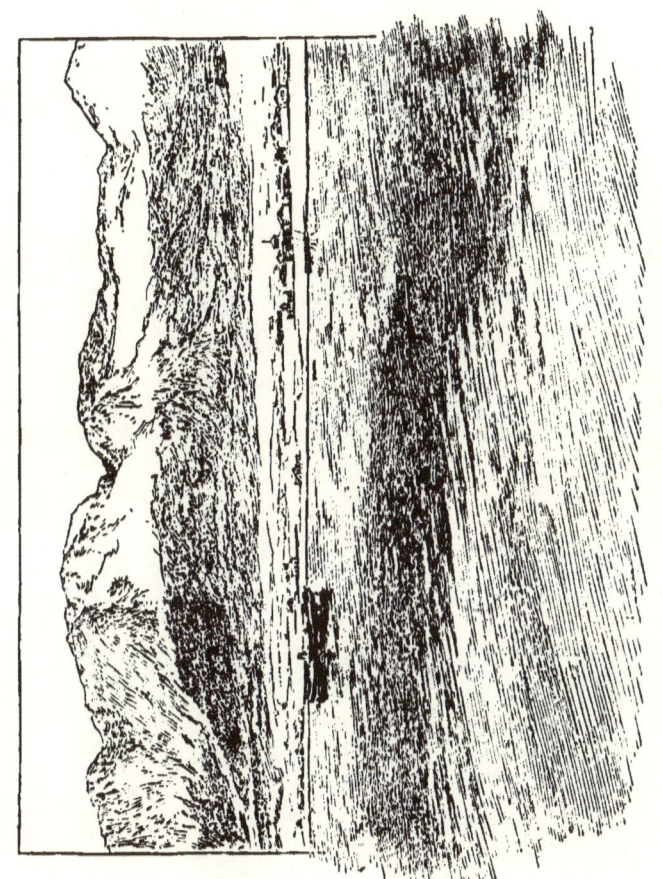

USHUAIA, THE CAPITAL OF ARGENTINE TIERRA DEL FUEGO.

be a well-sheltered harbor, where the anchor of a ship would get a right good hold on the ground. So, after sending a fleet to erect a lighthouse on the east end of Staten Island for the benefit of a commerce in which it had no part, the Argentine Government ordered the fleet to go around into Ushuaia Bay and establish a sub-prefectura. The building of such a station would tend to encourage the exploration and development of the island, so the government believed, and so the event is slowly proving. But just why the place should have been raised to the dignity of a capital is past finding out, for it was a sufficient check on Chilian aggression as a sub-prefectura, while the expense to the government is now several times greater.

I saw Ushuaia for the first time under rather unfavorable circumstances. The sky was overcast with storm clouds; roaring gusts of wind, laden with snow, came driving along at frequent intervals, and the region at the water level was buried under snow that was at no place less than two feet deep. It was on the 23d of May, just at the beginning of the antarctic winter. We had been steaming all the morning along the Beagle Channel, under the shadow, so to speak, of the glacier-covered range that overhangs the south coast of Tierra del Fuego, when at about noon the range turned away to the north from the channel, making a curve so that a half-circle of lowlands like the floor of an amphitheatre was left between it and the line of the range. Into the westerly side of this floor, where the waters could wash the feet of the lofty mountains, there projected a rounded bay, the mouth of which was well guarded, but not obstructed, by a low island and a long sandspit on the west. It was an ideal harbor, and, after what had been said of it on board ship, there was no difficulty in recognizing it as the site of the capital of Tierra del Fuego.

A little later we rounded the island and then the settlement came into view—apparently at that distance a single row of houses standing at the water's edge. Nor did a closer approach change the appearances very much, for although not exactly in a row nor washed by the waves, there was only about a score of buildings all told, and none of them was above a hundred paces from the bay.

And right curious these houses were. First of all, of course, was the capitol building, a one-story structure in the form of a right-angled ⊔ standing with the wings away from the sea.

This building was made of wood, and it was painted to that peculiar shade of red that in old times was so much favored by the Yankee farmer when he had put up a new barn. A little to the right of this stood the home of the Governor. This, too, was a frame structure, but it was in the form of a Central American *hacienda* —a low, rectangular affair, with a peak roof that ran down over all four walls to form a wide veranda on all sides. The rest of the buildings of the town can best be described by saying they were duplicates of the dwellings to be found in the mine camps of the United States. Every one had plain, unpainted wooden walls, and every one a corrugated iron roof. A few had garden plots enclosed with fences of split pickets, but the majority were unenclosed. They were all scattered along the narrow slope of one of the foot-hills of the great mountain range. This slope is in summer grassy.

Back of the scattered row of houses the first ridge had once been covered with a forest, but the trees for ten

rods or more up the slope had been subsequently cut
for fuel and other purposes, leaving a field of stumps.
Above the clearing the forest rose rapidly in solid rolling ridges until six hundred feet above the sea. Then
the forest thinned out, and in clumps and bunches of
brush spread up the mountain side for a few hundred
feet more, to disappear entirely at the edges of the glaciers and banks of eternal snow that were piled among
the rugged rocks clear to the crests three thousand feet
above the sea.

To add to the sombre aspect of nature incident everywhere to the winter season is the lack, in Ushuaia, of
sunshine. The Beagle Channel is in 55° south latitude,
so that in winter the nights are long and the days brief
at best, while even such lengths of days as they might
have in the open is cut down by the shadows of the lofty
crests. The sun does not get above these crests until
almost ten o'clock, and it disappears again soon after
two o'clock. Even then its face is so often hid by the
snow clouds above the crests that one may almost say
that the village in winter is shrouded in perpetual
gloom.

As a port Ushuaia showed a substantial wooden pier
over one hundred feet long, built by the government
for the use of its officials. At some distance from this
was a smaller and more slender pier, built by a merchant.
There was anchored in the bay the dismantled hulk of
what seemed to be a big, worn-out, seagoing tug. It had
really been a tiny cruiser, however. Another vessel of
a similar model, but much newer and well painted, was
a cruiser kept there at the call of the Governor, but just
what he might want to call it for did not appear. Moreover, the tubes in her boiler had gone wrong and she

could not have answered anybody's call. In addition to these two there was quite a fleet—say half a dozen sailboats of the sort used by Cape Horn gold-hunters—sloops and catboats from twenty-five to thirty feet long, while a tiny schooner that had once been used by the missionaries lay rotting on the beach some distance around to the west. The vessels afloat, as they veered to and fro at the ends of their long cables, gave some air of life to the harbor, an air that was increased by two or three Indian families, who were paddling about in the wretched little dugouts the missionaries taught them to make in place of their old-fashioned bark canoes of Viking model.

Here, then, in the score of mine-camp shanties along the beach and in two broken-down hulks afloat, lived the inhabitants of the capital of Tierra del Fuego. If the town itself was curious, its people and their manner of life were found to be no less curious when one came to get acquainted. Small and wretched as the place was, it had a complete outfit of the officials and assistants needed for the dignity and peace of the most populous territorial capital anywhere. There was a complete list of executive officers, with secretaries and servants; a complete list of judicial officers, with clerks and servants; a complete list of police officials, from a commissioner to a patrolman; a file of soldiers with commissioned and non-commissioned officers; a crew of sailors for the vessels, with the usual officers, a school teacher (male), and a matron for a girls' school.

The town had also six citizens—plain, every-day folks, not entitled to wear uniform. All told, the number of inhabitants was less than sixty. I went on shore to learn something more about the local government than what

I could see from the steamer. They told me that the Governor was in Buenos Ayres working for an appropriation to make improvements.

"Improvements in what?" I asked.

"Just improvements about the place."

"How much money does he want?"

"Who knows? He ought to have $20,000."

"What one thing, for instance, would he do with the money?"

"Well, there is the shed back of the Capitol, where the sawmill is. That ought to be enclosed to keep the weather off the machinery."

"Would that cost $20,000?"

"It should do so. You'd make it cost that if you were Governor and had to live here. Nobody gets pay enough to make it worth while staying."

"Will the Supreme Court sit to-day?"

"I beg pardon."

"Will any Judge hold court to-day?"

"Oh! Scarcely. What made you think such a thing likely?"

"When are courts held, then?"

"They are n't held. No cases to be tried."

"Not even a police case?"

"No. Do the people you have seen look like criminals?"

"Certainly not. Where can I find the school-house?"

"There is none."

"Where do they hold school, then?"

"They don't hold any."

"Why not?"

"There are n't any children here."

So the questions and answers ran about all official

doings, if that term may be used in connection with the life in the town as a capital.

The truth was that the executive department of the government had nothing to execute, so to speak. The courts had no dockets, the police had no beats to patrol, and no criminals to arrest. The soldiers did not even stand guard, nor had the sailors either a watch or lookout to employ them. Of all the government employees there was but one class that had any employment worth mentioning. The cooks and their assistants had to labor daily. Even these were well-nigh out of a job when I arrived. Owing to negligence on the part of some one in Buenos Ayres, the supplies of flour and about all other kinds of food had been allowed to run out. We carried thirty half-starved sheep to the settlement from Punta Arenas, and these were hailed with delight, because everybody there except the plain citizens was on short allowance.

I made a tour of the place, wading through snow up to my knees. I found three people engaged in useful occupations. One was a squaw, who was pulling the hair from an otter skin in the store run by one of the plain citizens. In the kitchen attached to this store an Englishman was getting dinner and a German was cutting meat for sausage. In all I saw three women in the place, but it was said three more could be found. There was not, they said, a heating stove in town, nor was there a cord of fuel in any one pile. The men were usually found standing in what might be called the sitting-rooms of the houses, or in stores conducted by the plain citizens. They usually had their hands in their pockets. All wore heavy sack coats, which were kept buttoned to the chin, while some had mufflers about their necks.

The plain citizens were composed of Englishmen, Italians, and Germans in equal numbers. Three of them were Argentine citizens, and the others were cosmopolitans. When, in the course of conversation, I referred to a trip I had made to some Colorado mining camps, the plain citizens with one accord brought out specimens of ores that I might pass judgment on them. When I protested that a brief residence in a couple of mine camps would by no means make a man a judge of ores, they thought I was over-modest. They all had specimens of gold dust, but aside from this there was nothing of value save a chunk of iron said to have come from a limitless bed, and a piece of ore from which a Buenos Ayres assay had obtained an enormous per cent. of nickel.

I asked about the gardens. They said that cabbages, turnips, carrots, parsnips, and a few other hardy vegetables flourished in the season. I saw cabbages and turnips as big each as a peck measure, but the potatoes were in no case larger than an English walnut. The wild grass of the region was said to be very nutritious, and the appearance of the fresh meat I saw in the stores indicated that it was so. One merchant, Mr. Adolph Figue, had taken up enough prairie land on the west side of the bay to carry 6000 sheep or more, and this he was stocking with every prospect of success, because the Rev. John Lawrence, in charge of the missionary station, had very fine flocks and herds in the same region.

The stores were established for trade with the prospectors and Indians. It will readily be believed that prices were high. The prospectors bought goods with gold dust, while the Indians traded furs, weapons, and models of their old-fashioned canoes for the goods they wanted. The traders found a sale for the curios on the Argentine naval transports that call there every three weeks. The stocks carried in the stores were liquors, navy bread and other cured foods, tobaccos, clothing, and cheap cloths, and miners' tools. The goods are named in the order of the demand for them.

When asked if there was anything there to interest a sportsman, one replied:

"No. We get all our game from the Indians."

The Indians did the only out-door work that I saw done on shore. There were goods landed from the steamer, and a gang of Yahgans from the Mission hauled them from the little pier belonging to the merchant up to the merchant's store, a distance of perhaps 150 yards. In spite of the depth of snow, they used a hand-cart for that purpose. I did not see a sled or toboggan in the settlement. If any one there knew how to make and use a sled, he did not, apparently, have the energy to use his knowledge. In fact, no white man seemed to have energy enough to do anything. As said, everybody stood about muffled to the chin and with his hands in his pockets. They gazed out of the window at the bay and the mountains; they gazed at the goods behind the counters in the little stores; they gazed at the blank walls and read for the ten-thousandth time ordinances and edicts issued by various officials and pasted up there. Doubtless all would have been glad to sit down—to gaze from comfortable arm-chairs instead of standing up to do it. But they couldn't do that. There were no arm-chairs, for one thing, and then the rooms, having no fire, were too cold for comfort when a man sat down.

On the whole, a more cheerless life than that of the people of this austral capital would be hard to imagine. They do not work. They do not read. They do not converse more than is necessary. They neither flirt, frolic, fight, nor fish. They have no interest in botany or zoölogy, and they keep no record in meteorology. Their interest in geology is confined to the finding of pay dirt, and they look for that in only the most desultory and cursory manner. A stay of three days is, in winter at least, enough to make any one agree that "nobody gets pay enough here to make it worth while staying." Even the chance of enclosing a shed at a cost of $20,000 would not keep a Yankee there much longer than the time needed to enclose a shed.

ON A BEAGLE CHANNEL RANCH.

From Ushuaia we steamed away east for thirty miles, and there found, as the sailors said, that the mountains on the north side had all fallen down. In place of lofty peaks and rugged crests of rock, snow, and ice, there were on the north side low, rounded hills, with luxuriant pastures and beautiful forests. South and west lay Navarin Island, and this was one huge ridge that reached far above the clouds. That is to say, the land on the north of the channel was open to the sun and sheltered from the fierce, cold storms that came from the colder regions south and west. The change of climate was remarkable. There was neither snow nor ice in sight save on Navarin Island and the distant mountain tops, and even then it did not descend within several hundred feet of the sea.

In the midst of this charming district, living on the

shore of a little bay that afforded excellent anchorage for our steamer, we found the Rev. Thomas Bridges, the founder of the Ushuaia Mission, but who for seven years had been engaged here as a ranchman and farmer. All of the pasture land in sight, and more, too—eight square leagues lying along the Beagle Channel—belonged to him. On the prairie-like Gable Island he had a flock of 4500 sheep that needed no other attention than an occasional visit and shearing in the season. On the mainland he had herds of cattle, a band of horses, and a great drove of pigs. He had miles of picket fences enclosing his pastures. He had a great garden patch on a sunny slope, where all the hardy vegetables grew in profusion and potatoes attained a size to make the Ushuaia product seem worthless. His house was a great, two-story frame enclosed with iron—in form and convenience like the house of an English country gentleman of wealth—though the appearance, due to the iron, was somewhat *outré*. There were sheds and storehouses near by, and a pleasant pavilion on the lawn that overlooked the bay. Afloat was a great lighter for carrying the produce of the farm to the steamers and the imported goods ashore, besides a regular fleet of small boats, cutters, and sloops, for pleasure and for visiting various parts of this estate, with its twenty-four miles of water front.

Nor was the interior of the mansion in any way behind the general appearance of the estate. There were rich articles of furniture, a library (probably the only one worth mentioning in Tierra del Fuego), pictures, and bric-à-brac. As a home, the house showed but one thing that could be criticised, and that was the room in one corner where clothing, food products, tobaccos, tools, etc., were kept for trading with prospectors and Indians, but that has probably been removed by this time to a separate building erected for the purpose.

The family of Mr. Bridges consisted of himself and wife, his wife's sister, two charming girls under sixteen, and three sturdy boys, only one of whom, a lad in his teens, was at home, the other two being on other parts of the estate. To aid these in the work of the estate, there was a small colony of Yahgan Indians living in little houses that were located behind a hill out of sight of the great house. The squaws had been taught to do housework, of course, and the men the heavy work of the farm. In addition, each male member of the family had a young Indian valet.

Ranching on the Beagle Channel (this ranch stands further south than any other in the world, by the way), is very profitable, according to Mr. Bridges, in spite of the high latitude and the distance from the market. The sheep yielded enough wool to net a gold dollar per head, in addition to which the increase of the flock that season had been 108 per cent. of the ewes. The care of his herd of cattle cost something, because at that time he had to have a man ride the range to keep the cattle from straying off up among the mountains, but when a fence, then in course of construction, was completed, the cattle would in every way rustle for themselves. The pigs, too, cost nothing. They roamed the forests, living on the tiny nuts the antarctic beeches produce, and certain vegetable and fungus growths produced by nature. This food produced most excellent pork for cured meats. Such labor as was needed was furnished by the Indians, who were satisfied with the food the ranch produced, and sufficient clothing for themselves and families, in lieu of cash pay. The long experience which Mr. Bridges had had as a missionary had taught him how to manage the Yahgans without friction and at small expense.

As to the market, the wool was shipped to England, via Buenos Ayres. The surplus pork, bacon, beef, and vegetables were sold right on the farm to the prospectors and wandering Indians, who came with gold dust and furs. The prices obtained were something to make glad the heart of any farmer, bacon bringing an English shilling a pound, and fresh beef sixpence. On the whole, Mr. Bridges must have an income not much below $8000 a year in solid gold from his ranch, besides the increase of his stock, and the improvements he is making in the estate.

The acquiring of this estate cost Mr. Bridges very little. The land was given to him by the Argentine Government under circumstances which show that he is an adroit man of business. In 1887 there was quite a stir in Buenos Ayres over the Argentine portion of Tierra del Fuego. The government had sent Don Ramon Lista, a traveller and man of letters, on an exploring expedition along the east coast. Herr Julius Popper, a German engineer and man of letters, had conducted a prospecting expedition across the island and had found gold in quantities around San Sebastian Bay. The stories and lectures of these two men filled the newspapers for some time. At the height of the interest Mr. Bridges, the missionary, arrived in town and delivered a lecture or two on the island as he knew it, and on the wonderful Yahgan tribe of Indians. Especial interest was paid to the Yahgans, and the populace became enthusiastic over the missionary who had passed so many years of his life in that out-of-the-way region. Taking advantage of this, Mr. Bridges said in the course of one lecture :

> Our life among the Yahgans has been eminently practical, with a view of leading them to cultivate the soil, keep cattle, build permanent huts, and live in a more orderly and settled manner. The improvement which has taken place in their condition since is wonderful. They have learned the arts of civilized life. They have acquired the skilful use of firearms, and some of them are splendid sportsmen. They are acquainted with the value and use of money, English or Argentine, a good sum of which is continually passing through their hands, as they prefer selling for money rather than bartering. They occasionally visit Sandy Point and the Falkland Islands, and are thus thrown in contact with a civilization which they are anxious to attain to.
> My object in coming to Buenos Ayres has been to obtain a grant of land in the Beagle Channel on which to create a farm, and employ native labor upon it, thus seeking to supply a want in reference to agricultural products which we have long felt, and at the same time insure the well-being of some of the natives.

Land on Beagle Channel did not then seem of much consequence to the people of Buenos Ayres, so Mr. Bridges, under their influence, got a water front twenty-four miles long as a gift from the National Government. It was the only stretch of land fit for a ranch on the channel, and he got it all.

An officer of the steamer I was on said the land was given under the impression that it was to be used by the missionary for the benefit of the tribe, and that even then Mr. Bridges would not have got it had the government known that the " wonderful improvement " in the condition of the Yahgans, of which the lecturer spoke, had been confined to a handful of individuals, while the tribe, as a whole, had dwindled from 3000 healthy heathen to a few hundred diseased beggars.

However, Mr. Bridges had told just what he came for —to get land "to create a farm and employ native labor," and so supply a want for agricultural products "which we (the missionaries, of course,) have long felt." Mr. Bridges supplies agricultural products for a price, and he employs some Yahgans, who, as he believes, are better off when sawing logs by hand into fence rails for his ranch than they were in the old days sitting around an open fire eating whale blubber and telling stories. As to the prices he charges, it must be said that he merely shows good business tact. They are always considerably less, even according to those prospectors who do not like him, than charged by Ushuaia merchants, though still from three to five times as much as charged at Punta Arenas (Sandy Point), in the Straits of Magellan.

The prospectors, disposed to criticise Mr. Bridges for making the best business possible of his farm, alleged, without offering any proof of their charge, that Mr. Bridges got his money for stocking the farm by taking clothing which generous people of England sent to the mission for gifts to the naked savages and trading it to the Indians for furs, which he sold for his own private benefit. I do not believe he did that. It appears from the missionary record (see page 56, *South American Missionary Magazine* of London, March, 1879, and page 39, February, 1881, for instance), that the missionaries did trade with the Indians for furs, and that the clothing which the Indians received was usually, but not always, paid for with either labor or furs. The missionaries did sell clothing sent out to be given to the Indians, but they made no secret of it, and the donors learned the facts in the magazine. The missionaries did not want to pauperize the Indians, they said, by giving gifts. But the profits of these trades went to the society. In 1881 Capt. Willis of the mission schooner in a letter spoke dolefully of the prospect for buying skins on the society's account, "as there are so many sealing vessels out." Capt. Willis spoke also (see page 233 of the magazine) of three canoe loads of Indians who "exchanged otter skins for clothes, and were eager for tobacco."

The missionaries should not be accused of misappropriation of goods simply because the thrifty society wanted to increase its cash income by trading at a tremendous profit with the Indians, for whose eternal welfare it had been created.

Of course Mr. Bridges has been trading with the Indians on his own account, but it was, no doubt, with goods purchased with his own money. One reads so much of the dangers and privations which fall to the lot of missionaries that the fact that they all receive good salaries is always overlooked. The salary of a missionary down there was never less than £120 per year cash, while he received his board and lodging free in addition, of course. Then there was land at Ushuaia where the missionaries could pasture herds bought with money they saved from their incomes. They naturally took advantage of their opportunities. They bought cattle and sheep which were carried there on the society's yacht. The climate and the pasture favored them. The herds and flocks increased. What with his lawful private trade and his lawful stock business while a missionary, Mr. Bridges, no doubt, had ample means for stocking his farm when he left the society's service to turn farmer that he might "insure the well-being of some of the natives." With his twenty-four miles of water front, his cheap labor—the cheapest, for the purpose, found anywhere—and his ready access to market, Mr. Bridges will, doubtless, become one of the wealthiest land-holders in the south part of the continent.

There is one other point which a captious critic might bring against Mr. Bridges, but is one the prospectors would not be likely to think of. Some of the land he now holds once belonged to a number of Yahgan families. Their title was not the indefinite one which a tribe might make to the territory it occupied, but a very clear title—a title that any civilized government would acknowledge. It was theirs by right of possession and improvement. The Yahgans had built houses and had fenced and cultivated this land before Mr. Bridges thought of getting it for himself. One would like to know that Mr. Bridges bought the rights of these Yahgans after he acquired title from the Argentine Government, and that he paid for them more liberally than he was accustomed to pay for labor on the mission grounds.

ON THE PRAIRIES OF TIERRA DEL FUEGO.

Mention has been made of the fact that although all the adventurers in the South Sea were ready to enslave and kill fellow-men found under other flags, and endure all sorts of hardships, as well, for the sake of gold, they nevertheless sailed right past Tierra del Fuego without a stop worth mentioning regardless of the sea beach and grass-root placers that were to be found at many points along shore. Almost equally curious is the fact that the Spaniards in the eighteenth century and the Argentines in these last years should have spent much money in planting colonies on the desert coast of Patagonia when north and east Tierra del Fuego, with a better climate and a soil very much better, lay idly awaiting appropriation. The parts of Tierra del Fuego, with the adjoining islands that made the old explorers shiver, were all to the south and west. The "most savage country I have seen" was found by Captain Cook on the weather side of the Andean range, where it rises south of the Strait of Magellan. All Tierra del Fuego, save for that west coast range, is a great alluvial bed, the work of floods operating during untold ages; and Tierra del Fuego is a triangle-shaped island almost as large as the State of New York. In the old-time mud lie the bones of old-time monkeys, kangaroos, and parrots drowned in floods in the days when Tierra del Fuego had a tropical climate. It is apparent that in old days there was a strait across Patagonia where the Gallegos River is now found, and there is a distinct break in the Andes there. So, too, on Tierra del Fuego there was a similar break running across from San Sebastian to Useless Bay. Both regions are rising rapidly from the sea also. But, unlike Patagonia, the low parts of Tierra del Fuego are well-watered prairies, while the foot-hills of the mountain range are covered with forests of saw timber.

In addition to this, the climate is, considering the latitude and the proximity to Cape Horn, marvellously good. The reason for this is, of course, found in the height of the mountain chain, and of the mountainous islands west and south. These fence off the storms that cover the mountains about Ushuaia with ice and snow. A snowfall of six inches is counted deep on the prairies, and if it lies forty-eight hours on the ground the circumstance is remarkable. On the other hand, there are sufficient falls of rain to keep the prairies covered with the most luxuriant grasses. Because frosts come in every month it is not a good farming country; but, on the other hand, it is rarely cold enough to freeze over the fresh-water ponds.

Probably Argentine has the best part of the prairie region of Tierra del Fuego, but the first attempt to take advantage of the rich pastures was made at Gente Grande Bay, opposite Punta Arenas. Mr. Steubenrach, the British Consular agent, seeing that sheep flourished on the more sterile plains of Patagonia, got a concession from Chili on the Tierra del Fuego side, and after erecting fences and buildings, carried sheep there from the Falkland Islands, " placing a missionary in charge of the farm." The hiring of a missionary was a diplomatic stroke. He was expected to civilize the Ona tribe of Indians living on the prairies and make shepherds of them. This work was begun in approved fashion. Pow-wows were held and presents distributed. The Onas in increased numbers came to the ranch, and made many signs of good-will. But they stole sheep by night, nevertheless—rounded up great bunches of them, which they drove away to some convenient spot, and then hobbled them by breaking their hind legs. In this condition the sheep could still feed and the Onas could feed on them at will.

Thereat the missionary held more pow-wows and argued the matter with them. He explained that eternal perdition awaited the souls of Indians who stole sheep. The Indians were not troubled by that prospect. Indeed, it is said, they wanted to know what awaited white men who took land from the Indians without paying for it, and they could not or would not understand the reply the missionary made to them. They seem to have been as obtuse in understanding points of law regarding land

titles as North American Indians have always been. So
they went on taking sheep in lieu of rentals for the land.

Finding that threats of future fire did not avail him,
the missionary sent to Punta Arenas for Winchesters and
men to use them. Thereafter the propagation of sheep
and the growth of barbed wire fence, and the slaughter
of Indians went on together in right merry fashion, for
everybody but the Indians and an occasional white man
caught napping.

The sheep business is spreading slowly, as all things
are done in Spanish American regions, but it is a sure
growth. It will eventually cover all the grass land of
the island, in spite of the Onas, just as it spread in
Australia in spite of the black fellows, and as cattle
spread in Texas in spite of the Comanches.

THE ONA INDIANS.

The Ona tribe is a distinct race inhabiting the prairie
region of Tierra del Fuego. The traveller who goes
around Tierra del Fuego in the Argentine transports is
sure to see several—children and women, as a rule, who
have been captured by the soldiers that make occasional
forays from two of the three stations that the Argentine
Government maintains on the island. One of these two
stations is at Paramo, mentioned in the chapter on the
gold diggings, and the other is at Thetis Bay on the
south-east corner of the island. At both of these
stations one may usually find a couple of officers and a
soldier or two having their families with them. The
Ona children are used as servants in these families, and
when the families return to Buenos Ayres they carry the
youngsters along with them. I saw a full-grown girl and

a half-grown boy, brother and sister, taken there in the steamer I was on.

In the city they get "a sufficiency of food" and a "semi-annual distribution of clothing."

It was the doings of a party of Ona Indians that gave Tierra del Fuego its name. The Onas have always inhabited the part of the island which Magellan first saw, and their habit of signaling one another by means of fires led them to make extraordinary smokes at the marvellous spectacle of the ships of the navigator. Magellan naturally called it the Land of Fire.

It is a curious fact that the Onas have been mentioned very little in the stories of Cape Horn travellers in comparison with what is said of the Yahgans and the other tribe of the region called the Alaculoofs. Nearly all of the early navigators fell in with Alaculoofs, but so far as I remember only Darwin and Fitzroy make special mention of the larger and strange tribe of the prairies of Tierra del Fuego. Cook did see some and he partly describes them, but he did not understand that a part of the clan he saw was, as his illustration seems to prove, of the Yahgan tribe and part of the Ona.

The reason the Onas were overlooked is made plain to the modern traveller. They were a land tribe; they did not make canoes and they had no horses. The Indians with canoes came off to the ships of the explorers. The Onas could not do so. Moreover, the explorers kept to the north shore of the Strait of Magellan, east of the narrows, because of the more sheltered anchorages there, and so they saw the Tehuelches of Patagonia, but missed the Onas.

People who know the results of white visits to aboriginal tribes will congratulate the Onas.

AN ONA FAMILY.

Modern explorers of Tierra del Fuego,—the prospectors and the plainsmen of Patagonia, believe that the Onas and the Tehuelches are of one origin. In proof of this it is alleged that the languages of the two are so much alike that the two tribes understand each other when brought together.

This brings us to one of the most remarkable facts in connection with the Onas. They do not build boats and neither do the Tehuelches of Patagonia, but considerable numbers of Onas have been found in Patagonia and may still be found there.

How these Onas got over to Patagonia without a boat is an interesting question, but it is not unlikely that they swam across on some hot day in summer at the first narrows in the Strait of Magellan. A strong swimmer could easily cross there at slack water, in spite of the low temperature of the strait.

The Onas in their native land have no horses. They have in these last years captured a good many from the sheep men, but they have eaten them as fast as they got them. Horse meat is the greatest of delicacies to them as it is to the Tehuelches. Their chief dependence for food is the guanaco that abounds in Tierra del Fuego and a prairie squirrel. In the chase they depend on bows and arrows and the bolas chiefly. But the Onas often kill the guanaco by surrounding a bunch and running them down. Thus the Ona has become, probably, the best cross-country runner in the world. One shepherd told me that often, when mounted on a first-class mustang, he had been obliged to chase an Ona five miles across the plain before he could get "within killing range of the thief," and even then the Indian was not unlikely to double or dodge and escape altogether.

The picture of an Ona Indian flying for life across the prairies with a relentless horseman in pursuit is something to stir the blood of the spectator; it would stir the blood of a citizen of "the boundless plains" of the United States in one way, and that of "the Quakers in the effete East" in another, however. But it is a picture often seen in these days in Tierra del Fuego.

The home of the Ona is as bad as any in the world. A saucer-shaped hollow big enough for a bed for all the family is scooped in the ground. In the little ridge about this poles and brush are placed, and over the weather side of the brush is thrown a skin or two. The fire is usually built just without, but near the door of the hut. It is more useful for cooking food than for imparting warmth. The Onas at night allow the fire to go out. To protect themselves from the cold they resort to a novel blanket. They all lie down on the ground with the children in the middle of the huddle, and then call their dogs to come and lie around and over them. It is a poverty-stricken Ona family that has not enough dogs to cover it out of sight. The dogs are a sharp-nosed but hairy lot, and they certainly keep the family warm.

The fact that all the tribes of the Cape Horn region build such wretched houses has always been taken as a proof of their lack of intelligence. How great a mistake was thus made in the case of the Yahgans has already been shown. The Onas, as will some day be learned, are also misjudged. The reason for building so frail a shelter is apparent on a brief consideration of their method of life. They are necessarily nomads. When the food of one spot was eaten they had to migrate. Now, the Onas had no horses or beasts of burden, as did the Tehuelches. They could not carry big skin tents about as the Tehuelches did. So they built a temporary shelter only. In the coldest weather a location near the seashore, where mussels and fish abounded, was usually chosen, and there they built larger and better wigwams. When they migrated to Patagonia and acquired horses they made skin tents. They did not make poor shelters from any lack of intelligence.

The skin of the Ona is remarkably white for one who lives all but naked in the open air. Their hair is black, but lustreless, and they have a curious habit of singeing off the hair so as to leave a tonsure on top of the head just where the North American Indian allowed the hair to grow long for a scalp lock. The face is oval, the eyes dark and pleasant, the cheek bones not too prominent, the nose sometimes quite prominent, and the mouth full and with regular but yellowish teeth. Because whiskers come late in life, and so are an indication of coming age, the men pluck them out, through a desire to appear young; but after thirty-five they let the beard grow because of the pain of pulling so many hairs as then come. They are remarkable for using combs made of whalebone. No other tribe near Cape Horn does that.

Their shoulders are broad and strong and the chests deep. The mothers have hanging breasts, but those of the maidens are well-rounded and firm. The arms and limbs are round and sinewy, but the stomach, especially after a square meal, is very prominent.

Of the capacity of the Ona's stomach, one story will serve. A girl of about fifteen, who was captured on a northern ranch, refused to eat for eight days, and then appetite got the better of her temper. A sheep had been roasted whole for the dinner of the rancher's family, but the Ona girl was allowed to begin on it, and seeing that her appetite was good, she was not interrupted. When she had finished, so they say, she had cleaned all the bones of the sheep.

For making a fire the Onas carry bits of iron ore, which come from an island in the Alaculoof region, west of Tierra del Fuego, and are obtained by barter with that tribe. Flints and agates abound in the Ona country, and these with the ore and a bit of dry fungus, always carried wrapped in a bit of hide or a bladder, enable the Ona to light a fire even in a rain-storm.

The Ona bows are made of native wood worked into shape with shell knives where civilized knives are not to be had, but so many prospectors have been killed by them in recent years, that the tribe is fairly well supplied with cutlery. Then, too, barrels drift ashore from Cape Horn ships, and the iron hoops are made into knives. The ships also supply materials for tips for the Ona arrows in the shape of whiskey bottles. Very fine points are made from glass by the Ona artisans. The arrows are made of a kind of reed, and are so light as to be well-nigh useless when fired against the wind.

Very little is known of the Ona language, save that it is as harsh as the Yahgan is liquid. Their religious beliefs, too, are unknown. When in distress, as when captured by the whites, the old cut long and deep slashes in the chest with any sharp thing at hand; but when once they find themselves well treated they become bright and cheerful and affectionate, and rarely evince a disposition to leave their captors. From what is said of these captives (who are in all cases held, as said, practically as slaves, in that they receive only food and clothes for their labor), it is plain that the Ona is an agressive warrior toward the whites only because of ill-treatment.

When the Rev. Bridges and the Right Rev. Sterling once made a journey across the island they had not one bit of trouble. They did not kill anybody, did not have any cause for firing a gun, or making either an aggressive or defensive movement. Damnable ill-treatment on the part of the whites is at the bottom of all the Ona aggressiveness—and Ona suffering.

The only effort that has been made to alleviate the sufferings of the Onas at the hands of the whites was the establishing of a Catholic mission near San Sebastian Bay. When I was there no success had been attained by the mission. On the contrary, a priest, who had gone with a guide to seek for the Onas, had failed to return, and when a party of sailors from the nearby sub-prefectura went to look for the two, they found their heads only. The Onas have been made to suffer so much that they will not now trust any one.

When prospectors have disappeared only their bones have usually been found, and these were always marked either with fire or human teeth. The Onas eat the whites they capture, hoping thereby to obtain the white man's valor.

In their fierce fight for their homes, the Onas have an advantage in the fact that the dividing line between the Argentine's and Chili's shares of the island runs through the heart of their country. Each white nation is very much opposed to allowing the other to invade its territory with an armed force, and so the efforts of the sailors and soldiers of either side must end near the line, if not on it. So pursuit of the Onas is always ineffectual. Nevertheless, the shepherd will drive them into a corner at last by extending his wire fences, and then extermination will come.

It is an interesting fact in medical science, that the Onas a long time ago discovered a sure and speedy remedy for the chief ill that Indians are heir to through association with the whites, in a decoction of the thorny bush that grows on the plains, and is known to science as *berberis*.

THE ALACULOOFS.

One tribe inhabiting the Cape Horn region remains to be mentioned. It is found exclusively among the islands west of Punta Arenas and Cockburn Channel. I wish that I had the facts for describing it. This is the tribe that has been mentioned so often by people passing through the Strait of Magellan. They were invariably called Fuegians by all who saw them, and were described in terms to indicate that they are the most wretched, the most filthy, the most degraded, and the most terrible beings on earth. As I said, I should like to know the facts, for these descriptions, except as to their appearance to a casual observer, are valueless. The Yahgans were described in equally severe terms.

On the beach at Punta Arenas the citizens pointed to a dismantled sloop that was hauled up to be sold at auction. She was a ragged thing, say twenty feet long. There was a large hatch amidships with splashes of blood on it, and a number of holes where Winchester bullets had come up through the boards from below. She bore the name of *Teresina B*. With four men as a crew and a cargo of tobacco, rum, old clothes, matches, hard bread, cheap cutlery, etc., she had sailed away from Punta Arenas for a trading voyage to the Alaculoof Indians. Her crew were bound, in a small way, on a voyage like that of the great Magellan ; they meant to

ALUCULOOF INDIANS.

get valuables in return for things of little value. When about forty-five miles south of the town they sent a man ashore in a small boat for wood and water, and that was the last ever seen of the man. The next morning three canoes loaded with Indians came in view. Thereat one of the white sailors urged the sloop's captain to make the Indians stay away, or at least to permit but two or three men in one canoe to approach at a time. To this the captain replied that the Indians were Christian Yahgans from Ushuaia, and just what were wanted.

"Very well," said the sailor, "you may do the trading. I'll go down below."

He went below and drew the hatch almost to its place and fastened it. The captain and the other sailor remained on deck to trade, the sailor sitting over the companion-way.

As the Indians drew alongside it appeared that they were Alaculoofs instead of Yahgans, and they dropped their paddles, and, grasping their harpoons, attacked the whites. Both white men were badly wounded by the first harpoons thrown. The sailor fell into the cabin, his head badly cut, and all life apparently gone. The captain had life enough to try to crawl down, but the Indians were on him, and he was harpooned to death.

Then the Indians swarmed on the sloop, and the man who had fled to the hold opened fire with his rifle. The Indians tried to get at him with their harpoons, but the white man's weapon was too much for them, and they had to flee.

This is the story the man who hid in the hold told after he got back to Punta Arenas, bringing the body of the captain and the wounded sailor. It may be true. The Indians have been swindled and openly robbed, maltreated, and murdered often by these Punta Arenas traders, and if they did not retaliate sometimes one would not think well of them.

Early in 1894 the Catholics of Punta Arenas established a mission station in the Alaculoof territory. Possibly this mission will do the Indians good instead of harm.

CHAPTER VI.

STATEN ISLAND OF THE FAR SOUTH.

WHEN the ordinary citizen of New York city hears any one speak of Staten Island the name at once recalls to his mind a host of pictures of ferryboats crossing a beautiful bay; a landing where vociferous men in uniform and rapid-transit trains await the rush of passengers; shady avenues leading over rolling green hills; charming cottage homes with grassy lawns and tennis courts about them; booming town sites; a sea beach devoted to fun that is hilarious rather than joyous; oyster beds and fishing smacks—a most remarkable conglomeration of metropolitan, rural, and alongshore life, and all within a half-hour's journey of the city which he proudly calls his own. To a few—to a gray-haired merchant here and there down town, a few grizzled watchmen about the shipping, sundry skippers of the ships where the watchmen are employed, all of whom have seen service in the sealing ships of twenty-five years and more ago—a reference to Staten Island awakens memories of an entirely different nature. Instead of the smooth waters of New York harbor they think of a boisterous sea; instead of leafy avenues, bordered by charming homes, they see only foaming surf, with dark and threatening cliffs ; instead of the pleasures of tennis court or the hilarious dance, they remember only the whizz of a hurricane in a ship's rigging, and work on deck when drenched by icy sleet and rain. The one knows only the Staten Island that bounds the south side of New York bay ; the other knows as well, perhaps is much more familiar with, that other American Staten Island lying more than 7000 miles away in the Cape Horn region.

No more lovely Indian summer day was ever seen than the first day of the Antarctic winter, June 1, of the year 1894, as enjoyed by the passengers and crew of the Argentine naval transport *Ushuaia*, as she steamed out of the east end of Beagle Channel and headed for the Strait of Le Maire, bound to St. John harbor, in the east end of the Antarctic Staten Island. The air was soft and warm, the water dimpled, the leaves on the waving trees ashore flashed in the sunlight, the distant snow-capped mountains rose through a dreamy haze. And so the conditions remained until the sun went down and the slender arc of the new moon appeared among the luminous mists of the western sky. To the passengers the prospect of a delightful night was all that could be asked, but the old salts shook their heads.

"You just hold fast all till midnight," said one to whom a passenger spoke enthusiastically of the weather. "To-night is the change of the moon, eh?" and he nodded his head toward the west.

Sure enough, by midnight a northwest gale fit to twist the life out of a ship was roaring over the water, and the little *Ushuaia* was pitching and tossing along like a Newport catboat in a cross sea. She was then in the Strait

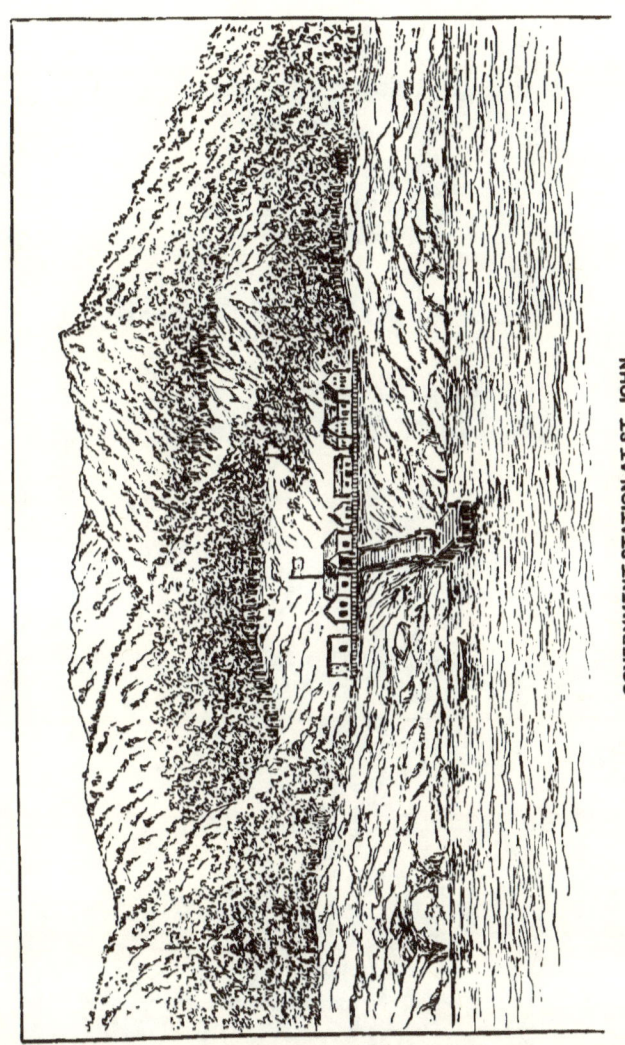

GOVERNMENT STATION AT ST. JOHN.
FROM A SKETCH BY COMMANDER CHWAITES, A. N.

of Le Maire, and a worse current for a contrary wind can probably be found nowhere in the world. It is a rush of broken water hurrying along at from five to six and a half knots an hour, while the tide rips, formed by the eddies off the capes on both sides of the strait, are something to make a seaman gasp. Luckily for us, we had a seaboat of a model fit even for a maelstrom, and with scarce a sea on deck we labored through the worst of it, and at daylight next morning the outline of "the rugged inhospitable Staten land was visible amidst the clouds" on the starboard bow.

Thereafter we cruised along, heading to the east, for several hours within a very few miles of the coast, and the passengers gathered on deck to gaze on such landscapes as only those who travel out of the usual way may enjoy. And certainly it was a view worth all the discomforts of a long and stormy voyage, for here is found the end of the mountain system of all the Americas. Cape Horn Island is, in a sense, the south end of the Americas, but the backbone of the hemisphere bends to the east at Mount Sarmiento on Tierra del Fuego, and running along the shore of that great island is broken by the Strait of Le Maire, as it was broken by the Strait of Magellan, only to appear again beyond the narrow water in the cliffs and ridges and gulches of Staten Island. It is not until one has been on or around Cape St. John, on the east end of this island, that he can accurately say he has rounded the southern end of the American continent.

It is true that at first glance one would scarcely recognize any relationship between the Rocky Mountain system and the ridges of Staten Island, but one does not need to be a geologist to recognize a certain similarity on a closer inspection. And nowhere will the similarity be recognized more quickly than when passing New Year's Islands, just off the north coast of Staten. Here on these islands, small as they are, the traveller sees a tiny picture of the plains of Colorado, below Pike's Peak, and if he will but land there, and wash a panful of dirt, he will find at the bottom the kind of dust that has made Cripple Creek famous.

As seen from the passing steamer, Staten Island is a continuous ridge varying for the most part from 2000 to 3000 feet above the sea. The sides seem steep and the tops are rounded. The snow line in June was about 1000 feet above the sea, but the use of the word line should not be understood to imply that the snow ended at any well-defined limit. Not all the crests 2000 feet high were white, and on the sides of the mountains the drifts and blotches of snow sometimes reached down to within 500 or 600 feet of the surf. Still, there was comparatively little snow below an altitude of 1000 feet, and not much bare ground above that limit. At a distance of five or six miles the colors of the uncovered parts of the mountains were dark grays and black. The rocks looked very like the rocky declivities one may see all along the Hudson, though in no other respect was the scenery like that on the Hudson. A closer view of the island showed that the darkest shades of the mountain sides were green rather than black, and were due to wide masses of vegetation, among which tree trunks could be distinguished with a glass. But there was no sign of animal life ashore.

Over the sea, however, as we steamed along, the air fairly teemed with antarctic life. Ducks in flocks a half mile long drifted and sailed hither and yon. The little Cape Horn pigeons, whose black backs and wings are most beautifully mottled with white, floated in scores and hundreds in the air about the ship, sometimes so closely that one could almost touch them with the hand. The huge white albatross, with its ten-foot spread of wings, careened up and down and around, as if for the pure love of the motion, while coal black gulls—the web-footed ravens of the sea—contested with their light-colored cousins for the refuse thrown from the ship. Then there were the penguins. Once, as we steamed along, we ran into a flock of them, and sent them diving from wave to wave—in on one side and out on the other—in a way that at first sight made the spectators think that they were a school of fish, short and thick, black on top, and with a white stripe on the side, skurrying away for life. Even now, as I think of them, I am haunted with a doubt as to whether, after all, when I thought I saw webbed feet and outstretched neck, I was not mistaken, so great was the resemblance of the fleeing penguin to a fish. And then there was a tiny kind of gull, the male of which was almost pure white—a bird that seemed little, if any, larger than a robin. It was a most wary and most sprightly little fellow, and it almost always preferred diving to flying. In short, nowhere in the whole voyage of the *Ushuaia*, of which the trip to St. John harbor was but a small part, did I see bird life so abundant, so varied, or so beautiful and interesting as off the coast of Staten Island.

By ten o'clock in the morning we were plainly approaching the barren, bold promontory that faced the giant seas at the east end of the island. The gale of the night before had moderated considerably by that time, but the nearer we approached the headland the more boisterous did the sea seem to be before us. To the passengers who did not know the place we seemed to be rushing into a tide rip more dangerous than anything we had seen, but just when we were preparing for the tossing that appeared inevitable, the frowning coast line opened. A fiord between the mountains was seen off the starboard bow, and we at once headed in for it. The tide rip off the east end of the island, a rip that has mention in all the coast guides and charts of the Cape Horn region, begins at this harbor.

As we entered the mouth of the fiord, we could see that on a rock jutting out from the westerly side was a building in form and apparently in size the exact counterpart of the six-sided peanut and candy pavilions one can see about the picnic and other resorts near New York. Its peaked roof was surmounted by a bulbous cupola like the top of a tower of a Jewish synagogue, and near by was a tall flagstaff from which the blue-white-blue Argentine flag flapped vigorously in the gale.

By and by we got pretty close under this rock, and then we could see some men in naval uniform standing on a ledge beside a little cannon, which they fired off just as we ran from the breaking waves that were dashing across the mouth of the harbor into the oil-smooth water within. The ship answered the salute with a roaring blast of her whistle, and then we rounded the crag where the pavilion stood, and found ourselves in what looked like a bowl-shaped bay, walled in by precipices so high as to make our vessel seem utterly insignificant. Then on one side of this bowl, fifty feet or so above the water, was seen a row of little light-colored wooden houses, built on a narrow bench on the mountain side. There was a flagstaff before the largest of the buildings, and a neat

picket fence before the whole row. From the centre of
this fence a stairway ran down the steep decline from
the bench to the beach, and from the foot of the stair a
narrow pier projected a hundred feet into the bay. There
were davits on both sides of the pier, with boats hanging
to them, and not far away was a big lifeboat of heavy
model lying at anchor. The grass that had grown below the water line of the lifeboat was so long that it
could be seen a hundred yards away as she rolled lazily
in the dead swell.

As soon as we had cast anchor a couple of officers and a
crew of sailors came down to the pier, and then rowed
off to us in one of the boats. There were enthusiastic
greetings between those in the boat and their friends on
the ship.

The little row of houses built on a cleft, so to speak,
in the side of the rugged mountains that border St. John
Bay is known among Argentine seamen as the "Sub-
Prefectura del Puerto San Juan del Salvamiento." It
was established late in the Antarctic summer of 1884. It
should be kept in mind that the chief object of creating
a Government post on Staten Island was for the support
of a light-house to guide ships bound around the Horn,
but a secondary consideration was the providing of a
place of refuge with a depot of provisions for the crew
of any ship so unfortunate as to be wrecked thereabouts.
It was estimated that from seven hundred to one thousand ships of various nationalities pass within sight of
Staten Island every year, and that before this light was
established about one in a hundred was wrecked there.
These estimates were wrong, but they had the effect of
establishing the station.

In the United States the crew of a first-class lighthouse

consists of three men. That of a life-saving station consists of a coxswain and not less than six men. To man the third-class light-house on Staten Island four men were provided, while in addition to the coxswain and crew of a life-boat there was a naval officer of the rank of a lieutenant, known as the prefect ; a second in command of a lower rank, a secretary to the prefect, a valet, a cook, a baker, and a file of soldiers.

Having learned this much while on the ship, it was with a great deal of curiosity that I climbed from the boat to the pier and walked ashore.

The foot of the bluff had been terraced with spiles to keep the seas from washing out the soil there, and it was said that a northeast gale sent an ugly swell into that part of the bay in spite of the shelter of the point on which I had seen the pavilion. Under such circumstances, the only perfectly safe anchorage for a vessel was further up the fiord around a bend. Although the *Ushuaia* seemed to be anchored in a bowl-shaped bay, there was really a passage through what seemed to be the western wall of the bowl, and a plan of the whole fiord as laid down on the chart was really of the shape of a sock.

The stairway up from the pier had a railway of wooden timbers, with a winch at the top designed for hauling up and lowering the boats, but it seems never to have been used. At the head of the stairs was a bell that had been taken from the English ship *Guy Mannering* that ran into the rocks not far away during a fog in 1892. From the stairs we went to the Governor's house. The Governor was at home in Buenos Ayres on a vacation, but his assistant, with the secretary, did the honors. They had a very good quality of brandy, and very good wine, also. The house was built of planed pine. It was somewhat in the form of a right-angled U, open toward the fiord. The house was ceiled instead of plastered, and was plainly but comfortably furnished. That is to say, it was comfortable for one who could enjoy that climate unmodified by artificial means. To a citizen of the United States the Governor's house was lacking in the one thing most necessary for comfort in a climate where cold and stormy weather is the rule and the thermometer never goes above 12° centigrade. There was no heating stove in it. With the exception of the cook, the baker, and one sailor, that entire crew lived day and night in a moist atmosphere, where the thermometer ranged from 30° to 40° Fahrenheit almost every day in the year.

From the Governor's house a trail led along the mountain side, across a roaring brook, with waters as black as those in an Adirondack stream, and off over the crest of the promontory that half closes the mouth of the fiord. The Governor told me it was a well-made road, and, except for a ten-rod strip across a swamp, it was paved with stone. In the swamp there was a stone here and there—almost enough to enable an active man to cross dry shod. For the last thirty yards before reaching the end of the promontory the trail was a narrow goat path on the crest of a precipice one hundred feet high, facing the sea. With the mighty waves from across the ocean thundering against the foot of that great wall, throwing their spray high over its crest, and at times sweeping pebbles from the pathway, with the solid water rising up as if to grasp the wayfarer, that is a trail of which one may well think with a feeling of awe as well as of delight.

On a level table of solid rock at the end of this path stood the little six-sided pavilion I had seen from the sea. It was built of wood, with an iron roof, and the three sides toward the sea were filled with window glass in frames that could be removed. Inside the pavilion and facing these window frames stood two benches like two steps of a stairway. On the lower bench was a row of three locomotive head-lights. On the upper were two head-lights with a ship's anchor light (Fresnel lens) between them. The little pavilion was the light-house of St. John's Cape, Staten Island, in the route to the Horn.

In a little room at the back of the pavilion were the materials for keeping the lamps clean and bright. The place seemed to be well kept. A small wooden shanty near by was the bunk-room of the four men who attended to the lamps. A telephone was in one corner of the pavilion, but the line to the prefect's house was out of order.

Returning to the little settlement, I found that the bakery was a log-house, and so was one of the storerooms. In store it is said that a sufficient supply of dry and salt provisions for six months is kept.

While looking about the buildings one of the sailors came to me, and, speaking in English, said he had heard I was from New York city, and thereafter for ten minutes I was kept busy answering questions asked with the eagerness of one who has a great longing to hear from home. By and by he was willing to talk of himself, though anxious to conceal his name, "because I do not want my people to know how I am living. They would rather I was dead than what I am." He had been the unruly member of a wealthy German family in New York, and had a great desire for the sea. He was placed on the schoolship *St. Mary's*, and in the spring of 1883, when almost ready to graduate, had had a fight with one of the ship's naval officers, after which he jumped over-

STATEN ISLAND OF THE FAR SOUTH. 147

board, swam ashore, and later shipped on the Yankee war ship *Nipsic*, which some time later sailed to Buenos Ayres. There he deserted her, and, having picked up a little Spanish, shipped in the Argentine navy as a full-fledged seaman, the navy department there preferring men who could speak English. He was afterward sent to Tierra del Fuego to man one of the stations established there in 1884. Then he went back to Buenos Ayres, where he readily got employment in a mercantile house because he spoke two languages, besides Spanish, fluently. He lost his job through dissipation after a while, and then drifted back to the navy. Once more he went to Tierra del Fuego, and there picked up a good-looking young squaw for a companion. When transferred to Staten Island he was allowed to take her along. I visited the strange couple in their home. It was a house 8x10 feet in size and 7 feet high. The frame was wood, and the covering sheet-iron. It had no ceiling of any kind. The furniture consisted of a bed, a chair, a table, a packing case, a couple of chests, and a heating stove for burning wood. And that was the only stove of that kind I saw south of Buenos Ayres.

The young man was an excellent penman, and so had what he called a soft snap. He kept the books and did the writing generally of the station, while the other members of the crew of his rank had such hard work to do as the station required. I asked him if he was ever homesick, and he said he was not, except when he happened to meet a Yankee, and that had not happened before since leaving Buenos Ayres. He was receiving $30 paper (say $7.50 gold) a month, with rations and clothing for himself and squaw. The squaw took good care of him, and did laundry work besides for the officers.

"I do not care for what you call civilization," he said. "I have everything I want that is within the reach of a poor man anywhere. I am very much better off than the workingmen in New York. Why should I not be contented? If I ever make a pile I'll go back, of course. I may take Cheenah there sometime, anyway, if I can do it without being recognized. She wants to go and I want to please her. But if I don't strike it rich, what do I care?"

I have given this much space to the young man, because it is the true story of a boy who ran away to sea, and so will be of interest to other boys who would like to run away as he did.

A tour afoot over the island would be interesting, though a journey of great hardship. The coast line is but a series of fiords and bays. Behind New Year's Island, on the north side, is a bay that sets in almost to the centre of the island. Another from the south comes almost to meet it, the waters being separated by a low neck of sand, say 300 steps across. The traveller can find here the wreck of an old tramway by which the Yankee sealers, say fifteen years ago, used to run their whaleboats from one water to the other. It is certain that this neck of sand did not always exist. The scientists say that Staten Island is rising rapidly—that some of the bays now too shoal for a ship to enter afforded good harbors in the days when the discoverers of the region were beating to and fro. However, these two bays are still fair harbors, and the sealing crews used them every year. One finds old kettles and vats used for trying out the oil of the hair seal and the sea lion, as well as of the whales that were once numerous. There is also an old shanty that would be useful still to any crew so unfortunate as to be wrecked there. A couple of goldhunters, who worked the sand on New Year's Island with success in 1893, used the old shanty as headquarters. A whale may be seen about the island now and then in these days. So, too, may a few seals and sea lions, but there are not enough to pay working as yet, although the hunt was abandoned there some years ago, and the game is slowly increasing.

To travel along the beach of the island is impossible, save for short stretches. The sea breaks against the almost vertical cliffs for the greater part of the way. The way over the mountains has been attempted occasionally. Singular as it may seem to one who sees the rounded contour of these mountains—a contour which one thinks would give a perfect drainage—the chief obstacle to a tramp overland is the long succession of bogs and swamps. There are bogs that are impassable to a man without snow-shoes, which lie at an angle of thirty degrees with the horizon, if one may believe the crew of the St. John station. The bogs are masses of moss, roots, and rotten vegetation that hold water like a sponge, and yield under the foot as slushy snow would do. Where the bogs are not found there are wide breadths of forests, and very interesting as well as impassable forests they are. At the sea level the trees may be from thirty to forty feet high, with slender trunks and flat, thick, interlaced tops. As one works his way up the mountain the trees are found to be smaller, but standing closer together and having the tops more closely interlaced, until at last, with a forest three or four feet high, one can almost walk on the flattened tops of the trees—one could so walk with the aid of Norwegian skees.

Since the fur and oil industry was destroyed, Staten

Island has produced nothing for export. That some part of the island could be devoted to sheep-raising there is little doubt. The Falklands, where M. Bougainville vainly endeavored to plant a French colony, now support about 2500 people, who are all well to do through raising sheep. The centre of Staten Island has the best climate, and, according to those who have climbed about the region, a ranch properly located would make its owner rich. An advantage which Staten Island has over the Falklands is in the supply of wood, but this, on the other hand, would compel the building of fences to keep the sheep out of the brush. Besides, there is so much good land for sheep in Tierra del Fuego yet unoccupied, that no one is likely to try to develop such resources as Staten Island may have for many years to come, unless, indeed, some one be found bold enough to brave the certain dangers of the seas for the sake of the gold on New Year's Island.

CHAPTER VII.

THE NOMADS OF PATAGONIA.

THE story of the nomads of Patagonia living east of the Andes—the Tehuelche Indians,—is, on the whole, more cheerful reading than that of either of the other tribes of the region. For over 350 years after they were discovered by white men they maintained an undisputed sway over their desert territory. They were visited by missionaries, but were never brought into the enervating subjection to them that ruined the Yahgan. They were physically and mentally a noble race of aborigines, and when at last they went down before a merciless civilization, they fell, man fashion, face to the enemy.

Brief space will suffice here for a resumé of what history tells of them. It was on April 1, 1520, when they first saw "men with faces like the snow." Magellan had happened into St. Julian harbor. They came with wonder to see marvellous vessels that brought him, and it is said that they tell around their camp-fires to this day of the trick by which he succeeded in loading two of their chiefs with chains that he might carry them away forever.

The Tehuelches were afoot, then, but it was not many

years before horses from the Spanish settlement at Buenos Ayres had spread to the Strait of Magellan, and so the explorers of the seventeenth and eighteenth centuries found them mounted. They were not a vicious race; on the contrary, they were of kindly diposition, and even playful when well treated, though their experiences with the whites eventually taught them duplicity, theft, and outrage. But their good dispositions did not attract white settlers, because the whole of Patagonia, east of the Andes, was a desert that seemed wholly incapable of supporting a civilized being.

However, the Jesuits came to them bringing the cross in one hand and apple-seeds in the other. The cross did not flourish, but the apple-seeds planted about the lakes in Western Patagonia grew into a great forest, that has produced abundance of fruit and much strong cider ever since.

Later still, at the end of the eighteenth century, Spain attempted to establish colonies at Rio Negro, Port St. Julian, and Port Desire. They did some little trading, but the Indians very properly mistrusted the good faith of the whites, and in 1807 Patagonia was once more abandoned to the natives, save for the one post on the Rio Negro known as Carmen de Patagones. This was maintained partly because of the great salt fields found on the desert near the town. But the terms on which it remained unmolested by the lordly Patagonians were exceedingly humiliating to the Spanish rulers of Buenos Ayres and of the settlement. The whites had to pay an annual tribute of cattle, knife-blades, indigo, cochineal, and other goods as rental for the Indian-owned land they occupied.

We read in the history of the State of New York

that in the days before the Revolution, the brave old Mohawks used to send a warrior, now and then, alone among the Hudson River and even the Long Island tribes, entering this or that village, walking in the midst of a group of the head men, and while they cowered in his presence, addressing them as squaws and denouncing them for this and that failure in their duty to the noble tribe he represented. In like manner, even until within twenty-five years of this writing, has a Tehuelche chief from the desert of Patagonia been known to ride alone down the main street of Carmen de Patagones to the plaza. Reining in his horse by the low-peaked stone monument still to be seen there, he would shake the great skin mantle from his brawny shoulders, strike the butt of his spear a ringing blow on the pedestal of the monument to call the whites about him, and then, in disdainful words and with imperious manner, ask why the tribute had been delayed. All of this the whites bore meekly and meanly. They could not fight the Indians successfully, and they were willing to submit to such treatment because of the profit in the trade they carried on with their red masters.

If any one wants fully to appreciate how degrading trade is to the human soul, let him read the stories of white traders among red buyers.

In modern times—rather in the nineteenth century, two efforts to convert the Patagonians to Christianity have been made, one of which is of especial interest to American readers, because undertaken by a citizen of New York at the behest of the American Board of Christian Missionaries of Boston. One Captain Benjamin Morrell had been on a sealing voyage along the Patagonia coast, through the strait and up the Chili coast, and on returning had brought an interesting story about the aborigines. The story was printed in book-form and the missionary society people read the book, and were thereby led to send out a couple of missionaries to look over the region and the people Morrell had described. Mr. Titus Coan, then a student at the Auburn Theological Seminary, and a Mr. Arms of Andover were selected. A sealing schooner took them to the Strait of Magellan, and on November 14, 1833, at the beginning of the warm season there, they landed. That they were kindly received and well treated scarce need be said. They brought a tent and a variety of articles, which were of the greatest value to the Indians, but they were never robbed. On the contrary, they were freely supplied with the best the Indians had. In return the missionaries did some work, such as sharpening knives, making wooden spurs, etc., but, on the whole, the missionaries lived on the charity of the Indians. Their experiences and thoughts have been preserved in a book entitled *Adventures in Patagonia*, by Titus Coan. They travelled about with a host that for a time was composed of Tehuelches or Patagonians proper, and of Onas who had come over from Tierra del Fuego. They had to live on such food as the country supplied, of course, and to endure the vicissitudes of the climate.

They remained only a few days more than two months, leaving the region in a sealing schooner on January 25, 1834. They had had enough of life with a nomadic race on a stormy desert like Patagonia. Horseflesh was not suited to their stomachs nor tent life to their inclinations. The Indians had told them plainly that no missionary could succeed who would not live Indian fashion, and that settled it. Of course these Patagonians had souls,

Mr. Coan was sure those souls were going to be lost—absolutely sure of it, unless, indeed, some one taught them "the way of life." But there were souls elsewhere in the world that needed saving, too—among the South Sea islands, for instance, where snow was unknown, and horseflesh was not esteemed a dainty. It would be much more comfortable to convert wicked South Sea Islanders than Patagonians.

As was said, for 360 years after Magellan's infamous disregard of the rights of man, the Indians of Patagonia in their conflicts with white aggressors held their own. It was a pity in the eyes of a humanitarian that there should have been conflicts, for all were utterly needless, but, on the whole, the Patagonia day was bright.

Then came the setting of the sun. The day of all the Patagonian Indians was ended. The "progress of civilization" demanded the extermination of the desert races. The pressure of Christian owners of cattle and sheep for new pastures demanded that the best of the hunting grounds of the Indians be taken. The frontier of settlements in Argentine had to be extended to the Rio Negro because cattlemen wanted the land, and the cheapest way to make the extension was by war. In these matters the civilized people of the Argentine have been as much like the civilized people of the United States as two bullets from one mould.

This war of extermination cannot be described here, but one feature of it may serve to give the reader some idea about its general characteristics.

It was not uncommon for the soldiers to take a stalwart Indian prisoner, and after tying him so that his struggles would be unavailing, to cut his throat slowly with a dull knife.

"I have often seen them haggle away at a Tehuelche throat—haggle and saw, while he writhed and begged for the stroke of grace, for full five minutes before the artery was severed and his life-blood made to spurt out on the sand. And while they tortured each victim thus, they would turn to any one not of their nationality and say, by way of apology for their cruelty:

"'He is no Christian.'"

So said a German to me in Buenos Ayres, a man who had been with both of Roca's expeditions, and of whose veracity there need be no doubt whatever.

Shocking as was the cruelty meted out to the Indians, only the sight of it could stir the indignation of the spectator more than the excuse for it which the soldiers gave—"he's no Christian." And yet, before the reader's feelings lead him to a bitter condemnation of the soldiers, let it be remembered that, according to the orthodox religious teachings in these United States of North America, there were in the air, about each group of those Argentine soldiers, numbers of evil spirits watching the torture of each unfortunate Indian—watching with eager malice the moment when the Indian's soul should be released, that they might bear it away to the realm "where the worm dieth not and the fire is not quenched." The soldiers tortured for five minutes, but these devils will torment each Tehuelche soul for all eternity. And, what is more, could the reader enter the precincts of the unfortunates and ask why the soul was tortured, he would get, word for word, the very excuse the Argentine soldiers gave:

"He is no Christian."

The home region of the Tehuelche is a section of the bottom of the South Atlantic Ocean lifted up where man can see it. There are salt lakes and beds of salts, left there when the sea-water was for the most part drained away. There are traces of ocean salts everywhere. It is an alluvial region; a well-driller would find many layers of sand, gravel, clays, etc., but no rock beds, save in a few places where volcanoes bubbled up, nobody knows when. The only volcanic rocks the traveller alongshore will see, however, are at Port Desire and south of the Rio Gallegos. At Port Desire the bluffs on the north shore are volcanic, while some leagues south of Gallegos is a range of volcanic peaks that show conspicuously above the plain. Elsewhere the traveller sees only a desert that is for the most part level, but has been worn into gulches along such streams as exist and shows, as one travels inland, a terrace-like formation. It is an arid desert for the most part, " but springs and fresh-water streams can be found every hundred miles or so. You will rarely have to pass more than one night without water if you journey from Punta Arenas to Buenos Ayres," as an official at Santa Cruz said.

But inhospitable as the desert seems to be, it has afforded during the knowledge of man subsistence for herds of guanacos and flocks of ostriches, probably the only beings that survived all the changes in the region since the days when monkeys, parrots, kangaroos, and elephants abounded in the unsubmerged parts. The desert seems to have been peculiarly well adapted to guanacos and ostriches, and the flesh of these with dandelions, bunch grass-seed, fungi, etc., seems to have been peculiarly well adapted to sustain a race of men that were physically magnificent. An official at Punta Arenas told me that the measurements of one hundred Tehuelche men, taking them as they came to the settlement, gave an average height of over five feet ten inches. When it is considered that some of these were half bloods, or men having had Argentine and Chilian fathers, the average indicates a great race. The missionary, Titus Coan, found a noticeable number of men six feet six inches tall in his day. Rarely, if at all, will such a one be found now, but the gauchos and others with whom I talked assured me that men of six feet three and four inches were quite common. Patagonia has always been a region favorable for developing the human frame, and in the days when the Tehuelches were horseless, and so had to outrun afoot, the ostrich and guanaco, there were giants beyond doubt among the race that averaged the tallest on earth. Their frames were not only large, but their strength was prodigious. A man in health could really drag a balky horse across the desert.

By the Indian standard they were a handsome race. The men showed intelligent, vigorous minds in their faces. Their foreheads were high, their noses of the Roman type, the nostrils not unduly expanded. Their teeth were simply perfect; so were their eyes. Those I saw in the settlements showed a heavy, stolid expression, but the gauchos said that look was not a good indication of their character; that when in their desert wilds the men as well as the women were a merry-faced, laughing lot. The young folks are everywhere bright-faced and of cheerful dispositions. The young women are said to be particularly attractive, having very light skins for Indians, beautiful limbs, firm and well-rounded breasts, heads poised like young queens, and faces that show a mingling of modesty and coquetry quite impossible to describe or catch with a camera, but nevertheless within the appreciation of even a blasé beholder.

A TEHUELCHE SQUAW.

Like many of their white cousins, the Tehuelche girls continually chew gum—the exuded and hardened juice of the incense bush that abounds on the desert. So, too, do the Tehuelche men, for that matter, and they say it preserves the teeth. Certainly no people have finer teeth than the Tehuelches.

It is impossible to give anything like an accurate estimate of the number of red inhabitants of Patagonia, either now or at any period since the days of Magellan. The Rev. Titus Coan thought the Tehuelche tribe numbered 1000 in 1833. Don Ramon Lista, an Argentine writer and explorer of good repute, says that when he was among them just before the war of extermination they numbered 500 warriors, or nearly 3000 souls all told. There are now a few at Coy Inlet, a few hanging about each settlement, and a few along the Andes—perhaps 500 all told, according to the gauchos.

For an estimate of the Tehuelche mental calibre we can readily resort to their mythology, fables and proverbs of which, fortunately for ethnologists, a number have been preserved. The scientific world is especially indebted to Don Ramon Lista, who was careful, when among the Tehuelches, to collect as much of what may be called their literature as possible. As examples, here are two Tehuelche fables :

THE FATE OF THE BOASTER.

A fox challenged a stone to run a race. The stone begged to be excused.

"Let us run down the slope of this hill," insisted the fox.

"I am very sorry, but you had better keep out of my way."

"You think to overtake me? What foolishness! I run like the wind."

"We will run," said the stone.

The fox darted away like an arrow. The stone began to roll, and then to jump and to jump, until it wounded to death its rival just as he was arriving at the foot of the hill.

THE REWARD OF A DESIRE FOR VAIN DISPLAY.

A panther met a fox wearing a crown tuft.

"What a beautiful ornament you wear! How did you make it?" said the panther.

"Very easily," said the fox. "I cut open the head with a flint, and then introduced into the wound the beautiful plumes of an ostrich."

"How admirable! I wish to go through the same process. Would you take the trouble to do it for me?"

"With a thousand pleasures."

And the fox rasped the head of the panther till the skull got thin, and then broke it in with one stroke of the flint.

So the panther died.

Here are three proverbs:

The dog follows the fox and kills it, but then comes the panther and kills the dog.

Nothing spurious can be good.

The little feather flies more swiftly than the great one.

In his religious beliefs the Tehuelche is as interesting as in other matters. There is one good god and from him all good things come. He is so good and kind that he is never offended. He does not require worship from the Indians, but according to the gauchos they have a ceremony of thanksgiving peculiarly interesting. In the early summer, when the young of the guanaco and the ostrich are numerous and easy to take, ostrich eggs still to be had and pasture is at its best, the Tehuelche cacique gathers his clan and decrees an offering to the good god. Thereat a young mare is lassoed, brought to a convenient spot, and there thrown down and secured on her back so that she cannot thrash around with her hoofs. Then all the people gather around while the man who is handiest with a knife draws his keenest blade, slashes open the breast of the mare, cuts out the heart, and holds it, still quivering, up in the presence of all, that it may become the offering by all of a living heart to the god to whom they give thanks.

They believe in evil spirits and there are medicine men and medicine women among them. Curiously enough, the medicine women are commonly young and the handsomest of their clans. These medicine mixers drive away evil spirits by incantations, but if the ordinary medicine fails, then all the men assemble, and, mounting their horses, ride furiously around the camp, firing guns into the air and waving their war-like implements about their heads. Apparently here is a field in which the Salvation Army missionaries would be very successful. The home of the soul after death is in the sky—somewhere in the blue vault they see by day, and the road to it lies by the way of the glories of the west at sunset. Of old they used to burn all the effects of the deceased that he might have them in the other world, but now a small outfit of horses and dogs is sufficient.

With them the witch and the sorcerer are stern realities, but the Tehuelches never torture their supposed witches to death. The desert air never trembles with the moans of old women whose misfortune it is to be sullen or insane. But when one cuts his hair or trims his finger nails the clippings are carefully burned. So, too, are all effects left behind when moving the wigwams. The witch is supposed to obtain a devilish power over any one when she can get hold of any such part of him.

In dreams—"when the heart sleeps, the mind sees a glimmer of the things to come," they say.

In music the Tehuelche is not much of an artist. The skin of a guanaco stretched over a hoop or bowl makes a drum. The bone of an ostrich leg, with holes cut into it, makes a sort of flute, which in turn is used to make the sinew cord of a bow to vibrate with a tum-tum noise.

The Tehuelche year begins in September, and the lapse of it is noted by the position of Orion. The four seasons are known as the fat time, or the fall; the cold time, the season of new grass, and the season of ostrich eggs. The moon measures the months, and one word serves for the name of the day and the sun.

In his astronomy the Tehuelche has named the Southern Cross the track of the ostrich, and therein has shown himself superior to the whites in at least one matter. The milky-way is the path of the guanaco, and the clouds of Magellan are the guanaco wallowing places, while Mars is the carancho, a conspicuous, eagle-like vulture common on the desert.

Following the tendencies of the age, the Tehuelches have become republicans. There are chiefs now, but in the old days the chief was a deal more of a ruler than now. In these days the chief is to the clan what the ablest and most experienced of a party of hunters in the

Adirondacks is to his associates. He knows the woods and woodcraft better than the rest, and the rest therefore listen to his advice. In the quarrels over trivial matters in camp the head man will often serve as peacemaker, because where a quarrel spreads a division of the clan follows, and the chances of success in hunting are greatly diminished. It takes a good many people to draw a circle around a bunch of guanacos in an open desert.

The marriage ceremony begins with an exchange of presents between the bridegroom and the girl's parents. Then a small tent is erected for the young couple and they are placed in it until night, when all the people gather around as big a fire as they can make near the tent. As the fire burns up at its brightest the males, beginning with the chiefs and ending with the boys, dance, in sets of four, while the squaws look on critically. The dress of the dancers includes a breech clout, a sash about the shoulders, and two feathers in the hair. The divorce ceremony consists in leading the woman back to the tent of her relatives, a ceremony rarely known, however. As the head of a family, the Tehuelche is kind and considerate to the woman and very affectionate to the children. They pet and fondle and kiss each other and use words of endearment. Sometimes they quarrel in the family, of course. There are white men a plenty—even Americans, alas, who beat their wives. So there are Tehuelches who do so.

On the other hand, although the story of it may seem like a fable to the reader, the truth is, that hen-pecked husbands are found in as great proportion among the Tehuelches as among the whites. But, on the whole, it is agreed by all who know the Tehuelches that in their homes they are the happiest people imaginable.

A CIDER FESTIVAL.

The one vice—rather the root of all evil—among the Tehuelches is the love of liquor. Robes, weapons, horses, daughters, and wives will all be exchanged for rum, and there are traders crossing the desert every day of the year seeking out their camps to sell the stuff to them. Then, too, there are apple orchards on Lake Nehuel-Huapi. In the season great festivals are held at the orchards. Then the apples are made into cider in skin-lined pits, and the fermented stuff is consumed in vast quantities. The Tehuelche, when drunk, becomes quarrelsome, and murders are then common, although the squaws hide all weapons before a festival begins.

The weapons of the Tehuelche are like those of the gaucho—lassoes, bolas, and knives. They also make bows and arrows, spears and what the gauchos call "the lost bola." The lost bola is simply a stone of convenient weight at the end of a three-foot cord. It is intended for battles only, and is called lost bola because when thrown it is not usually recovered again. The effective range of this lost bola is ordinarily 100 yards, and in some hands twice that. Iron bolas are the favorites, because being smaller for the weight they have a longer range, and because, too, they are more easily seen and recovered after a cast across the dull-colored desert than pebbles are. The Tehuelches carry guns and pistols to some extent, but chiefly for use against the spirits.

Because of his use of the bola the Tehuelche is, in a sense, a sportsman as distinguished from a pot hunter. The game has a running chance for life. However, the usual way of capturing game is for the men to draw a circle about a bunch of guanacos when pumas and ostriches are often enclosed and killed. When on the march the women with the pack train serve as a part of the enclosing circle.

The tent of the Tehuelche is a large affair. It is what would be called in this country a shelter tent, or a lean-to open in front. It is of rounded exterior, like the fourth part of an orange. It has a frame of forks and ridgepoles, and is covered with guanaco skins. Other skins serve to divide the interior of the tent into rooms. Whole families and their guests go to bed in a single room in the out-of-the-way parts of the United States, such as the mountains of Kentucky and West Virginia, but the Tehuelches are modest enough to divide their sleeping places so that parents and children, boys and girls, and guests are separated by curtains of horsehide. For beds they have cushions made of coarse blankets stuffed with guanaco wool, and they know the comfort of pillows, which are made of soft skins stuffed with guanaco hair.

They are very modest in dress. From the time they are five years old they wear a cloth secured about the loins by a belt. To this the women add a gown in these days, and the inevitable robe of guanaco skins, while the men and women both wear the robe and boots made of the skin of a colt's hind legs. The old style of boots stuffed with straw that gave the name of Patagones to this really small-footed race was abandoned soon after horses were introduced.

In sexual morality, it is said, when the subject is first broached to the gauchos, that the Tehuelches are a bad lot, but when one asks for details he finds that in their natural state they were by no means lascivious. They have been corrupted terribly by the traders who swap rum for furs, but all the whites agree that the Tehuelche women were by nature modest and delicate, and, when compared with other aboriginal women, at once most patient, bright, cheerful, and helpful companions, and faithful as well.

For cooking the Tehuelches use the long steel bar common among gauchos for suspending a roast over the fire. The gauchos say the Indians are always in such a hurry to begin eating that time to cook a roast through is never allowed. The outside of the meat will be crisp, and even burned, while the centre is still raw. No matter; steaming slices are slashed off, and, dripping with hot juices, conveyed to the mouth. But having tried some of these slices myself, I can advise the reader to wait a like opportunity before condemning the Tehuelche's taste in roasts. Besides that, one must keep in mind that they are greedy only after a long fast, and that under such circumstances even the lordly white man has been known to eat half-raw meat. They also carry big kettles for boiling, and a rather better outfit of dishes than the gauchos use. These things they get of the whites in exchange for ostrich plumes. In the old days they used to broil their meat on the coals, and even now they fill small animals with hot stones and then bury them (hides on) in the embers, and so make a right good dish.

They are called dirty—even vile—because they oil themselves all over with the marrow of ostrich bones. As a matter of fact they are in most matters cleanly. They bathe daily when near a lake or stream (the men separate from the women), and when the floor of a tent is by accident fouled the careful squaw always cuts out the earth to a depth of two inches and throws it away. They are also called dirty because they eat the viscera of animals, the lungs, stomach, etc. They also eat un-

TEHUELCHES IN CAMP.

born guanaco kids and unhatched ostriches. One can tell about such doings in a way that will make the Tehuelches seem to be a very disgusting lot. And so the descriptions generally run. But when one remembers some kinds of food the most civilized white men eat, there is found to be very little difference in such matters between the two races.

Indeed, when one has seen these Indians—has noted their self-restraint, their dignity, and gracefulness of looks and bearing, their gentleness and consideration one for the other, the utter lack of servility among them; more than all, when one has noted the brightness of their minds, the ease, for instance, with which they learn a foreign language and grasp ideas entirely new and foreign to their environment and habits of thought—one all but loses patience with the pride of race and egotism of religion that have named them savages.

A visitor to the meeting place of the Société d'Ethnographie of Paris, sees upon the wall above the President's chair this motto:

Corpore diversi, sed mentis lumine fratres.

The truth of that motto is never more apparent than in a contemplation of the Indians of Patagonia.

CHAPTER VIII.

THE WELSH IN PATAGONIA.

A MOST remarkable colony is that which the Welsh have made in Patagonia. Rarely, if ever, in the history of the Americas have emigrants from the old country been surrounded by conditions and circumstances so discouraging as those to be described in this story of that colony, and rarely, if ever, has a colonizing project originated as did this the Welch colony that is now flourishing on the banks of the Chubut River, 750 miles southwest of Buenos Ayres. Although one must really see the country to appreciate fully what the colonists endured and have achieved, yet I fancy that some of the facts are of sufficient human interest to make the story fully worth the telling.

The colony is known by the name of the river on which it is located—Chubut. It was formed by immigrants who left their homes, paradoxical as it may seem, because they were patriots. They were all Welshmen, who, because the laws of Great Britain have compelled the use of English in Welsh schools since the year 1282, when Prince Llewellyn fell, determined to found a colony in such an out-of-the-way part of the world that they could, unmolested, perpetuate the mother tongue of

Wales. The prime mover in this matter was Dr. Michael Jones of Bala College, and he was assisted by Mr. Lewis Jones, who is now a resident of the colony.

These gentlemen looked the maps of the world over, and they read the descriptions of all the unsettled parts which travellers out of the way had written, the ultimate conclusion being that no habitable country in the world could offer such complete isolation as the Patagonia region of the Argentine Republic. There came a time afterward when they began to doubt whether the land they had chosen was really habitable, but it was then too late to turn back.

An appeal for a grant of land was made to the Argentine Government, and that is an appeal that is never made in vain by any colony acting in good faith to any Latin-American Government. It is true that efforts were made to dissuade the Welshmen from going to Patagonia, but those efforts were intended for the good of the colonists. They were asked to take the fertile lands of the north instead of the desert of the south. No one but the promoters of the colony believed that any settlement could exist in the desert, and never did promoters come nearer to losing heart and yet succeed.

It was on July 28, 1865, that the Welsh pilgrims first landed in the region they had chosen. At that time the whole of Patagonia, between Rio Negro and the Strait of Magellan, was in precisely the same condition that it was when Pedro Sarmiento's colony starved to death in the strait, when Cavendish discovered Port Desire, and when Darwin explored a part of the remarkable Santa Cruz River. Nor was that all. War was incessantly waged between the people of the republic (who were pleased to call themselves Christians) and the people of the desert plains, who were called savages by the self-styled Christians. And the savages, as has been told, had the best of the fights. The whites occupied one settlement on the Rio Negro, but only by favor of the red men. What could a handful of Welshmen, unused to plains life and wholly ignorant of savage warfare, do with such fierce warriors?

The time came, however, when the Welshmen were asking each other, " What would we have done without the Indians ? "

As said, it was in the last week of July, 1865, when the Welshmen first saw the land where they intended to perpetuate their mother tongue in its purity. July in Patagonia is the mid-winter month. A sailing ship took them to the southeast corner of New Gulf, a nearly circular bay in the coast, seven hundred miles southwest of Buenos Ayres. Here it put them out on the gravelly beach, gave them some food and water, and then sailed away. There were 150 souls all told. How utterly alone they were, and how far away from civilization can be better appreciated when we remember that in those days no merchant steamers had yet gone down the coast to pass the Strait of Magellan, and that the only white men living south of the struggling settlement on the Rio Negro were a disconsolate gang of convicts, guarded by an equally forlorn squad of soldiers in a stockade on the strait just mentioned. The Welshmen were separated from all civilization, even the Argentine kind—a kind to which they were not accustomed—by the stormy sea on one hand and by hundreds of miles of desert on the other, a desert that was utterly impassable save by the Indians, who alone, in those days, knew where the widely-separated springs of fresh water were to be found.

Nor were their immediate surroundings any more cheerful than a contemplation of the region that lay between them and the far-away settlement on the Rio Negro.

They had landed on a pebbly beach near the foot of a low, white alluvial cliff into which the elements had eaten holes large enough to be called caves. Beyond the cliffs the arid desert, a mixture of sand and pebbles, rose in sweeping undulations to a crest perhaps six miles away and four hundred feet above the sea. They were walled in by desert ridges. There was not a green thing in sight, but only ragged brown desert brush and an occasional yellow, dry bunch of grass. There was neither house nor hut for their reception or shelter, and, worse than all else, there was neither stream nor pool nor spring of water fit to drink anywhere within fifty-one miles. That was the kind of a country to which these 150 Welshmen came to plant a colony that should live by agriculture.

The Pilgrims who came to Plymouth Rock because they could not make the world elsewhere worship according to the dictates of their consciences, had a tolerably bleak time of it according to the orators on New England Society days, but if one wants to hear stories of real hardships endured by pioneers, let him go to Chubut and talk to one of the older Welshmen.

The first thing done was, of necessity, to dig a well for water. They found water, and the well is still there. A drink from its depths will carry a Yankee cowboy back to his old haunts on the plains of Southwest Kansas and No Man's Land, instantly; that is, it will carry his thoughts there. He will say "gypsum" or "alkali" with something verbally stronger still, as soon as he gets his mouth empty. Indeed, one need not look five minutes anywhere around New Gulf to find plenty of gypsum. Nevertheless, the water would support life after a fashion, and the Welshmen turned from the well to make shelters of the caves nature had provided.

From the work of arranging their scanty household goods in the caves these pioneers went forth, not to sow and plant, but to make a road. They were in the region where they were to find homes, but the actual home sites —the farms of 240 acres that were to be theirs—lay fifty-one miles away over and beyond the crest of the desert amphitheatre within which they had landed. They had to mark the trail lest they get lost, clear it of brush and level its irregularities, and then they must needs transport themselves and their belongings over it to the banks of the Chubut River.

And all this they did to find at last that, save for a deposit of black loam in parts of the valley of the stream, they had come to a land as desolate as the shores of New Gulf. The desert walled them in. The wells filled with alkali water. The north wind was like a blast from the furnace in which Shadrach, Meshach, and Abednego fell down, and almost every wind came laden with a brown fog of sand. They had sought isolation; they had found it with a vengeance.

Nevertheless, these Welshmen—and they were all miners, too, and not farmers—began work to make homes and farms. They laid out a capital city, which they named Rawson in honor of the Argentine Cabinet officer who had interested himself in their behalf. It was a sorry capital then, but duplicates of it can be found in the Texas Panhandle. It was a town of dug-outs and mud huts. There was no timber for houses.

They planted gardens. They looked the region over. They began to learn how to hunt the guanaco and the ostrich that roamed over the desert.

And then came the Indians, the huge-framed Tehuelches, to whom the early explorer of the region had given the name of Big Feet (Patagonians). It was a notable day in the history of the settlement, but not a day of bloodshed. The Tehuelches and the Welshmen became friends at once, partly because the Indians, on learning why the whites had sought the isolation, comprehended the matter in a way that made them feel a brotherly regard for the intruders such as they had never felt for any other whites. The Welshmen had come to find entire freedom in the desert, and that was something the freeborn son of the desert could appreciate.

That was an excellent beginning, but only a first victory. There were many other foes on the desert. There were the panthers, the great, lean, sly cats that are called also American lions. They swarmed on the uplands and by night came to the settlement for the blood of horses, cattle, and sheep. There were locusts in clouds that obscured the sun. There were wild geese, ducks, and coots from the river—the winged pests were in legions. It was a waterless region and uninhabitable for man beyond the valley of the stream, but in the thorny brush of the desert millions of nature's allies in her warfare against man found breeding places.

For the first year the colony was to be supplied with provisions by the Argentine Government. The contract was faithfully kept. The colonists hoped to raise enough food for their own use after that, but their hopes failed. The hot winds destroyed the few results of their labors which birds and beasts had spared. Nevertheless, they held on for another year, the government supplying their needs, although, meantime, more colonists had come. Then came another failure of crops. The reader will say it took a lot of pluck to hold on after that for another year. So it did. These Welshmen were full of it. Not only for another year, but for another, and another still—for six weary years those men fought the gaunt wolf that stood at their doors. Then came prosperity, but with leaden footsteps.

That the colonists did not perish absolutely of starvation was due first to the persistent care of the Argentine Government. Uncle Sam was counted generous when he gave to every immigrant 160 acres of land. The Argentine Government not only gave these immigrants 240 acres of land each, on the condition that they improve it somewhat and live there two years, but it established a commissary department in the colony, and for nearly ten years gave free of cost all supplies of food and clothing needed to keep them alive, and as late as 1877, when crops had begun to flourish well, still extended a generous helping hand. This was done in spite of the fact that these Welshmen were avowedly clannish. They had come to establish a Welsh colony, and had obtained permission in advance not only to preserve their own language, but to govern themselves and to live free of taxation. Under the terms of the original concession, they were of value to the Argentine nation only in the fact that they were to break up and cultivate so much wild land. They could not have been made to fight for the land of their adoption even against an invading host of Brazilian monarchists. No government was ever more generous to colonists than the Argentine.

Goods were sent to Chubut by the ship load. But more than once the ship went wrong, and the goods were lost. Then came the time of dire distress when only their good friends the Tehuelches could save them. The Welshmen were starving on several occasions when the Indians came down the river and brought succor— guanaco, and ostrich, and panther meat in abundance, with skins for clothing. As the corn of the Massachusetts Indians saved the Pilgrim Fathers, so the meat of the Tehuelches saved the Welshmen. But the Tehuelche Indians have not now to mourn, nor do the Welshmen now hang their heads in shame at the mention of any King Philip. White men made war on the Tehuelches and exterminated them, but no Welshmen, though the colony was then self-supporting, took part in that hateful enterprise, and when the red remnant were forced at last to give up the fight, they came down to the Chubut River and surrendered to the fair-dealing white men, who had called them brothers and meant what they said. More pitiful still, when one brave old chief, wounded to death, was breathing his last in Buenos Ayres, he smilingly looked about him and said:

"I am going to the Welshman's heaven."

As said, for six years, the colonists struggled against failing hopes, eating only the bitter bread of charity, struggled to maintain themselves where they could perpetuate their language in its purity. In 1871 came the turn in the tide. A dam was built across the Chubut River in that year, and an irrigating ditch taken out. Of course they did not finish the canal in one year. It was a ditch thirty-six feet wide on top, eighteen on the bottom, and six feet deep, and year by year they lengthened it out. When the water kissed the warm, dark soil, it was like the kiss of the maiden on the lips of the grateful beast in the fairy story. The desert was transformed into a blooming garden.

And here is an interesting fact. For six years the colonists had eaten no bread, save what was given to them. They would, therefore, get clear of that evil first of all. They sowed wheat and barley, and they sow little else to this day. Whatever may happen, the Chubut man will never again have to ask for bread of anybody.

However, as said, progress was slow. The first ditch was not well located, and when an unusual drought came the water of the river did not reach the ditch, and the crop failed in spite of it. Then, too, there were the wild pests at all times—the locusts and the wild fowl. Even after eleven years of irrigation—in 1882—there was a failure from the drought. But that set them to building a greater ditch, of which they all now make boast.

About five hundred settlers came out in the early years of famine, but the number dwindled to less than two hundred in 1871. In 1880 the result of irrigation had swelled the number to eight hundred, and in 1885 there were double that number. In 1880 the settlers were scattered along the valley for about twenty-five miles from the mouth of the river, and there was a sort of a village at each end of the settlement. The houses were, as a rule, even then mere huts. Wagons, and carts, and horses were had in sufficient number. In fact, the Government at Buenos Ayres had provided all of these things. But the abundant harvests of 1880 and 1881 gave a boom to the settlement which the failure of 1882 only checked temporarily. The colonists went up stream to a valley thirty miles long beyond a narrow cañon and took up land there. It was there that the head of the great new ditch was located. They have since gone to a third still higher. They have, in fact, taken up all the available land for seventy miles along the river. They have 270 miles of main irrigating canals. The largest has a cross section measuring 75x9x36 feet, and the whole 270 miles cost £180,000. There are 3250 people in the settlement.

Some of the details of their condition from time to time remind one of the Yankee frontier settlements. They began their religious life in the colony with union services, and got on comfortably until they prospered. Sectarians floated in on the waters of the irrigating ditch, so to speak, and there was a burst of zeal in building up denominations that brought a growth in church outfits quite equal to that in the area planted—rather larger, in fact. Among the 2000 people of 1883 there were two independent congregations with ordained ministers, who held regular services in chapels, of which "the walls were baked brick, the roofs were wooden, with a layer of mud on top, and the wooden benches had good backs to them," as one of them described the places of worship. They had also a stone-walled chapel in a third place, and held regular services in schoolhouses in other places. The Methodists had a brick church with an ordained minister, at Rawson, and held services in the upper valley. The Baptists had a fine chapel at Frondrey, one of the little villages that sprang up, and an ordained minister for it. In fact, there were, in all, seven ordained ministers in the colony, and in 1884 the Episcopalians brought out the eighth. Every one of these had his 240 acres of land, and every one worked his own farm and got rich, as his neighbors did, raising wheat.

It is a significant fact that up to 1884 the colony did not have a single physician. It scarcely needed one. Still some one was sure to break a limb every two or three years, and the colonists were right glad when, in 1885, a man with a diploma came there and took up the usual allowance of land.

In 1883 a number of Welsh prospectors came from Australia to Chubut and went as far back as the Andes. They found several croppings of lignite, which at first were thought to be good coal, and that made a stir. The stuff is now used for fuel to some extent in the houses, and it is to be found that five tons will serve for about two tons of Welsh coal.

Then they found gold and went to work filing claims. The gold, however, lies only thirty-one leagues from a port on the Chili coast where a German steamer calls once a month, so that the diggings, which include placer as well as quartz workings, will hardly benefit Chubut save as a market for produce may be created. About $50,000 gold has been invested in the workings. The Yankee traveller is sure to be informed, too, that "a Texas cowboy named Marshall has a store at the camp, and he says the diggings beat California."

Then it was observed that the desert plains above the upper parts of the inhabited valley swarmed with guanacos as the desert plains of New Mexico once swarmed with antelopes. Droves of from 5000 to 7000 were seen. It was rightly argued that sheep could live where the guanaco did. The Chubut colonists are going into the wool business, though slowly, and this is certain to be the greatest source of wealth to the colonists in the future. Bunch grass grows on the uplands. It is in scant quantity, but it is there. Water flows through the valley. The man who has water can hold all the sheep that can feed on the desert back of his farm, and that means at least two thousand. Sheep thrive wonderfully in the pure air and on the dry gravel of Patagonia. Everywhere along the coast the shepherds boast that every sheep is worth a gold dollar a year clear profit, besides the increase in the flock. But this statement should not lead any one to go to Chubut to begin life, because all the available land in the valley has been taken up.

Meantime, after irrigation brought crops, the subject of transportation had agitated the colonists. The mouth of the Chubut River had an impassable bar. Nearly all freight, previous to 1885, was either brought to New Gulf and carted thence over the old trail to the valley, or else was brought in tiny sailing vessels which, at the time, when the melting snow on the head waters made a freshet in the river, could work in over the bar. The surplus grain had to be shipped out in the same way. There was a weary and an expensive haul by the one route; by the other, a tedious and expensive waiting for high water. In 1885, a company was formed to construct a railway from the valley to New Gulf, and the Argentine Government granted a charter, and gave a subsidy of 204 square miles of desert land. I guess the subsidy is n't worth much, for there seems to be no way to get water on it. They even carry water from the Chubut valley to supply all employees along the line, now, but a road of a metre gauge was built, and a very good road it is, considering that English stock and materials were used.

Building the road involved the making of two new town sites—one on the gulf and one at the railroad terminus. That in the Chubut valley has been built up, but half a dozen wood, iron, and mud huts are all that can be found at Madryn, on the gulf. Still Madryn is an interesting town. It has a ruler, appointed by the President of the republic. He is called the Prefect. His district is a sub-prefect, and he is a sort of an autocratic Mayor. Lieutenants in the navy get all such appointments in Patagonia.

Madryn also has a Captain of the Port and a squad of sailors to help preserve the dignity of the Prefect, and the Prefect has an assistant Prefect, who ranks a little below the Captain of the Port. Outside of the official group, but on excellent terms with it, is the railroad group. This includes an agent, who is a well-educated Welshman, and a telegraph operator, who is the charming daughter of the agent. To rank with the non-commissioned officer and the Jack tars of the official group there is a foreman and a gang of railroad trackmen. Then there are two lighters afloat in the bay for the transfer of freight to and from the Argentine naval transports, which come down from Buenos Ayres once in three weeks. These lighters are excellent sea boats, instead of having the models that lighters in New York have. One is a schooner and the other is a sloop, and five men man the two.

The railroad has prospered moderately. It has 5000 tons of wheat to carry from the colony every year, besides some small packages of ostrich feathers, guanaco skins, and products of Indian workmanship. It carries in dry goods, groceries, and hardware, and several passengers a month pass over it each way. A train runs over the road every time a ship comes to port—say once in three weeks. In fact, the company is going to extend the line up the valley. The people living seventy miles above the end of the road want better facilities for shipping their wheat, and they are going to have them. This branch of the road will very likely have a train once a week to accommodate local passenger traffic. In case the gold mines develop half the wealth they are expected to, the railroad will be carried right away up to the diggings.

Patagonia railroad building is not expensive. All Patagonia between river valleys is everywhere ballasted with proper gravel for a road-bed, and is so nearly level that the ties can be laid, as they were laid on Texas lines years ago, right on the natural surface without turning a shovelful of dirt. As compared with some Yankee railroads, the only railroad in Patagonia is no great affair; but when compared with some others it leaves them out of sight, because it pays dividends as well as develops the country.

To sum it all up, here was a colony that might well have been called a failure before the people reached their destination. It was called a failure by about every impartial observer who visited it during the first ten years of its existence. Nevertheless, in spite of the drought, in spite of alkali, in spite of homesickness, in spite of all the myriad drawbacks to which it was subject, it prospered at the last, and is now worth millions sterling.

But alas for Dr. Michael Jones of Bala College! Alas for Mr. Lewis Jones, now of the colony! They planted their hosts in the uttermost parts of the earth that the shade of Prince Llewellyn might flourish and his language be spoken in its original purity forever. So the shade did flourish and the language was spoken for many years, but when prosperity came there was an influx of other tongues, along with an Argentine Governor and an official staff. Spanish was the language of the Argentine, and was necessary for all official business. Under the Argentine law every child born in the colony was a citizen of the republic, and it was a republic of which even the descendants of Prince Llewellyn did not need to be ashamed. The Welsh youngsters, indeed, have grown up to look with pride to the broad blue and white stripes of the flag under which they were born. They are children of the desert—and they love that desert—love it so well that they never lose an opportunity to speak in its favor ; and they speak of it with the soft vowels of the Castilian, rather than with the consonants of the Welsh.

CHAPTER IX.

BEASTS ODD AND WILD.

LET no sportsman or amateur naturalist be deterred from visiting Patagonia by the discouraging words of Darwin. When that famous naturalist had climbed the porphyry hills back of Port Desire, and, gazing away over the brown mesa, had seen little worth mentioning even by a naturalist save "here and there tufts of brown, wiry grass," and "still more rarely some low, thorny bushes," he went back to his diary in the cabin of his ship and wrote " the zoölogy of Patagonia is as limited as its flora." If Patagonia be compared with some parts of the tropics where the forests resound continually with the cries of birds and animals, where butterflies and humming-birds fill the air, and the insects are seen or felt in countless thousands, then, comparatively speaking, the fauna is limited. And yet there were—and are—some forms or life in Patagonia—insects, for instance—which, if Darwin had happened along at the right time, would have made him think the country about as full of life as it needed to be to keep a human being on the jump. There are as many mosquitoes and punkies (gnats) in Patagonia as in any game country I have seen in the two Americas, but the absence of this sort of life at certain seasons is one of the advantages which it offers to the sportsman, if not to the naturalist. For the hardy seeker after the thrills of the chase, with incidental trophies, Patagonia offers inducements quite the equal, all things considered, of any other wild part of the earth.

Of the animals a sportsman could find there the first in point of numbers is the guanaco. My first view of the guanaco was from the companion-way of the steamer in which I coasted the land. It was hanging in the rigging about the mainmast. The ship's captain had been away on a hunt, and had killed two, which were brought on board and hung up while I was writing in my diary down below. I afterward saw guanacos cantering over the hills unsuspicious of danger, and also fleeing toward a far country because certain that danger was near. They were even seen from the deck of the steamer as she ran down the coast. Although certain settlements have driven these animals from three or four old-time haunts, their number in Patagonia is like unto the number of antelope that used to range over parts of the United States. They are seen by the thousand.

In form and habits the guanaco is a very interesting beast. After a man has hunted it a while he comes to think it a model of beauty and grace, but at first view, even on the plains, it seems to the majority of people ridiculous. "It is like a long-legged calf with a neck three times too long," to quote the words of a Yankee sailor I found in Santa Cruz. As a matter of fact it has the body of a goat, but it stands from three to four feet high when full sized. The neck seems to be as long as the body, while the legs, which are as long as those of a deer, are really thicker, and seem thicker than they are, at least in winter, because of the length of hair. The color of the body of the full-grown beast is the red of a red cow, but the pelage is wool rather than hair until the animal is well on in years. However, the pelage of the legs is hair at all ages. In youth the wool is a light, almost a fawn color. At all ages the color of the back shades into white on the belly, while in extreme old age the guanacos are said to turn almost white all over. The track of the guanaco is something like that of a deer, though much larger, while the foot is peculiar in that it has at the under side a very prominent cushion, which projects below the protecting, forked hoof as the foot is lifted into the air, and which at all times probably supports the main weight of the body, making the step very light on the stony desert. The hoof is but a shell surrounding this bulbous cushion. The cushion is covered with a rough but yielding skin, which, though rough, is not calloused as the foot of a barefooted man comes to be.

When Darwin was in Patagonia he wrote some pages about the guanaco, paying considerable attention to its swiftness, its peculiar shape, which indicated that it was really the humpless camel of the South American desert, and its curious cry when alarmed, the exact neigh of a horse. But more interesting than all this was a habit which he believed it had when about to die. Along the Rio Santa Cruz he found the ground under the brush actually heaped up with the bones of the guanaco. Animal after animal had crawled in under the brushy shrubs, and, lying down upon the bones of others that had come there before it, had breathed its last. He also noticed that when a guanaco was wounded by a bullet it immediately headed for the river. The same habit was observed on the Rio Gallegos, but in no other place than these two valleys.

With Darwin's words as a text, Mr. W. H. Hudson, whose *Naturalist in La Plata* is the most interesting work on natural history ever written, has taken the trouble to reason out the cause for what he says "looks less like an instinct of one of the inferior creatures than the superstitious observance of human beings, who have knowledge of death and believe in a continued existence after dissolution; of a tribe that in past times had conceived the idea that the liberated spirit is only able to find its way to its future abode by starting at death from the ancient dying place of the tribe or family, and thence moving westward, or skyward, or underground, or over the well-worn immemorial track, invisible to material eyes."

With this uppermost in mind, I made haste on reaching Santa Cruz to ask the gauchos and other citizens for horses and a guide to the nearest guanaco cemetery, but they did not understand me. So I got Hudson's book and showed them the picture of the dying guanaco, and translated as well as small knowledge of Spanish would enable, his touching description of the animal in the place of skulls. By and by they understood, and with one voice said:

"It is not so."

"But the bushes and bones are there—thousands of skeletons."

"Without doubt."

"Why, then, do you say the guanaco does not go there to die, or to escape an imaginary evil? Why does he go there?"

"It is very simple. We stand now in the lee of this

house because the wind is very cold. Almost one winter in three the wind is much colder—there is a terrible winter. There is much snow, and ice over the snow. Every place on the mesa is covered. To escape the cold storms the guanacos seek the shelter of the bushes. The storm continues many days. They can find no food ; they cannot leave the shelter. So they die of starvation, one lying over another. Every plainsman has seen a thousand dead guanacos under the bushes after such a winter, not only here but in the cordillera as well."

However, though the guanaco does not have a dying place, it has a lot of characteristics sure to interest those who are lovers of natural history. Like the North American buffalo, it has wallowing places. On the plains of Patagonia, as on those of the Western States, great saucer-shaped hollows are seen in which the guanaco lies down to roll in the dust, but the Patagonian wallows are often much larger than any I ever saw in Kansas or Texas. The gauchos say this is because the guanacos resort to them in considerable herds—from thirty to one hundred—and at night sleep in them standing, heads out, in a ring, while the kids stand within the circle. This habit protects the young from the wild-cats and foxes. The guanaco has no effective defence against the assault of a panther save in flight. The old male guanaco with a herd of females to defend will fight when a panther attacks him unless the attack is immediately fatal. The canine teeth of the guanaco make a bad wound, and it can kick like a mule, but the panther is so quick and strong that the struggles of its victims are always hopeless.

In the right season each tough old male gathers a

harem of from thirty to fifty females, over which he presides in lordly fashion, and in one respect the old fellow is a very good head of a family. He leads the females into the hollows, where the grass is most abundant, while he remains on the highest knoll of the vicinity keeping watch for the enemy, and contenting himself by browsing on the scant herbage he finds about him. At times, however, the guanacos live in vast herds, and then all the older males remain on the higher knolls as sentinels. Their sense of smell is very keen. It is well-nigh impossible to get within half a mile of the sentinels by travelling down wind—some say they can smell a party of hunters that is a full mile away, and even more up wind. If approached carefully on the lee side one may get very close, however, and then the action of the sentinels is something that makes the gauchos laugh. The way the old bucks prance and jump stiff-legged and paw the air and neigh horse-fashion is one of the funniest things the plainsmen see.

But, like the antelope, the guanaco is full of curiosity. With a little flag or even a handkerchief a man, after concealing himself on the lee side of a herd, can toll them within pistol range by simply waving the cloth in the air at brief intervals. It is likely that the animal distinguishes colors, for the use of two or three flags of bright but different colors excites them much more than one white flag will.

When a herd is fired at with a gun (something that happens rarely in Patagonia) the report excites, but does not necessarily start the beasts running. Indeed, the sight of the smoke may draw them toward the gun. The wounded animal, if able to run, invariably plunges down the nearest declivity, and in the mountains this sometimes means a drop of hundreds of feet. If the animal is one of the leaders the whole herd with it will follow, sheep fashion. A gaucho, who had guided an English hunter from Punta Arenas up into the cordillera, said one shot of the Englishman's rifle one day killed over a hundred guanacos in this way. They all plunged over a lofty precipice. There was a camp of Indians in the vicinity at the time, and the result of the shot made the white man a very great medicine man in their estimation.

Guanacos can climb a mountain or run on a narrow ledge as well as a goat. Though found on the sea-beach, they also feed clear up to the edge of perpetual snow, and are quite at home in either locality. Their food is grass and twigs, but they are not found in the woods, save only as the natural parks along the foot-hills of the Andes might be called woodlands. Even there they avoid going into the clumps of trees.

Guanacos, when taken young, are readily tamed, and for two or three years, or until they get their full growth, make very pleasing pets. They are fond of being caressed, are very playful, and will thrive on any food suitable for sheep or cattle. But in the mating season, after the third year, they become so vicious that it is dangerous for women and children to keep them about. The females are then particularly ill-tempered toward women. They show their dislike by jumping toward the person that excites their anger and striking with all four feet at once. They also spit to a distance of five feet an acrid substance at the objectionable individual. If they knock one down, they will bite as well as jump on him.

The flesh of a guanaco that is under three years of age

is very good; that of a yearling or under is delicious, and killed in the early fall, it is fat and tender; to my taste the young are the equal of any venison. The old ones are tough and rank. The Indians do not kill the old ones unless driven to it by starvation, as during a long storm. To the Indian, however, the guanaco is the mainstay of life. From the hide of the full-grown animals he makes his tent, and from the skins of the very young—preferably those of the unborn—with their silky fur he manufactures the great blanket-like wraps that form his distinctive dress. The skin of the hind legs is readily turned into an easy boot, and the skin of the long neck is dressed and cut into strips which form cords for the bolas, straps, and bridles, and horsegear generally—in short, serves about all the uses of leather. In the sinews of the back the squaws find excellent thread, and in the wool a material admirably adapted to weaving blankets and filling mattresses and cushions. Nor is that all, for the bones serve various uses, and the marrow is used in place of vaseline, as well as eaten.

Judging by the good qualities of the skins I have seen, the hide of the full-grown guanaco would make an excellent leather, well adapted for valises and such uses, while that of the younger ones would serve admirably for fine footwear and gloves. Skins bring from 25 to 50 cents gold each in the market at Punta Arenas.

A curious kind of ball accumulates in the stomach of the guanaco. It looks something like a stone, but can be readily broken. It is said to possess medicinal qualities, and there is a ready market for the stuff at the settlement.

Next to the guanaco in interest if not in utility is the panther of Patagonia, the *felis concolor* of the naturalist,

Nowhere in the world does the great tree-climbing cat reach greater size or accumulate more fat than on the treeless deserts of the far south. Specimens from eight to nine feet long over all are frequently seen. Though, perhaps, rather lighter in color, they are in all other respects exactly like the panthers of the United States. How it happened one cannot even guess, but the panther is known very much better in the desert than in the United States. Rarely can one read a story of the panther in the States without seeing something about its terrible ferocity toward human beings, while the stories of the panther that comes out of the woods to play with the lonely wayfarer as a cat plays with a mouse, that it may at last crush and eat him, are enough to make the flesh of the unlearned reader creep on his bones. On the desert of Patagonia there are more panthers in proportion to the area and the numbers of other kinds of animals than in any other region of the world. The lonely wayfarer is not often found there afoot, but men have been on the desert unmounted, and the panthers have come to play around them, too. But it is not as a predatory cat that they come. It is as a playful kitten. Individual panthers play by themselves—old ones as well as young—by the hour. They will chase and paw and roll an upturned bush, or a round rock, or any moving thing, and lacking that will pretend to sneak up on unwary game, crouching the while behind a bush, or rock for concealment, to spring out at last and land on a hump of sand or a shadow. Then they turn around and do the same thing over again.

When it is in this frame of mind if a lone human being comes along the panther is as glad to see him as a petted cat to see its mistress. It purrs and rolls over before him, and gallops from side to side, and makes no end of kitten-like motions, and all because of the exuberance of its youthful spirits. I know that the average reader, accustomed to the Fenimore Cooper sort of novels, will think this an exaggeration, but the plainsmen of all Argentina call the panther by a name that means "the friend of man," and that too in spite of the havoc it makes among their sheep.

This name, "the friend of man," applied to a beast elsewhere counted ferocious, arose from an incident well authenticated in the history of Buenos Ayres, though I have no doubt that other instances of the kindly disposition of the panther toward the human race have served to perpetuate the title. In 1536 the people of Buenos Ayres, then a town of 2000 inhabitants, were reduced to the point of starvation because of a war with the Indians. One writer, Del Barco Centenera, asserts that 1800 of the 2000 died of hunger. The dead were buried only just beyond the palisades, because of the danger from Indians, and in consequence many beasts of prey came to feed on the thinly-covered bodies, a circumstance that added greatly to the terror and distress of the people. Nevertheless, hunger increased so much that many ventured out into woods along the river seeking edible roots, and with some success. Among these was a young woman named Maldonada, who, getting lost, was found and carried away by the Indians. Some months later, peace having been restored, Don Rui Diaz, the Captain of the soldiers, learned that Señorita Maldonada was alive, and thereupon he persuaded the Indians to restore her. He did this, not to relieve her from her slavery, but that he might punish her for what he believed to be her treachery. He thought she had deserted to the Indians, and so he condemned her to be tied to a tree three miles from town and left there to be eaten by wild beasts. This was done. After two nights and a day soldiers were sent to bring in her bones for burial, but to their great astonishment she was found unhurt. She said a panther had remained with her, and had driven off the jaguars and other beasts of prey that came to destroy her. The following sentence is from an old history of the town, and is given in the original for the benefit of those who read Spanish because of a pun in it.

De esta manera quedó libre la que ofrecieron a las fieras; la cual mujer yo la conoci, y la llamaban la Maldonada, que mas bien se le podia llama la Biendonada; pues por esta suceso se ha de ver no haber merecido el castigo á que la ofrecieron.

Freely translated this means:

In this manner she that was offered to the wild beasts remained free; the which woman I knew, and they called her Maldonada (ill-bestowed), whom they could better have called Biendonada (well bestowed), since from this happening it was seen that she had not merited the punishment she had received.

The kindness of the panther does not protect him from the assault of man, however. A war of extermination is everywhere waged against the race. Mr. W. H. Greenwood, a sheep-owner whom I met at Santa Cruz, had killed over 1000 panthers single handed, but in talking of the matter he said panther killing could not be called sport. When started by horse or dogs it runs with tremendous leaps a short distance. It gets tired out quickly, and then leaps into the middle of the largest clump of thorn brush at hand. There it sits up and snarls and looks like a fierce cat. It will claw the life out of any dog it can get hold of very quickly, but the moment a lasso drops over its neck it gives up, and lying down, shed tears as if it knew and dreaded its fate. Panthers are knocked in the head with the bolas, and even stabbed to death with knives by the shepherds, though this last act is really dangerous. The panther will not leap from its crouching place at a man, but if the man ventures in reach the beast may claw his life out, and he may not, too.

As the sheep ranches spread over Patagonia, the panthers are killed off as vermin. The flesh is freely eaten by everybody in Patagonia. Some like it roasted best, but most people prefer it boiled. Roasted it tastes like young pig. It is particularly esteemed because usually fat. The Patagonia plainsmen, as well as the Indians, consume fat as an Eskimo does. This is not because the weather is cold, as the arctic explorer imagined, but because they live on a meat diet exclusively. Vegetables supply the constituents to civilized folks which lean meat lacks. The fat meat is sufficient of itself.

Of the hunting habits of the panther many stories are told, and from these one learns that it is about the laziest hunter in the world as well as the most playful. It creeps up slowly on the guanaco herds, picks out a fat one, and then with quivering fur and flaming eyes it leaps at its victim. Two mighty bounds, no more, no less, and it lands on the back of the guanaco, and with a sweep of its right paw it dislocates its victim's neck. Down the two go in a heap, and then the panther tears open the neck of the guanaco and drinks the hot sweet blood that gushes out. This done, the carcass is usually covered up with brush, as if for future use, but as a matter of fact the condors or other carrion birds usually pick the bones.

That, at least, is the story of a panther's attack when it is lucky. Half the time the guanaco hears or smells its enemy in time to leap away in safety. The panther never chases its game, even when it gets so close as to tear bloody stripes in its flank.

At times the panther finds the herd feeding in the open, where no shelter behind which it can reach its prey is to be had. Thereat the wily panther lies down on its back behind a bush that may be afar off, and claws the air, first with one paw, then with another, and then with both. Up will come its hind legs next, or its tail will stand erect, with the tip waving from side to side. These motions are something guanaco curiosity cannot resist. The guanaco comes to the decoy by starts and hesitating runs, but it comes, and so meets its death.

It is a fine savage, the panther. Shepherds told me of losing from forty to one hundred and twenty sheep in a night, the mother with young cubs being the most destructive—not that she may feed her young, but because she is then most playful. She kills for fun. The guanaco is the panther's staple food, but horses, sheep, and young cattle are all liked by it. Indeed, no living being of the desert except man escapes its appetite for murder, one may say, for it claws down the whirring partridge as she springs from her nest, which it afterwards robs of its eggs; it kills the ostrich as he sits on his nest, and then, after hiding his body, it returns to the nest and eats the eggs with gusto; it snatches the duck or the goose from its feeding place at the edge of a lagoon; it crushes the shell of the waddling armadillo; it digs the mouse from its nest in the grass; it stalks the desert prairie dog (*Vizcacha Lagostomus Trichodactylus*), and, dodging with easy motion the fangs of the serpent, it turns to claw and strip out its life before it can coil to strike again.

And yet, with all this, it makes a charming household pet. I never heard of one being kept longer than three years, but none of those described as pets was ever killed for personal harm done to or even ill-temper shown toward a human being. The shepherds and gauchos agree that the panther is always a kitten at heart, so far as man is concerned, but it has an instinctive dislike for dogs and love for colts and lambs. These failings, in spite of good training, will sooner or later get a panther into trouble on the ranch, and then even the wife and children plead in vain for its life.

If it be thought interesting that a tree-climbing cat like the panther should flourish on the treeless plains of Patagonia, then it is remarkable that two kinds of the colored man's choicest game, the 'possum, should thrive in the same locality. In regions where there never was a tree, and never will be one naturally, the 'possum, with its prehensile tail dragging uselessly behind it, lives as comfortably, and makes just as good a roast, as ever it did where the pawpaws grow. That it has lived thus for ages on the treeless mesa no one need doubt; but when by chance one is transported from the plain to a region of trees, to the valley of the Rio Negro, for instance, the old tree-climbing instinct is found as strong as ever. A mother 'possum that had ten young ones as large as rats, was once taken from her nest to a plantation with trees, and straightway, without any hesitation, she climbed nimbly up, carrying her family with her in the usual fashion—clinging all over her back and sides. Nor had the use of her tail been forgotten.

So much for the ordinary 'possum. There is another sort found that is no doubt indigenous, and it is of a kind to make the eyes of a colored brother bulge with astonishment, for it is at maturity the size of a small meadow mole. There are bushes on the desert large enough to serve these little fellows as trees, and they are, therefore, able to follow their instinctive desire to climb and hang head down by the tail, but the spectacle of one of the little 'possum mothers climbing about a desert bush with her tiny young clinging to her is one of the most interesting sights in nature.

Another animal that is at least in one respect allied to the 'possum is the coypu. It might, perhaps, be called an aquatic 'possum because of its hairless tail and its habit of carrying its young on its back. The naturalists, however, say it is more like the beaver than any other North American beast, and it certainly has a remarkably beautiful pelage. Its flesh is very good to eat, but it is chiefly hunted for the fur. The feature of this animal, however, that at once attracts the attention of a stranger is the location of the nipples of the mother on her back instead of on her breast and belly, as in ordinary mammals. When seen swimming about with her young on her back, as is her custom, the nipples are found above the water line extending in a row from shoulder to hip, where the young can nurse as they are carried along.

Of the weasels, one kind is described as much larger than those in the United States. They travel in packs like wolves when hunting, and are said to have the most malignant and devilish faces of any beast of the desert. All birds and rodents that get within their grasp are torn to pieces in savage fashion.

Along the Andes many Virginia deer are found, but it

is only near the forests. They emit a rank odor from the leg glands that is said to be fatal to the desert snakes. The gray fox flourishes everywhere and grows to a rather larger size than in the United States, but he is remarkable for being very short-winded. At least, he is easily tired out. A race of a few hundred yards with a desert horse uses him up, and he falls a victim to the well-nigh unerring bolas of the plainsmen. He is not often killed by the Indians, for he is not fit to eat, but the shepherds slay him at sight because of the number of lambs he kills in the season.

Then there is the skunk, a counterpart in all respects of the skunk of the States. Skunks are very numerous in all parts, and often serve the Indians as food when larger game fails. It is an interesting fact, too, that the Indians capture them when young and make pets of them. There is rarely a collection of wigwams on the desert without a couple of tame skunks playing about.

The skunks, when tame, seem in all respects inoffensive. The gauchos I met when told that a skunk's bite is supposed in parts of the United States to cause a malady akin to hydrophobia were incredulous. They had never heard of such a thing.

Any reference to the animals of Patagonia that omitted the armadillo would be noticeably defective. It is an animal with habits that must interest an amateur naturalist greatly. There are two forms of the armadillo. Roughly speaking, one is like a hairy guinea pig with a pointed turtle shell over its back and head, while the other is like a thick turtle without any breastplate. The former is very rare even in its haunts on the Andes. The latter is everywhere abundant. As described by all who have seen it, the latter will eat and get fat—very fat—on anything from grass roots to decayed fish or cattle, from an ant to a poisonous serpent, from strawberries to rats and mice. In the wilderness it roams about by day because the cats of the desert persecute it most at night. Near the settlements, where, by the way, it thrives best, it is abroad at night, because man persecutes it in the day. Slow moving, as it seems to be when the traveller sees it at sunset, it overtakes the serpents of the region in a fair race, and kills them by squatting on them and sawing its body to and fro so that the edges of its protective shell cut the snake to pieces. It captures mice by sneaking on them cat-fashion and throwing its body over them like a trap. It grubs for worms; it robs nests of eggs and fledglings. Now, although it eats a great many things that are repulsive to civilized tastes, the armadillo is itself a most delicious article of food for any human taste, civilized or uncivilized. In my journeys as a reporter of *The Sun* I have eaten nearly every kind of fish, flesh, and fowl served between Ivigtut, Greenland, and Ushuaia, Tierra del Fuego, but found nothing quite so much to my taste as an armadillo baked in the embers of an outdoor fire on the desert of Patagonia. Nor was my judgment in the matter influenced by hunger, for my first armadillo was served unexpectedly after a plentiful repast of good beef roasted on a spit. It is said that armadillos are not found south of the Santa Cruz River. They are indigenous north of it, but the river's current is an impassable barrier to keep it from spreading south.

All travellers familiar with the desert regions of the United States are at once struck on reaching Patagonia with the remarkable similarity between the two countries. No one could object to the transplanting of armadillos to the prairies and deserts of the United States. They prefer animal food; they are good scavengers. They do no harm to crops, but on the contrary aid materially in destroying insects and other crop enemies. Indeed, they are so valuable in this respect that the Agricultural Department, which imported bugs of one kind to destroy others that were ruining California orange-growers, might well take into consideration a proposition to import armadillos.

Space is lacking even for brief reference to other animals. There is one thing, however, about the majority of all the desert animals that must strike the traveller as the most remarkable thing in nature. The big guanacos, the tiny rodent, half a dozen different kinds of mammals, besides birds, all live without water. I do not know this to be true, but every plainsman with whom I have talked said it was so. The panther, of course, finds a substitute in the blood he drinks, but there are others that do not have even a liquid food. They live on flesh or on the herbs that are never noticeable for having juices in them. Still, the matter is not without a parallel in the United States, for the prairie dogs, the rabbits, and the reptiles of such regions as the Panhandle of Texas and the Colorado Desert live in like fashion.

On the whole, Patagonia is one of the parts of the world for the hardy lover of nature to see when he goes a-travelling. The zoölogy is, indeed, about as scant, numerically, as the flora; but here, as in all other things, there is a universal law of compensation. Whatever may be lacking in the count of kinds is more than made up in the interesting characteristics of those to be found there.

CHAPTER X.

BIRDS OF PATAGONIA.

ALL things save song considered, the ostrich is the most interesting bird of Patagonia. There are really two kinds of ostriches in the territory, one at the north and one at the south, but in the eyes of an ordinary spectator they are all of one species.

The traveller will see them from the deck of the steamer as he approaches shore. From a distance they look like a flock of overgrown gray turkeys running around the desert. The angular gait of a turkey in pursuit of a grasshopper is theirs. That the ostrich existed in the days when sunny tropical skies hung over Patagonia is a fact well known to paleontologists. There are ostrich bones in the old clay beds of the region with those of the glyptodon and the monkey, but the monkey was wholly extinguished in the cataclysms of the early ages, while the ostrich, being better able to adapt himself to new conditions, survived, and is even now almost holding his own in the fight for existence on the desert, in spite of the onslaughts of the puma, the wild-cat, the fox, and the still more ruthless hunters who have human blood in their veins.

Just how it is that ostriches have survived can be understood by what the Patagonians tell of them. Thus the birds feed on flies, grasshoppers—about all the insects that appear in their region—and they do this from the moment they break their way through their egg-shells. They are able to make their own living from the first. Then, too, they are brought into being in peculiar fashion. The old cock bird has a harem of several hens, and he is in some respects a marvellously good head of a family. He builds a nest for the harem, and the hens take turns in depositing their eggs in it until it is full. Nests having forty eggs in them are not uncommon. When the nest is full enough the old cock takes possession, and sits on and cares for them until they are hatched. Meantime the females go wandering about the plains having a good time, and, incidentally, laying eggs where there is no nest—eggs that are called "strays" by the gauchos, and remain fit to eat for many weeks after they are dropped.

When the eggs are hatched the male looks after the brood—leads them about where food is most abundant, and keeps his eyes open for the ever-near dangers. Although the young birds do not at first recognize an enemy in the predacious beasts and birds that surround them, the old cock remains with them sounding "a loud snorting or rasping warning call" whenever he sees a danger, until the youngsters know the dangers for themselves—a very short time sufficing.

The habit which ostriches have of sticking their heads into the sand, leaving the body exposed to danger, has often been mentioned in books and used as an illustration of what a fool will do. But when one comes to study the ostrich in its home on the desert the habit does not seem at all foolish. Indeed, it is a wise provision of nature for the safety of the bird in a region where hiding places are scarce. When a brood of young ostriches is warned by their guardian they instantly fade out of sight. Gauchos told me that they had surprised broods of more than a score, of which they were able to find no more than three or four, and yet those birds had no more shelter for hiding than was afforded by a dozen or so of small bushes. Squatting motionless, with his head in the sand, the ostrich is so near in color like the sand and the scant herbage that grows there that even experienced hunters fail to see him. His body looks like a gray desert bush—so much like it that a man may look at without recognizing it. When looking for young ostriches the gauchos examine every bush within many rods of the spot where a brood disappears, and so find very often that what seemed to be a bush was wholly or in part a young ostrich. With its head up, of course, the ostrich would be at once detected. With its head in the sand it often escapes even the keen-eyed fox, the gauchos say.

Ostriches readily learn the habits of their persecutors. When Patagonia was first discovered by white men the aborigines were afoot, and the ostriches, being hunted by men afoot, were accustomed to flee at the sight of a man afoot. The Spaniards introduced horses on the pampas and at first the ostriches were not greatly frightened by a man riding. Very soon, however, they found the mounted man dangerous. For some hundreds of years only mounted men pursued the ostriches, and they at last got to a point where they did not fear a man on foot. Then came a great flood of emigrants to Buenos Ayres—chiefly Englishmen and Italians, both classes everywhere the avowed and open enemies of innocent bird life. These took guns to slay the ostrich, and straightway a man afoot once more became an object of terror, while the smell of powder smoke, it is said, will set the pampa birds running away when the gun is at a distance of two miles.

Further than that, a ranch owner is found here and there who will not permit ostrich hunting on his grounds. The birds quickly learn where they are safe and gather from surrounding districts in great bands, leaving the hunted grounds bare. And what is more remarkable still, the very birds that will flee for their lives when started by a man on the hunted grounds will show not the least concern at the approach of a man when they are on safe ground.

That they are readily domesticated may be inferred from this, and so their plumes may be obtained without killing them. But not many are kept so, because the old cocks are often ugly and will attack even men accustomed to feed them.

Because the ostrich, though having wings, is unable to fly, it furnished such sport on the desert as may rarely be found elsewhere. Consider the healthful dash of the athletic young men and women when hunting on Long Island. Remember the old time southern planter, when with thorough-breds and yelping hounds he ran to death the long-winded red fox. And then there are the races across the Colorado plains in chase of a coyote or an antelope or a deer. The game is worth the struggle then, and the struggle is worth—how can one estimate the value of such a mad chase? It is simply glorious, but there is a race better still—the race for the life of an old cock ostrich. With both wings drooping if he be at the south, but with one up and spread like a great sail if he be at the north, he stretches out his neck and flees away. The sportsman has no need to urge a well-broken desert horse—it will turn into the hot trail and stretch out in pursuit till the speed sends a gale whistling past the ears of the rider and the dust from his heels lingers above the mesa like the smoke from a flying express.

Nor is the thrill in the race alone, for there are pitfalls in the shape of burrows where a misstep will send the rider flying sure enough, while gullies and gulches with perpendicular walls lie here and there across the trail. The bird with widespread wings will land in safety after a jump over a precipice, but rider and horse must stop short on the brink or plunge to certain death.

And when the bird is overtaken he is never shot to death. The sportsman must loose the bolas from his waist, and, swinging them with whizzing speed around his head, launch them forth at the right moment to tangle the feet of the bird before it can dodge the blow. Men pay good prices in the States to see a Capt. Brewer knock down a pigeon at thirty yards with a scatter gun, and they probably get the worth of their money, but what is the skill of a pigeon shooter compared with that of the man who can strike a running ostrich with the bolas at a range of sixty yards?

Among the gauchos the chase of the ostrich is known as "the wild mirth of the desert."

The ostrich can swim after a fashion, but the water in cold weather numbs its legs until it is barely able to crawl out on the bank after crossing a stream. The Indians take advantage of this and drive the ostriches to water in cold weather.

Once upon a time a milk-white ostrich appeared

among the gray birds that roamed about to the south of Carmen de Patagones. Its conspicuous color at once drew the Indians and gauchos after it, but for some reason their attempts to kill it failed, and within a few days the belief that it was the god of the ostriches was spread among the hunters, and thereafter their superstitious fear of disaster made them avoid it altogether. It was seen for some years, but the unsuperstitious panther probably got it at last.

Both the eggs and the flesh of the ostrich are counted good eating, the wings being the most approved part of the flesh.

Next in point of interest to the ostrich are the various kinds of wild fowl. It is with a curious feeling that the traveller sees ducks singly and in flocks come hastening toward his steamer on the Patagonian coast instead of flying from it in wild alarm. A steamer passes each way along that coast once in three or four weeks, but the curiosity of the ducks is not satisfied by that, nor does such shooting as the steamer officers do serve to frighten them to a noticeable extent. I have seen a flock that had been driven away when one of its number had been shot return again to hover above the spars, and so lose a second and even a third individual.

Then, too, in the harbors flocks of ducks fly up and down and often alight within easy gunshot of the landings, while a gunner in a boat can have all the shooting he wants without the trouble of rigging up blinds or using decoys. In fact to kill ducks was too easy when I was there. The number of ducks seen was not prodigious. There was no wild celery or wild rice for food along shore. It was, indeed, difficult to see what they found to feed on about the harbors, but enough were there to keep a shooter busy. This refers to the months of April and May, and the people said it was the same the year round.

The best sport with a gun, however, is to be had with the geese. There are two varieties, and both are quite numerous enough to satisfy any one, even about the harbors. On the lakes—both salt and fresh—back in the interior they are found really by the million, and so, too, are the ducks. Around the harbors the geese frequented the low marshes and the borders of the lagoons that were filled with water at high tide. No one among the population had a decoy, and the birds were wild enough to get up at very long range if a man approached them openly either on foot or on horseback. They are much swifter on the wing than they seem to be, and so a sportsman could find use for any grade of skill that he possessed. On the other hand, the tenderfoot would not be obliged to go away without a trophy. It is an open country, so that the birds can be seen a long way off, but there are bushes enough behind which one may creep within easy gunshot range.

As trophies the geese found in Patagonia are remarkably beautiful. The Antarctic gander is snow white, with a bluish bill, while the female is colored and mottled in a way that makes her little, if any, less attractive to the eye than a North American wood duck. The ducks, on the other hand, are not especially beautiful. The teal is about the handsomest of the lot.

Black-necked swans are common enough, the bodies, save for the head and neck, being entirely white. So, too, are swans that have black heads, necks, backs and wings, with snow-white breasts. This is a most beautiful bird, and when roasted gaucho fashion over an open fire is said to be the best eating of any bird of the south end of the continent.

The swans, geese, and ducks are all found on the lakes 7000 feet or more above the sea, as well as on the seashore. The lakes form their favorite breeding-places.

Another bird sure to interest the sportsman is the Patagonian prairie chicken known as the tinamou. It lives on the most arid desert as well as near the streams. There are two varieties. The larger one is known as the rufous and the smaller one as the spotted tinamou. Both give as good shooting, and are as good to eat as prairie chickens or quails, and as game they are not materially different from their North American cousins. But the spotted fellow has peculiarities. The cowboys, when a flock is started, make a dash at the birds with yells and howls that simply unnerve the game. The birds squat down and permit themselves to be lifted up in the hands, and then, after a gasp or two, stretch out as if dead. If in this case, however, the bird be released from the hand, it springs away with a partridge-like whirr that is startling even to the experienced. More curious still, when the number of charging gauchos is enough to surround the flock, and the noise and excitement is in consequence great, the birds are actually frightened to death. The gauchos are a heartless lot as a class, and many birds that are only simulating death are mutilated in the most cruel fashion.

We now come to the birds that are interesting to the naturalist as distinguished from the sportsman, although the list of edible birds has been by no means exhausted. Of these the gulls, cormorants, and penguins will first attract the attention of the traveller. The Cape Horn pigeon, a gull the size of a pigeon, is the most beautiful picture in black and white I ever saw. It hovers about the ship in the most friendly fashion and with never a quiver or flop of the wings sails right into the teeth of the hardest gale—rising or sinking at will. But when caught in a flaw of wind near a wave-crest it gives a few energetic wing beats, and then is away again as easily as before.

The ability to sail directly into the wind with wings held extended and without flopping, which all seagulls possess, can nowhere be more readily studied than on the Patagonia coast.

Here, too, one sees the albatross, the largest of sea-birds. With its gray and white plumage and a spread of wings of from eight to ten feet (the sailors said specimens of fifteen feet spread were found), it is a remarkable sight for the inexperienced traveller. Captain Cook, when near Cape Horn, found the albatross made a very good meal, so that it was preferred to any meat the crew of the *Endeavor* had, but in modern times the sailors believe that killing an albatross will bring disaster to a ship, even more quickly than spilling salt brings bad luck to some shore folks.

The penguin is interesting because it flies through the water as some birds fly through the air. It beats the water with its muscular wings, which, by the way, have only short and hair-like feathers on them. The penguins are good to eat in spite of a fish diet, but are not sought after by any one in Patagonia. In the Cape Horn region the Indians pursue them eagerly.

Then for the Yankee traveller who is interested in bird life, there are the shore birds that nest in the Arctic region, even in Greenland—but at the call of the migrating instinct hurry away south when the northern winter comes, to land at last on the desert shores of Patagonia. There are at least thirteen varieties of shore birds that do this. That is a most remarkable journey. There are other birds found in north Patagonia in the winter time that go away south in the summer, but how far south they go no one knows. When I was in the Beagle channel I made diligent inquiry about the birds going away south, hoping to learn something to indicate whether or not South American birds visit the unknown-regions of the Antarctic continent, but the people down there had never been interested in such subjects as bird migration. In fact, I am conscious that such subjects as digging gold and raising sheep are of interest to many more people in the United States than anything that can be said of birds, unless it be the market value of bird skins.

However, there are some doings among Patagonia birds still to be considered, because they are strange as well as beautiful. For instance, there is a spurwinged lapwing that dances, what Spanish-Americans call a serious dance, such a dance as a quadrille.

"The birds are so fond of it," says one who has seen the dance often, "that they indulge in it all the year round, and at frequent intervals during the day, also on moonlight nights. If a person watches any two birds for some time—for they live in pairs—he will see another lapwing, one of a neighboring couple, rise up and fly to them, leaving his own mate to guard their chosen ground ; and instead of resenting this visit as an unwarranted intrusion on their domain, as they would certainly resent the approach of almost any other bird, they welcome it with notes and signs of pleasure. Advancing to the visitor, they place themselves behind it ; then all three, keeping step, begin a rapid march, uttering resonant drumming notes in time with their movements, the notes of the pair behind coming in a stream like a drum roll, while the leader utters loud single notes at regular intervals. Then the march ceases; the leader elevates his wings and stands erect and motionless, still uttering loud notes, while the other two, with puffed out plumage and standing exactly abreast, stoop forward and downward until their beaks touch the ground, and, sinking their rythmical voices to a murmur, remain in this posture."

That ends the performance. One kind of the rails has a different gathering. It is a long-legged bird, with a body as big as the ordinary barnyard hen. These birds always have a dancing platform in the shape of a smooth piece of ground, well concealed in the tall grass or reeds near the water they frequent. The invitation for the dance is a loud cry repeated three times in succession by one bird. They are a fun-loving race, and instantly gather at their old resort when the call is heard. The moment they reach the open ground they spread their wings, elevate their heads, and open their mouths. Then, with vibrating wings and yells as of lost spirits, they rush from side to side. From piercing shrieks their voices descend to moans and cries that sound like human beings in mortal pain, and then once more screams of anguish arise. It is the song and dance of the rail, but the performance sounds like the voices of men and women in the hands of demons.

The black-faced ibises mentioned by Darwin as a common species at Port Desire have a most remarkable song and dance, so to speak, in mid-air. As they fly along toward the roosting-place at sundown they will, without warning, dash themselves toward the ground, twisting and gyrating about in all directions, to rise again in like frenzied fashion, while they scream in wild glee, albeit their voices are anything but cheerful to a human being.

On the lagoons south of the Rio Gallegos is found a kind of a duck that has a curious performance in the air, also. The birds in small flocks rise to a great height and then divide into two lines, which alternately separate and come together, while all whistle and call in the happiest manner. As the two lines close up together they strike each other with their wings with a sound something like the spatting of hands at a minstrel jig. The performance may last an hour.

Let no one infer from what has been said here of songs and screams that the desert is a noisy place. It is, on the contrary, distinctively the silent land. One may ride all day and yet hear nothing but the beating of the horse's feet and the brushing of his own feet against the bushes. Even the fierce wind does not whistle or even sigh through the brush. In this land the birds, save only the water fowl, are as a whole silent or low-voiced. To one who has heard the constant and tremendous noises the birds of the tropical forest make the contrast is something wonderful.

Of the other birds that the traveller may see a brief space must suffice. Condors, with an eight-foot spread of wing, are common in the Andean region, and are rather numerous at Port Desire and among the rocks up the river there. The carancho is a great white-breasted bird, that is something like an eagle and something like a buzzard; it is everywhere abundant. Seated on the top of a bush on the gray-brown expanse of the desert, it is a most conspicuous object to the eye. Both con-

dors and caranchos follow the panther, to feast on the
game it slays for fun. The shepherds say they watch
these birds when hunting panthers, and where a number
of them gather somewhat excitedly, they invariably find
a panther hiding near the dead carcass of some animal.
Both kinds of birds, too, have the faculty of seeing
when an animal of any kind is from any cause so near
to death as to be unable to defend itself, and so gather
to tear the unfortunate beast to pieces while yet alive.
In the old days, when Punta Arenas was a convict station, the prisoners often escaped to the desert singly or
in twos or threes. Hardy ones were known to work
their way at times to the Argentine with the aid of
Indians or even alone, but the majority fell by the way.
Their fate was pitiful. With the lack of food and the
gnawing of thirst, their strength gave way until they
could but stagger on with faces to the north. And as
they staggered came shadows circling over the sand
about them. Then the shadows became substance in
the form of black-winged condors and white-crested
vultures of fierce aspects and an eager hunger for living
human flesh. The unfortunate would rouse himself to
shout and hurl stones at this devilish host—for a time
with success, but sooner or later he would stumble and
fall, and then they came and tore him to pieces.

Remarkable as it must seem to the reader, parrots are
found in the forests of the Andes as far south as the
heads of the Gallegos River. They can be taught to
talk, too, and are, in fact, very much like tropical parrots in all respects. They exist in the Rio Negro region
in great flocks.

There is but one species of bird there, they say, that
does not fear the feathered cats of the air, and that is a

species which one naturally would not expect to find in Patagonia at all—the humming bird. It does not seem to be a region of flowers and honey, as we commonly expect a humming bird's resort to be, though it abounds in insects such as humming birds like, but both flowers and honey are there, and so, too, are several kinds of humming birds in the summer season.

As has been said, let the Yankee tourist who is a lover of nature visit Patagonia, if only to see and study the birds. We Americans generally ask when something is proposed for us to do whether it will pay. I am not sure that even a Yankee could make money out of a tour through this desert, but if any one has made his pile high enough so that he can afford to go away and see some other part of the world, let him travel out of the way—go to Patagonia and Punta Arenas instead of Paris.

CHAPTER XI.

SHEEP IN PATAGONIA.

AT the port of Gallegos, I had a long conversation with Edelmiro Mayer, Governor of the Patagonian territory of Santa Cruz. The greater part of this talk was devoted to the sheep business, the one productive industry of the region that now pays a profit to all having capital in it. Of the stories that he told a few will serve as samples illustrating the growth of the sheep business in this new country.

John Hamilton and James Saunders, British subjects, went to Patagonia in 1885, arriving there with £500 each and a thorough knowledge of the sheep business. They bought some land and rented some more from the Government, and expended the rest of their money in a flock of sheep, uniting their funds as partners. As time went on, and they were able to sell wool, they invested their gains in more sheep and more land. In the season of 1893 they sheared 42,000 sheep and were the owners of fifty-eight square leagues of land, of which twenty leagues were paid for in full, and the mortgage on the rest was in such shape as to give them no uneasiness. By the estimate of Gov. Mayer the sale of the wool from the 42,000 sheep in 1894 paid the owners just $42,000 gold clean profit above all the expenses.

Another Englishman—I have lost his name—went to Patagonia in 1886 with no capital save his knowledge of the sheep business and a good reputation. Having abundant testimonials as to his character and qualifications, he got sheep and the use of land on credit: a capitalist was found to grub stake him, as the miners say. In 1893 this man sold out his accumulations for £26,000, and with his wife and children went back to England to live like a lord.

I saw a man at Gallegos who had gone there to work as a carpenter. He did not have $10 when he arrived—in fact, he went there in the steerage of one of the Government transports. He had been in Gallegos less than three years, and he had a family to support out of his earnings meantime. Nevertheless, he was the owner of 1000 sheep, of which two thirds were ewes. In the ordinary course, as matters run, he will be a man of independent income in five years.

There are three sailors in the country, who, within five years, were wrecked on the coast and landed with nothing but the clothes on their backs. They went to work on sheep ranches, and now have several thousand sheep each.

"And how many men have gone into the sheep business and failed?" said I, when Gov. Mayer had told of these things.

"Not one."

"Have any big companies tried it?"

"Yes, down on the Chili territory."

"Have any of them failed?"

"Not yet. On the contrary, all have paid big dividends, but, of course, a company may be made to fail by its manager. The business in the hands of individuals of moderate means is just now the best in the world. It is better than 100 per cent."

"I should think everybody in Buenos Ayres, Valparaiso, London, and every other money centre dealing with this region would be rushing into it, then."

"The country is filling up rapidly, but of course capitalists are generally shy of a business that offers such big dividends. Besides, one must learn the sheep business if he would get rich at it, even here."

"How much land remains now for the capitalist to buy?"

"In Santa Cruz territory there are to be had 2500 square leagues of strictly first-class land. It will carry more than 1000 sheep per league, and it is held by the Government at from $2500 to $3000 gold per league, according to location. You can find about 12,000 square leagues more of fair land that can be had at prices considerably less. It would perhaps prove a better investment in the long run. The territory has about 12,000 leagues of worthless land—lava beds, etc., utterly barren —almost too poor to support a guanaco.

"Of course, a very poor man cannot buy even a single league of good land, and he does n't need to buy. One ought to have some capital with which to buy sheep, but the land can be rented for periods of, say, ten years, subject to purchase at a stated price. If one can raise the money for the sheep, the land need not trouble him. The rental of the best land is but $20 gold, per year for a league."

"What is the cost of sheep now to a man who would invest?"

"From $2 to $2.50 gold per ewe. Rams cost from £2 each up to any price you want to pay for fancy stock. The ordinary ram at £2 is the one to buy now."

"Then, for a fair beginning, how much capital should a man have?"

"Five thousand dollars gold."

"But how did the sailors, with neither capital nor a knowledge of the business, get on?"

"They accumulated both by hard work, and it still can be done readily. The sheep owners are always glad to hire sober young men who are ambitious to learn the business and willing to endure the incident hardships. Their terms are not very attractive perhaps. The learner signs a contract to work for four years. The first year he gets no wages in cash. His food and shepherd's outfit are supplied, but he must clothe himself. The next year he will receive from £2 to £3 per month, and the last year from £4 to £5 a month, according to his ability. He must be a first-class man to get £5, however. Meantime, if he has any capital, he can keep as many sheep of his own as he wants, not to exceed 1000 to begin with. These he may pasture on the owner's land, and the owner furnishes the rams to run with them. He may also keep the increase of this flock of sheep on the owner's range, so that at the end of his four years' apprenticeship he not only may have his experience, but he should have not less than 7000 head of sheep. That, of course, is for the youth with capital to start with. With no capital he would get on slowly, for his wages will not buy many sheep."

"In the United States the presence of young men ambitious to become owners of herds very often serves to deplete the holdings of those who are capitalists," said I. "These young men sometimes gather calves that do not belong to them and re-mark full-grown animals. Are you troubled so in Patagonia?"

"Not yet. We have read about your rustlers, but have had no experience with them, though sheep are more easily stolen than cattle."

"Are you ever troubled with drought?"

"Not in southern Patagonia. This country is really a desert, and yet it is well watered ; by which I mean that there are plenty of lakes and springs south of the Gallegos, although the region between these waters is either very like a shingle beach or a rock-strewn waste."

In Punta Arenas everybody seemed able and willing to talk about sheep. Men who owned large herds were in all cases enthusiastic over the present outlook of the business, but their figures were a trifle less booming than those of Gov. Mayer. Thus one man who was manager for a French company owning something over 100,000 sheep, with the necessary horses, said that they made three francs on every head clear of all expenses from the sale of wool alone. The increase of the lambs averaged about 90 per cent. of the ewes, and this was an additional profit. When told that estimates made up the coast called for 100 per cent. increase, he replied that that could be had only where labor was abundant enough to care for the lambs when first dropped. The lamb at birth does not know anything—not even its own mother. Even on finding her by accident it does not know where to get its natural nourishment, but is as likely to suckle a lock of wool as the teat. Such helpless beings need great care, though after a week or so they require no more attention. The long-wooled varieties of sheep are in favor. The lowest average of wool sheared is said to be 7 pounds per sheep. A printed table of statistics which the manager carried showed that the average yield in 1889 in all the Argentine was 4.4 pounds, while that of the United States was exactly that of the lowest yield of his flock—7 pounds. His range was considered poorer than the average, but it had sustained two sheep to the hectare—one sheep on an acre and a quarter of the range.

The great difficulty that owners of large herds had in making profits, he said, was in finding laborers competent to do the work.

The one disease to which Patagonia sheep are liable is the scab. This is kept under by dipping them in various kinds of baths, the expense for the bath running from $80 to $90 gold per year for every 1000 sheep. The next greatest expense is for the killing of panthers. Every shepherd carries a carbine, and must be supplied with all the cartridges he wants. These rifles sell for less money in Punta Arenas stores than in New York gun-shops, but the annual expense for rifles and cartridges on some ranches is very great.

Foxes and a species of wildcat make havoc with the young lambs, and so these must be exterminated, too. What with hunting down vermin and looking after the sheep to keep them on the range and to dip them for the scab, the French manager had to employ a man for every 2500 sheep in his flock. On the whole, his flocks, numbering a little over 100,000 sheep, cost the company 200,000 francs per year, while the sale of the last clip yielded 500,000 francs, and the price was not high. In his judgment, it would be a very poor business man who, after starting with a good outfit and 1000 ewes on the

Patagonia range, did not attain an income of $20,000 gold a year at the end of ten years.

This being the most conservative estimate of the profits of sheep-growing in Patagonia, the picture, as a whole, is certainly enchanting. It will probably remind some readers of the days, something like twenty years ago, when the profits of the cattle business in Texas, New Mexico, Oklahoma, and other grass-and-water countries were setting people wild. These readers saw great mansions built and furnished in a style to make merchants smile and artists weep—built out of the profits in cattle. They saw men go into the cattle business one day with no capital but a broad-brimmed hat and the next, so to speak, saw them draw certified checks for tens of thousands of dollars. Patagonia sheep are now just where Texas cattle were when the owners began to reach out from the green bottom lands of the Arkansas and the Platte, the San Augustine plains of New Mexico, and the Rio Grande Valley of Colorado. It is not in the nature of any business to pay 140 per cent. or more profit per annum for any length of time. I do not doubt the figures of either the manager of the French company or Gov. Mayer, but the conditions are now of a kind that cannot last.

In connection with the profits of the sheep industry must be mentioned the effect of rag money on the prosperity of the sheep owners. In both Argentina and Chili the national money was at so great a discount when I was there that a gold dollar would buy from $3.75 to $4 paper, according to the fluctuations of the market. Because of this depressed condition of the currency, both countries had about the cheapest labor to be found anywhere. That is to say, when the currency was inflated and its ability to purchase gold fell there was little, if any, increase in the number of dollars paid to ranch hands per month. Now the sheep owner sells and continues to sell his wool in Europe for gold. He exchanges as much of this gold as he must for paper with which to pay his men ; but because the paper dollar has become worth only 27 or 28 cents in gold, he can now pay off his men with less than one-third as much gold as was formerly required. So far as food is concerned, the workmen are unaffected, for they get nothing but meat and a ground root called farina, with Paraguay tea to drink, but for their clothes they must pay four times as much as formerly, because about all the cloth of the region comes from Europe.

The homes and the home life of the sheep owners and sheep herders are well worth describing in connection with what has been said of the great profits the careful and industrious owners may make. I visited one of the best ranches in the territory of Santa Cruz. It was located three miles below Santa Cruz city, and was the property of two brothers of English blood, born in the Falkland Islands. The Falklands being full of sheep and no more land to be had there, these brothers took their inheritance and went over to Patagonia. They selected their range when choice could be made anywhere, and so got two valleys running into that of the Santa Cruz. No matter how dry the season, therefore, they were sure of grass for their flocks, and no matter how severe the blizzards of winter, the sheep would find plenty of shelter under the hills and steep banks and in the lee of the clumps of brush that grow on low ground. The brush, too, was in sufficient quantity and of a size to serve as fuel and for building corrals. It was as good a location as one could ask for.

On the tongue of moderately high ground, where the two valleys united to enter that of the Santa Cruz, they built their house. It was a mansion for that country. The walls were of vertical boards battened with thin strips, and the roof was of corrugated iron. This structure was divided by wooden partitions into four comfortable rooms, of which two contained two beds each, one was a general living room and kitchen combined, and the fourth was a store-room. All but the last had good wooden floors. There was a good wrought-iron cook-stove in the main room, and a table and chairs that had come from a furniture factory. The beds, too, were of factory make, and there were sheets as well as blankets on them. There were a few photographs on the walls—portraits of relatives and friends—and everywhere a profusion of grocery and tobacco-store lithographs. All these things could be seen when the doors were closed, because there were windows with glass in them, and the glass was kept clean. There was a broom in the corner, and the floor showed that it was used regularly. In short, here was a house that was neat and comfortable.

I ate dinner with the brothers. We had mutton roasted over an out-door fire—the best kind of roast—with fresh-baked bread, Yankee hard tack, and coffee with granulated sugar and Yankee condensed milk in it. Knowing something of ranch life as it is ordinarily found in Patagonia, I said to one of the brothers:

"I do not believe there is a sheep man in Patagonia that lives more comfortably than you."

"I fancy not," he said. "We have about everything that we want, and do not mean to starve for the sake of saving sixpence extra."

Thereat an employee who had been a sailor, and had

turned shepherd with good success, rolled his eyes expressively toward a bright-colored lithograph on the wall above the table. The lithograph was a picture of a pretty girl leaning over a farm-yard gate in a way to show her well-rounded form to advantage, while her skirts were so short that she was at least in no danger of tripping on them when she walked. Jack's gaze lingered on the fair form for a minute, and then he said :

"We have everything that the soul could long for, except society. You can't get the kind of a wife you want to come to this country."

"I 've heard," said I, "that the Tehuelche girls are pretty and coquettish in their manners, and not at all averse to marrying stalwart young white men."

"That 's so,' said Jack. "I know. I tried it. I gave an old buck six horses for his daughter, and she was the prettiest one in the whole tribe. We were married Tehuelche fashion. They killed and ate half the horses I gave for her, and made a dance, and the medicine man shook his rattles over us, and put charms around our necks to keep the devils off. That was the swellest Patagonia wedding of the year, I 'll lay five pounds. So we set up housekeeping. Then the old buck, and the mother, and the grandmother, and the sisters of the grandmother, and the brothers and sisters of the buck and of the mother—Lord ! the whole tribe came to visit us. It took ten sheep or a horse a day to supply them with grub. I stood it for a month, and then I got a divorce."

"That 's an interesting incident. How did you manage the divorce business ?"

"Took my Winchester, and run the damned outfit to the other side of the Cordilleras."

I saw half a dozen sheep men in Gallegos. They had

come to the settlement partly on business and partly for the pleasures of society. With a dozen villagers they were seated at a large table in the dining-room of one of the hotels. A huge kerosene lamp overhead afforded fair light—enough at least to show that the crowd was unshaved, unwashed, and squalid. Each man had a tumbler at his elbow. A fat, round bottle that held about a gallon of claret was passed along at frequent intervals to keep the tumblers full. All but one were drinking wine. The exception was an Englighman, and he took whiskey. Half the crowd were playing cards, and there were kernels of corn in little heaps as chips before each player.

"This is a great game," said Mr. William Clark, formerly of Salem, Mass., a ranchman, who acted as my guide. "You play it, eh? Of course you do. Why, man, they've only corn for chips, but they are winning and losing a hundred dollars and more every game."

"So? To judge from their dress they could n't afford to lose fifty cents."

"Of course they could n't, but they 're rich—most of them. Each red kernel is a dollar chip, each white one twenty-five cents. This is a great country."

"So it is. Is that old fellow with a ragged shirt at the head of the table one of the rich ones?"

"You bet he is. Ragged, eh? Well, rather; but he 's the proprietor of this hotel, and owns ten thousand sheep besides."

"And the swarthy old pirate alongside with the big heap of reds—who 's he?"

"You call him a pirate? How did you find it out? That 's just what he is. He lent me a hundred not long ago, and charged me two per cent. a month. He 's the

Government blacksmith. He only gets $30 a month, but he has hundreds of dollars loaned out at two per cent. a month. Big pile of reds, eh! You call him a pirate? That's just what he is."

On further inquiry I learned that three men playing at the table with the landlord had incomes better than $2000 gold a year, while the rest were employees on small wages paid in paper, the best-dressed man being a servant on $20 a month. Four had been well educated and two could barely read. Apparently they were all enjoying themselves, and I asked Clark if they were. He looked at me in astonishment.

"Why, man, of course they are. What more could you want?" he said.

The sheep man does not want anything more.

Mention has been made of a man who sold out his holdings in Patagonia for £26,000, and then went home to England to enjoy the proceeds of his labor, only to find on arriving there that he was unable to enjoy himself as he had expected to do. This family had lived in Patagonia only a very few years, but the life in a mud hut, where there was not a single restraint of civilization, had changed their habits and thoughts so much that they were utterly out of place among their old friends. To keep her house clean and herself was a burden for the wife, even when she had servants to help her; to wash and shave, and wear a starched collar, made life intolerable for the husband. The latent wild instinct in both had asserted itself until it was beyond control, and they returned with joy to the savage freedom of the desert.

And so it had happened to every sheep man living among his sheep that I met or heard of, except the two brothers near Santa Cruz. That there were other exceptions, I have no doubt, but they were mere exceptions. The ranchmen of Patagonia are almost to a man educated and by their youthful training refined. Some, as said, are university men, but, as a class, they live lives, that, to people of culture and refinement, seem utterly savage. They become so accustomed to this manner of life that they will endure no other.

The desert is a strange region. It is forever bleak, barren, and monotonous to the eye. With its piercing winds and blizzards on the one hand, and its fierce heats and thirsty wastes on the other, it is apparently the most inhospitable region in the world. But it takes hold of the heartstrings of men, strips off their thin veneer of civilization, teaches them joys of which they had heard only such faint rumors as may come in dreams, and so holds them fast. "Such things were and are in men; in all men; in us too."

CHAPTER XII.

THE GAUCHO AT HOME.

"WE would rather hear the bird sing than the mouse squeak," is a common saying of that most interesting class of men in South America known to the world as gauchos, and it is the saying which, better than all others originating with them, gives an insight into their character as a class. To this may be added the book definition of their name. Gaucho, in the Spanish-English lexicon, is a term in architecture "applied to uneven superficies." The gaucho is the cowboy, the shepherd, and the plainsman of the prairies and deserts that extend from the Rio Grande do Sul in Brazil to the Andes and from the Grand Chaco forests of the Argentine to the Strait of Magellan. He is an out-of-doors citizen of somewhat "uneven superficies."

My first view of a gaucho was had on Flores Island, the quarantine station of Uruguay, a place where nearly all the passengers bound on the English steamers for the River Plate, during the yellow fever season, are obliged to stop for disinfection and observation. We had been on the island a little over a day when a steer was butchered to renew the fresh meat supply. Nearly all the passengers went to see the beast suffer, among

GAUCHOS AT HOME.

the rest a Brazilian naval officer, en route to a station in the Missiones. After a little time he came to my room, asked why I had not been at the killing, and added :
" It is now the best time to go. The killing was nothing—a gaucho put his knife into his throat and it bled to death—but now the gauchos will have an *asado*. Did you ever in your life see an *asado?* It is of the finest of meat. They will roast the ribs of the cow by the fire."

Near the buildings set aside for the use of the third-class passsengers from Brazil we found a number of gauchos preparing to roast the ribs of beef over a small open fire—a fire so small that the coals and ashes occupied no more space on the ground than the ribs would have covered. The rib piece was threaded, so to speak, on a slender but stiff bar of steel five feet long. The bar was thrust into the ground so that the beef was inclined like a shelter tent above the blazing fire, and there it remained for about two hours, being turned occasionally by the gauchos.

Although this was the first time I had seen beef roasted in just that fashion, I was much more interested in the gauchos and certain other things they did than in their roast of beef. Had the officer not told me the men were gauchos I should very likely have mistaken them for sailors. The Nantucket whaler, fresh from a three years' cruise in the Pacific never showed a sweeter roll in his gait, than did these South American cowboys as they fetched to alongside the fire or veered off in search of fuel to keep it burning. Nor was the resemblance in the gait alone, for every man of them wore a belt with a knife, the handle of which was just where the man's hand would find it in the shortest time. Then, too, the hats of the gauchos were of the nondescript sort, and all worn easily on what a sailor would call the northwest corner or some other corner of the head. The leg-gear, however, was by no means nautical. Jack always loved flowing trousers, but not flowing as these were. At first glance the gauchos seemed to have brown zouave trousers with white leggings at the ankles, but a closer inspection showed that they wore rather close-fitting cotton drawers in place of trousers, and that in addition their legs were clothed from the ankles up with a length—say three yards—of wide brown cotton goods. One end of this piece of goods was tucked up through the belt and spread out across the small of the back. Then the other end was brought up between the legs, tucked up under the belt and spread out across the belly until its edges touched or even overlapped the edges of the rear end. That is all there was of it. The stuff bagged down between the legs in a fashion that made the wearer the most ridiculous looking man, in my judgment, on the continent. The nearest approach to it in North America can be found in the trousers with flaps in front, which the good farm wife used to make for her husband in the old days. It is true that the Yuma Indian of the Colorado desert wears a short length of cloth in something after the same fashion, but he draws the ends through the belt until they hang down before and behind, leaving the middle to fit close to the body, in which fashion he appears to be wearing a short skirt.

"What do they wear that cloth bagging between the legs for?" said I to the Brazilian.

"You are to remember," he replied, "the gaucho lives on the plains where no tailors find themselves in order to make clothes à la mode, eh! And the gaucho cannot himself to make trousers and he cannot himself to put what you call them—the patches over the holes in the trousers where he sits in the saddle. But he can to buy cloth and to wear one end between him and the saddle to-day and the other end to-morrow and another part to-morrow—past to-morrow. Caramba! The cloth never can to wear out in much time, but it can to cover the holes behind in his trousers. Is it not true?"

Caramba is a Spanish word meaning in the American language "gosh." It is in common use among South Americans of all classes, a fact worth mentioning, perhaps, for the reason that the gauchos have no more forcible word for use even under circumstances that would lead an American cowboy into the most sulphurous depths of profanity.

Ridiculous as the gaucho appeared when seen on Flores Island surrounded by houses and people dressed suitably for a summer stroll on Broadway, he seemed a very different being when I came to meet him in Patagonia. A hawk mounted on a smooth walnut perch in a city museum does not seem quite the same bird that it does when it snatches a partridge from under the jaws of a snarling fox on the edge of a thicket in the Adirondack wilderness. To see the gaucho at his best, that is where he will be found most interesting, one must go where he lives utterly free from all restraint, even the restraint of association. Such a place is Patagonia. This great southern desert gives perfect freedom to its roving sons. It is a wondrous solitude. One rides away from the valley of the stream in which he has left his ship, until the crest of a hill shuts out the view of the water, and then finds himself alone utterly. Pebbles red and brown, that have been rounded by the waves, with the gray and yellowish sand of attrition, are under his feet. On every side are scattered clumps of stiff, gaunt gray bushes. Further away the land rises in knolls and ridges. Seeking for a change in the landscape, one rides to the top of the highest crest in view, only to find that the ridges he saw before had apparently moved on. At any rate, before him stand ridges and knolls of precisely the shape he had looked at on first scaling the mesa. Turning around and looking back, the ridges and knolls just seen in front are found duplicated. One may ride for hours with never a change in the landscape which the ordinary eye can detect. It is an unvarying gray wilderness. It is as silent as it is desolate. The wind blows strong in the face, but it does not whistle, neither does it make a rustle in the bushes, unless it be a gale. The brush does not even bend or sway under its impulse. It is, save to the most observant, usually a lifeless desert. The faint chirp of a desert sparrow, called by the Indians, mouse bird, because of its color and its habit of running over the sand as it dodged behind a bush at the strange sight of a human being, would not be heard by the ordinary traveller, and unless the ostrich or the guanaco were stumbled upon by accident, no sign of life would come to cheer either the ear or the eye.

Nevertheless, when once a man has learned the secrets of the desert and its savage joys, he returns to it as to the arms of some fierce sweetheart, finding there a spell, an elation that makes all other kinds of life seem insipid. Nature has in store many undescribed and undescribable pleasures for those who can return to live a natural life in the wilderness.

It is in curious fashion that many of the gauchos of

Patagonia have gone to the wilderness to live on the bounties of nature, and it is a curious life they lead there. A ship is driven ashore on the Patagonian coast either by real accident or purposely, that her owners may collect the insurance. Of her crew, should they escape, at least one will become a gaucho. They will all reach one of the settlements, where a chance to take service as sheep herders will be offered them. Several will enter this service and so learn the simple arts of the plainsman —to ride a mustang, to roast meat on the steel rod that leans above a fire of small brush, to throw the lasso and the bolas, to hold the fur robe called a quillango about the shoulders while galloping across the desert in the teeth of a gale. The shepherd life seems good for a time, in spite of the steady diet of mutton, with only an occasional change to guanaco meat, the ribs of a panther, or the wings of an ostrich. By and by, however, this life palls. Why should one be tied down to one spot when the whole wilderness lies before him and nature will there supply every want? Why should one take orders when he can follow his own free will? Why mix in the quarrels and envying and strifes of the head station when silence and safety and peace may be found beyond the range? The shepherd becomes a wild gaucho.

And then there is the soldier stationed on the frontier. In the old days he was like a break-water to stop the Indians who in waves came to whelm the scattered settlements. Now there is peace, but the old forts are still manned.

"So many officers are martinets," the soldiers will say, "and at best it is a dog's life in the barracks. Let us be wolves instead." The soldier turns gaucho, sometimes without waiting for the formality of a discharge.

Last of all there is the lad who is growing to man's size in the officers' quarters of a frontier post, or in the general store of the frontier settlement. The desert calls to such boys every day as the sea calls to the children on Nantucket beach. They have lassoes and bolas as the Yankee boys have skates and baseballs. They are riding mustangs before the New York boy is trusted on a tricycle. Meantime the gaucho is ever before them with his swagger and dash, his hearty laugh, and his quick anger. Mothers may frighten their children when babes in arms by saying, "The gaucho will carry you off," and may tell the older boys that the gaucho is the personification of all that is ribald—the desperado of the plains—but as the leaders of the *courriers du bois* of Canada were the sons of French gentlemen, so the chief men of the gauchos are of what is called good family. I saw one of that kind—an Englishman by birth. He wore on his shoulders a poncho—a small squaw-made blanket with a hole in the middle through which he could thrust his head. On his feet were potro boots, a sort of foot-gear made of the skin of the legs of a colt. About his waist was a belt that carried a knife, of which the handle was silver and the blood-stained blade a foot long. He was unshaved, unwashed, and ungroomed. But he had on a suit of fine silk underwear, "because, don't you know, I can't get used to the beastly scratching of furs and flannels."

The outfit of the Patagonian gaucho is simple and not expensive. With one good horse and three dogs he can start, but a swell gaucho may have a score of horses and a dozen dogs. To these he must add a good saddle, with numerous saddle-cloths, which are usually nothing but small blankets woven by the Tehuelche squaws from guanaco hair and wool, purchased or stolen at the ranches. Equally necessary are the quillangos, the great fur robes made by sewing together the skins of young guanacos. With two or three of these the gaucho can pass the night comfortably in the lee of a bit of brush even when a blizzard is raging. The water-proof canvas sleeping-bag lined with fur would be warmer and lighter, but the gaucho will have none of it because his quillangos serve as overcoats by day.

The weapons of the gaucho are simple, and with one exception inexpensive. They are the lasso, the bolas, and the knife. The last, having a carved silver handle, may cost as much as $25 gold. The lasso is a horsehair rope. The bolas have been described by every writer who has visited the River Plate, but it may be worth telling here that the reader can make them for himself by taking either two or three round balls of iron an inch and a quarter in diameter, or two or three round stones of two and a quarter inches in diameter, and securing to each the end of a stout cord three feet long. Then tie together the other ends of the cords, making a good big knot in doing so. To use the bolas, grasp this big knot and one of the bolas, and then after whirling the free bola or bolas about the head to give them speed, hurl the whole outfit at any target handy. If the novice does not crack his skull in his earlier efforts to master the bolas, they quickly become an effective weapon with a range of twenty yards. After considerable practice a healthy man can achieve a range of thirty yards, while fifty or sixty yards may be covered by the man of exceptional skill. The gauchos tell of ranges up to 100 yards, with a two-ball out-fit made of iron. It may be so.

Having these weapons, the gaucho commonly scorns all others.

"I am astonished to learn that you do not carry a good revolver," said I to a gaucho who talked English fluently.

"And I am astonished to hear people like yourself think one of any use to us," he replied.

"But I have heard that you gentlemen of the plains have misunderstandings with each other, and that you then fight to kill."

"It is true."

"Would not a good revolver be a handy thing to use in self-defence at such a time?"

"It would indeed. To defend oneself—why, I suppose nothing could be better for that. But we do not fight so. To think of shooting a man when—Bah! Pardon me, my friend, but I can see you have never felt a man's flesh give as you drove your steel home."

The story of the life of the half-wild gaucho on the desert is full of adventure. The gaucho's day begins with the capture of a horse from his herd. It is literally a capture, for the plains horse, no matter how well trained, hates the draw of the cinch. Where a man travels alone one of his herd must be securely staked out over night, that he may be able to round up and load the rest, if there be loads. Sometimes the precaution of staking is of no avail, for there are wild horses all over Patagonia, and the joy of their lives is to stampede a tame herd, especially a herd with mares in it. For this reason mares will sell for a dollar or two each, where stallions or geldings of less strength are sold for ten or more.

When the horses are packed and attended to, breakfast of coffee, possibly, and cold meat left from the last repast will serve, but the usual bill of fare is a cup of *maté*, the tea herb of Paraguay, and a pipe of tobacco. The morning appetite of everybody in Spanish America seems to be that of a man who has been on a spree the night before. Some bitter bracing drink is all that is wanted. Then the *maté* pot is slung to the saddle, a last look is cast over the camp ground to see that nothing is left, the finger tips touch the cinch to see that it is tight, and then the gaucho swings into the saddle.

The gaucho born to the life is of the very best class of riders. Drunk or sober, asleep or awake, over the smooth mesa or across the broken ground of a gully, the gaucho sits in his saddle as easily, as securely, and as comfortably as a New Yorker sits in a cross seat of an elevated train car that has no other passengers. And yet the gaucho's seat is apparently insecure, for his legs dangle about in a way that would be simply shocking to a Central Park riding master, and one has to see the gaucho's mustang jump sideways and land stiff-legged, while the gaucho's legs are still dangling, and to see the look of absolute unconcern on the gaucho's face when the mustang jumps so again and again, to thoroughly appreciate him as a horseman.

The gaucho once mounted, where will he go and how will he pass the day? One may as well ask the first question of an Indian or of a guanaco feeding in a gully. He will go where the whim takes him and stop where night finds him. He has absolutely no reason for taking thought for the morrow, and he takes none. He will pass the day galloping easily across the desert, in the main, with mad dashes this way and that as the dogs start an ostrich. He will dismount to break the neck and disembowel the bird when overtaken or when tangled up by the bolas. He will chase a young guanaco, as well, and when an ostrich has started from under his horse's feet, so to speak, as often happens at a certain period of the season, he goes back on its track after killing it, because he knows it was on a nest when started, and that in finding the eggs he will find a delicacy of the desert.

The Patagonia ostrich egg is a huge affair, equal in weight to more than half a dozen hen's eggs. The gaucho breaks a hole in one end to let the steam escape, and then stands it in the ashes at the edge of the fire and lets it roast. Of course, it must be turned occasionally. Because these eggs are a hearty kind of food they are usually eaten at the gaucho's evening dinner. And the gaucho dinner is a tremendous affair, so far as quantity is concerned.

Having galloped over the plains all day, with, perhaps, a stop for luncheon, a cup of *maté*, and a smoke at midday, the gaucho is hungry when night comes. But, although he may have more meat than any three men may eat, he will not have enough to satisfy his appetite. This is not because the gaucho is a glutton, but because a meat diet does not fully satisfy the demands of the human system. The Indians eat fungus of various kinds, grass roots and seeds, and berries in the season. The gaucho will gather the berries because they are everywhere abundant. He will pick up a handy bit of fungus, but will not go out of his way to find it. The bunch-grass seed is too small a matter for his happy-go-lucky soul. So he is always hungry at night, and never satisfied entirely unless, indeed, he chances to kill a good fat panther. The fat of the young panther is the most satisfying food of the desert. To tell just how many pounds of young panther meat a gaucho will eat would be to throw a doubt over this whole narrative in the minds of readers not posted on such matters

However, with his guanaco, his ostrich, and his panther meat, with his *maté* cup after, and his pipe after that, the gaucho is contented, if not entirely satisfied.

Out of the day's captures he will keep the skins of the ostrich, for the feathers are worth 50 cents gold a pound in the settlements, and he sells them that he may buy more *maté*, some more silver for decorating his saddle, and some ribbons and candy to carry to a more or less attractive squaw. The money left after the purchase of these necessaries of life is used in buying a jag of the largest size obtainable with the resources at command. That is to say the gaucho gets drunk whenever he goes to a settlement. Getting drunk is the one civilized habit to which he clings to the end of life. In all other respects the Patagonia gaucho is a picturesque savage, the Arab of the Southern desert, who passes his days in wandering from oasis to oasis.

These gauchos of Patagonia are only one species of a class. There are gauchos, as has been intimated, on the cattle and sheep ranches. They are much more frequently seen by travellers than are the Patagonians, because they gather at the pampa railroad stations, and may even be found in certain quarters of Buenos Ayres. They wear their distinguishing dress everywhere, and so may be recognized readily. As seen from a railroad train they look like slouching loafers. The ordinary traveller see the gaucho at his worst. In fact, the gaucho has seemed to be such a worthless dog to so many travellers, and so many travellers have written and printed their impressions of the gaucho that he has in these later years learned that all foreigners regard him as a pretty hard citizen. Now, the gaucho is above all things a man of pride, and even of vanity. He wants to appear well, especially before strangers, and so it has come to pass that to call a gaucho a gaucho is to insult him.

Strangers should always avoid insulting a gaucho until after they have got the drop on him with right good guns. The gaucho is the handiest man with a knife in the world, and his estimate of the value of human life is as low as that held by any class of men.

"What does it matter? Many beautiful horses die," he will say when he hears of the death of a friend.

"I was in a gaucho saloon up the river one day last summer," said a Buenos Ayres man to me, "when a Frenchman looking for a ranch to buy came in. He wanted to smoke and had cigarettes, but no matches. And what was very much worse for him, he did not know the etiquette of the occasion. With cigarettes in hand, he placed one in his mouth, and then in politest terms asked the favor of a light from a gaucho who was puffing a cigarette stub, possibly a little more than a quarter inch long. So far he had done well. The gaucho said, 'with pleasure,' and the Frenchman was soon puffing his cigarette. Then he made a well-nigh fatal error. Instead of returning the worthless stub with thanks he dropped it on the floor, intending, as he said afterwards, to ask the gaucho to do him the favor of taking a fresh one. But he did n't have time enough to even open his mouth. Dropping the stub was an insult. It implied that the gaucho had been smoking a too short stub. Caramba! That Frenchman was impaled on a twelve-inch blade before he knew what was to happen."

Not only is the gaucho written down as a desperado; he is called the laziest of men, and in proof of this charge is cited the fact that he will saddle a horse and ride half a mile rather than walk forty rods. But the truth is that in his peculiar field he will work down any other kind of man. Give him horses and set him to branding cattle. He will begin his day's work by saddling the horse before the peep of the longest day of the year, and then will drink a cup of coffee, mount, and go to work. For seven hours he will gallop about the excited herd, whirling and throwing the heavy rope, downing the cattle with marvellous precision, and then out of the exuberance of his spirits gallop against the stronger bulls as they flee from the hands of the marker to send them rolling over and over in a cloud of dust. At the end of seven hours or so he will want what he calls breakfast—a few pounds of boiled and roasted meat will suffice, and if he have a couple of bullet-like loaves of bread the size of his fist, known there as *galletas*, he counts it a feast. This eaten, and a cigarette rolled, he mounts and continues the work for seven hours more. And that is not an extraordinary day, either. A ride of 100 miles in a day is not counted great by a gaucho, while seventy-five miles a day for a week, during which three camps will be made without food or water, is a matter of frequent occurrence. In short, the gaucho does any work that anybody can do on a horse, and he does it in a quantity and with a good humor that are astonishing. Attending to cattle is not hard work in the sense that ditch digging is hard, but a cowboy's life is not one of ease in either North or South America.

The home life of the gaucho of the pampas can be duplicated on the plains of New Mexico. The walls of his house are almost invariably sun-dried blocks of mud, and the roof is a flat layer of mud over brush, supported on the crooked trunks of willow trees usually found in the valleys of streams. For the roof, a thatch of the long pampa grass is also common. This is much better, because it is tight until it rots. The mud roof leaks in time of rain so badly that the family moves out of doors. Fact! The floor is the earth as the builder found it. There may be two or three rooms, but one usually suffices. Here the gaucho and his family, and his mother or his wife's mother, and a sister or two pass their lives. A few skins of cattle and panthers and deer will serve for a bed when a blanket has been thrown over them. A brazier may sometimes be found, and on this water is boiled to make *maté*. The food—meat of various kinds only—will be boiled and roasted over the open fire built without or under a simple shelter in the wet season. There is often no table, and chairs are scarce. The food, if served on a table, is simply heaped up on a platter or dish of some kind, and each one makes a grab at the heap. As often as otherwise each helps himself from the pot or the roast as it hangs over the fire. One jabs his fork into a convenient spot of the roast—forks are common on the pampas—and with a clever stroke of his big sheath knife cuts off a slab of meat. One end of the slab is flipped into the mouth when an upward stroke of the knife divides the slab, leaving a fairly convenient piece in the mouth. Watching a family of eight or ten—men, women, and children—squatting around a fire, simultaneously flipping the ends of slabs of meat into their mouths, and with upward strokes of keen-edged knives cutting away the slabs and leaving the mouth full of the steaming roast, the whole group talking and laughing continually, meantime—that is one of the most interesting, if not the most pleasing, experiences of a journey in the Argentine Republic. The traveller who visits a gaucho family must needs join in the feast, following the fashion of his host, and it is a fact that more than one tenderfoot has sliced off the tip of his nose in an effort to cut off his mouthful of meat only.

In his social and home life the gaucho is, as one would expect from what has been said, an affectionate husband and father for the most of the time, with occasional outbursts of temper when he treats those dependent on him with great cruelty. Dancing is the favorite amusement of the sexes when together, and the gaucho is then— and at every opportunity, in fact—a most persistent gallant, and a successful one, too.

Next to an intrigue, the gaucho loves to gamble with cards and play billiards. He is altogether too excitable to make a gambler fit to compete with the cold-blooded professional from the Rocky Mountain mining camps, but he nevertheless acquires great skill in the manipulation of a deck of cards, and he educates his eyes until he can detect the slightest marks on the back of a card, and so recognize the hand of an opponent. Indeed, cheating is counted as a mark of superior skill in playing any game of cards. The gaucho would be greatly astonished as well as angered if called a rascal for cheating.

At convenient distances across the pampas, and at

every railway station, will be found the gaucho saloons. They are mud-walled huts, of course, but larger than the homes of the gauchos. The walls will be found occupied with various Government ordinances relating to affairs in the district, and especially to the sale of liquors. With these will be great, crude lithographs, representing events in the last revolution, or some other fighting scenes. Mingled with both ordinances and lithographs are the tiny pictures that come with the packages of cigarettes on sale everywhere. These cigarette pictures are of a sort to make a North American, or even a North American manufacturer of cigarettes, gasp. They contain illustrations of, and conversations between, men and women that are almost always indecent, and invariably of a sort of wit that makes the gaucho scream with laughter.

The pampa saloons sell but two kinds of drinks that are reasonably pure—rum and beer. The beer is made in the suburb of Buenos Ayres—Quilmes—and Quilmes beer is good. The native rum is consumed in vast quantities by the gauchos, but it is not popular with ranch owners simply because it is cheap. One would as soon expect to find Stock Exchange brokers working the growler after a day's business as to see a pampa ranch owner bring out a bottle of rum.

The liquor glasses of the pampa saloon are peculiar. They are water tumblers in shape and outer dimensions, while the capacity is that of New York whiskey glasses. The amount of glass in one will make it weigh nearly half a pound. A more compact or better shaped missile for a saloon fight would be hard to find.

Gaucho etiquette, as already intimated, is a matter

demanding the closest study of the stranger. That the gaucho is hospitable, and in his way generous, need not be said. The stranger who enters a pampa saloon will be asked to drink, without fail. If he wishes to drink he should say so, and when he has swallowed his potion should ask the other fellow to have something. But if he does not wish to drink he need not do so, provided he knows how to refuse. The correct form of refusal is to say :

"Many thanks, sir ; many thanks. I have had all that I wish to drink, but will you not give me the pleasure of paying for the drinks for yourself and the gentlemen, your friends ? "

To this the gaucho will reply by declining with thanks, and the matter is ended comfortably. It is an offence to decline bluntly to drink, because in the gaucho's mind such a refusal could only come from one who felt himself very much above the company assembled.

There is one kind of a drink, however, which no one should refuse without first, as said in another case, getting the drop with a good gun on the other fellow, and that drink is *maté*. The drinking of *maté* among the gauchos, and among all Argentines for that matter, is like the smoking of the calumet among North American Indians. A small gourd is nearly filled with the powdered herb, and then boiling water is poured in to fill the cup. This done, a silver tube with a strainer at the bottom is poked into the decoction, and the drinker sucks the liquid up through the tube. Now, as soon as the tea has been sucked out the tea-maker fills the gourd once more with hot water, and passes it to the next person in the group, and so on. The one gourd and the one tube must serve for all the company. It will try the stomach of the inexperienced traveller to take the tube into his mouth wet from the lips of a drunken gaucho, but he had better do it with thanks and look happy. It is better to put a vile tube in the mouth than to receive a keen knife blade in the belly. And those are the horns of the dilemma often presented to the man who interviews gauchos in their native haunts. And of all things it is the worst insult possible to wipe off a mouth-piece before taking it into the mouth.

Though ignorant of books, the gaucho is a keen observer of nature. He is a thinker, bright, too, if not a deep one. His terms and sayings ought to be gathered into a book for the instruction, as well as the amusement of his fellow-man. He calls the chase of the ostrich the wild mirth of the desert. The panther is "the friend of man," because it has been known to defend men from the attack of the more vicious jaguar, and because it often comes to purr about solitary travellers on the pampas, as a tame cat might do. The rattlesnake, a species not known in Patagonia, however, is the bell snake. The dragon fly is "the son of the southwest gale," because that wind often brings clouds of these insects. There is a huge and fierce spider on the hotter pampas that does not hesitate to attack man—a most repulsive and fearsome being. The gauchos have a weird song in which they tell of an army of these that came to attack a city, and although the men of the town fought bravely, all were routed and overwhelmed by the terrible foe.

They say that horses know an Indian camp by its smell when many leagues down the wind from it, and are stampeded by the odor, because in the old days the Indians were predatory. They say that pampa deer kill a venomous snake by running around it and exhaling an odor from the leg glands that eventually suffocates the reptile. Many people affect not to believe any of this class of gaucho stories. But ever since there were gauchos, they have been drying the stomachs of ostriches, and after powdering the stuff have been taking it for disorders of the stomach, while it is only within late years that pepsin has been on sale among civilized people as a remedy for dyspepsia.

The worst feature, all things considered, of the character of the gaucho is his cruelty to animals. Cattle herding or growing on the range is naturally and inevitably blunting to the finer feelings of the herders. In the States, as in the Argentine, it is made a cruel business by law. The law provides that range cattle must be branded, and branding is infamously cruel. From branding cattle to deliberately torturing them for the pleasure of seeing their sufferings is but a step. I have known an Oxford graduate to skin a fox alive—so great is the degrading influence of cowboy life. But the gaucho does not become degraded in this respect; he is born so. Of the gaucho's religion, a sentence will suffice. He would be insulted were one to tell him he was not a Christian—meaning a Catholic—but he has never heard of the Sermon on the Mount, and is as incapable of appreciating its doctrines as is a Yankee preacher who believes in the foreordained damnation of human souls.

Compared with North American cowboys, we find that there are more rough riders among the gauchos. They do not practise so many fancy tricks, such as riding in quadrilles, but they can hang over the side of a horse to escape a bullet, or still hang on to the horse when dead. They know not the glories of a Stetson hat, with its band of gold braid, but solid silver saddle horns and stirrups and plaitings on saddle flaps are their delight. They have not that provident ambition which turns cowboys into bankers and statesmen, but they have a hearty contempt for a shallow pate, they hate a horse thief and lynch him with fierce glee, and they despise the man who kills with a bullet as one who is a coward and who misses the most ecstatic thrill of delight that comes to a man hunter—the delight of feeling the thrust of the knife that cleaves the victim's heart. They may be savages, but they are not animals. They laugh and sing, dance and flirt, gamble and drink, race and fight, work and endure, and so long as they do not lose their horses—so long, to use their own figurative expression, as they do not lose their feet, they never see a dull day and rarely feel a sorrow worth the mention.

Among the great variety of books in South America now accessible to readers of English the majority refer in one way or another to the Argentine Republic partly because it is a leading nation there, but chiefly because Buenos Ayres is, as its people say, "the Athens of South America." Nearly all these books have been written by Englishmen, and it is to English writers that Americans commonly look with confidence for information about many other things, and in many other matters, than those of geography. Because of this tendency and trustfulness of American readers I think I cannot do better, in concluding this sketch of Argentine gauchos, than to quote a sentence from a work entitled *Argentine, Patagonian, and Chilian Sketches*, by Mr. C. E. Akers. He says (page 115) : " The native gaucho, too, is not a very highly interesting individual."

CHAPTER XIII.

PATAGONIA'S TRAMPS.

A NUMBER of surprises await the traveller who visits Patagonia, but probably none is greater than the sight of the tramps sure to be found at almost every port. There is nothing especially surprising in the quality or grade of the tramps; they are the same uncleanly loafers that offend the eye on the highways of the United States, but to find them on the desert and tramping from place to place, that is remarkable.

For, consider what Patagonia between the Rio Negro and the Strait of Magellan is as a place of human residence. The settlements are hundreds of miles apart. One who rides from place to place cannot travel in a straight line, but must go hither and yon to reach the springs of sweet water, and even then, in many places, the known springs are from 100 to 130 miles apart. In very many parts of the desert, only the best horses and men can stand the terrors of thirst and heat by day and of thirst and cold by night.

Worse yet, it is for the most part a trackless desert. No wagons are used, and the hoofs of the unshod horses that are occasionally taken over the route do not leave a trail that any one can follow. Nevertheless, in spite of all this—in spite even of the fierce storms of sleet and hail—tramps are to be found at about every settlement, and in some way they get on from place to place, seeing the country in true tramp fashion, and living on the food and wearing the cast-off clothing and drinking the liquor they beg from the more or less industrious people found in the region. I say more or less industrious people advisedly, for the reason that tramps are found not only among the ranches of the energetic sheep farmers, but also in the wigwams of the Indians.

I got my first view of a Patagonian tramp at the first Patagonian port I entered—Madryn, on the shore of New Gulf. The Captain of the Port had a United States wife, and, on learning my nationality, made me at home at his house. While I was in the parlor talking to a number of people a man came to the open door and knocked. The Captain's wife came to the Captain and said:

"There is that vagabond again." Then she asked me if I had expected to find tramps like the Yankee article in Patagonia. I followed the Captain out in order to see the fellow, and found a man with unkempt red hair under a badly worn soft hat, a face that was of a pinkish red color and blotched with big freckles, a thin, sandy moustache, and thin, sandy beard, a coat and trousers but no shirt or socks, and a pair of shoes that were almost devoid of soles. In the presence of the official he was meek and deprecatory. He wanted to make an explanation, but the official would not listen. A naval sailor was called and ordered to put the tramp into a lockup. Thereat the tramp brightened up greatly, and walked away talking cheerfully in very bad Spanish to the sailor.

Then I learned something about the tramp. He had appeared at Madryn some weeks before that, saying he had come from Buenos Ayres on a ship. He was looking for work, too. Still no ship was then in from Buenos Ayres, and when ranch work was offered to him he said that it was a kind of work that he could not do. He loafed about Madryn, sleeping in the lee of one house or another, and begging food first of the few families there and then of the seamen who helped to keep up the dignity of the Government establishments. When people began to treat him coolly he wanted some one to take him to a little settlement sixteen miles away along the shore of the gulf. No one would do it, so he started away afoot. He had just returned from that settlement when I saw him.

"What will you do with him?" I asked.

"Give him some breakfast."

"And then?"

"He will have dinner. In the morning, after coffee, he must go."

There was but one route for him to travel—the little railroad that led to the Welsh colony of Chubut. It was a route fifty-one miles long and without water, but no one doubted that he would walk it without trouble. I guess he did n't walk it, however. The one train of this road came to town next day. I saw the tramp standing beside it while the crew were busy with their work. There were in the train some open box cars, and some that could be easily opened. While I was looking at the crew the tramp disappeared and I saw no more of him, although I was in Madryn two days longer. I think he beat his way to the colony in a freight car, tramp fashion. The Welsh colony is sixty miles long and has some thousands of inhabitants, all of whom were once poor, but have now at least enough to eat and to wear. They remember when they were poor, and they will give food and cast-off clothes even to this vagabond.

Still there was a mystery about the fellow. I wanted to learn how he got to Madryn in the first place, but all that he would say was that he had come in a ship, which was obviously untrue, unless he had come from some small sailing vessel beating along the coast. But that seems an impossible explanation of the matter, and the mystery remains.

When in the course of time I reached Rio Santa Cruz and went ashore I found a drowsy-looking white man sitting on the beach talking to a native Argentine of mixed blood. The white man, though somewhat sleepy, was indignant, to judge by his expressions and accent. Seeing me he stopped his flow of profanity for a moment, and then said :

"Beg pardon, s-s-stranger. Are you English?"

"No, I'm a Yankee," said I.

"Glad to—hic—hear it. That's whi'-whi' man's country. S-s-see tha' ship?" (Pointing to a brigantine anchored in the stream.) " S-she's English. S-so 'm I. T'—hic—t' 'ell with her. I'm one of her crew. Th' Captain lef' me—hic—here becau' drunk. S-s-said this bes' place for me ; going t' leave me here."

"Oh, I guess not. He's got to carry you back to London, or wherever the ship cleared from."

"Lonnon be damned. I'm from S-s-sandy Point. Wish t'—hic—'ell I was there now. Tha' 's God's country, eh? 'F 'e don' take me 'board to-ni', going walk S-s-sandy Point surer 'n fate."

Finding conversation with the sailor growing more

difficult with each sentence, I asked the Argentine man about him, and learned that he was originally one of a crew of a ship wrecked on the coast of Tierra del Fuego several years ago. The crew had in some way reached Punta Arenas, or Sandy Point, as the English call it, in the Strait of Magellan, where most of them had found life so pleasant that they could not tear themselves away for any length of time. This man had been sailing in the fleet of little traders that have Punta Arenas for headquarters, but had signed articles on the brigantine, and was in duty bound to return in her to England. She had come into the Rio Santa Cruz for a cargo of wool, and was then well-nigh loaded. The men, of course, had been obliged to come ashore for the wool with small boats, and as a result this man had been able to get drunk. He had been worthless as a foremast hand, and so the skipper had taken advantage of his drunkenness to get rid of him.

"Well, will he walk to Punta Arenas?" said I.

"Y' are dam' ri' I will," interrupted the sailor.

"Who knows?" said the native, with a shrug of his shoulders. "Many of them try it, as he will. Not many arrive there."

The last I saw of this fellow was on the evening of my last day in Santa Cruz. He was curling down to sleep on the lee side of a bunch of bushes. He was rather drunker than when I first saw him. He had been drunk every day while I was in port, and this, too, though penniless.

Down at the Rio Gallegos I found two more English-speaking tramps. Both claimed Punta Arenas as their home, and both spoke of it as the chief centre of the world's delights. Both were miners, they said, and they had come from the low-tide diggings a few leagues down the beach. Both had been sailors at one time and shepherds at another, and both were about as worthless as any vagabonds I ever saw. They were there during all the time of my stay, and they took pains to speak to me at every opportunity. They said each day they were going to start the next day for the strait colony, but I guess they remained where they were until the authorities forced them away.

That the tramps were numerous enough at Gallegos to be considered a public nuisance was evident from the fact that copies of a tramp ordinance were posted conspicuously in the bar-rooms. This provided that all persons found within the town limits who were without occupation or employment or means of support, and any one found begging should be arrested by the police, and on conviction before the Justice set to work "on any public improvements that the magistrate may direct for not more than two months."

I called the attention of one of the tramps I met to this ordinance.

"I twigged it the first day," he said. "I have n't done much but lie around and twig things since I came, but I 've got an occupation. Yes, sir, I 'm a miner, and I 'm here to buy horses for the outfit down the beach. Just as soon as I can get a herd of $50 horses together at $20 each I shall cut this town dead."

Inquiry at the various ports showed that professional tramping in Patagonia had developed from a variety of causes. In the north the old-time professional loafers simply extended their journey from the capital city to the Rio Negro. It seems that cattle and sheep breeding have in some way a strong tendency to make men over-hospitable. On the pampas of the Argentine, in the sheep stations of Australia, and among the ranches of the American prairies the wayfarer is not only welcome, but is made to feel that he is so. In the United States the abuse of this hospitality has pretty well destroyed its old-time heartiness. The Yankee ranchman now wants to know the character of his guests before making them welcome. In the Argentine known loafers are invited in. Men are found there who own horses and ride about from ranch to ranch, never doing a stroke of work from one year to another, and yet are made welcome at a single ranch table for weeks and months at a stretch. I have never heard of such a custom elsewhere, except in Australia. These pampa vagabonds have extended their routes to the Rio Negro ranches since the destruction of the Indians made it possible to settle the Rio Negro valley.

Next came the tramp element to the Welsh colony at Chubut. These Welshmen were supported absolutely for six years, and in part for ten or more by the Government. As a rule, the Welsh were of too sturdy a make to be injured by the charity, but some were overcome by it. They learned the desert routes from the Indians. They even strolled away with wandering bands of Tehuelches and became desert nomads.

Then, when the Welsh had prospered and were able to employ laborers on their farms, there were disagreements between masters and men, which ended in the men going away, anywhere to get clear of the hated employer.

When I was at Gallegos I fell in with William Clark, formerly of Salem, Mass., of whom mention has been made, who owned a fine ranch up the river. Clark had only two days before left his ranch to come to town, and the first thing he told me was that he had been entertaining a citizen of the United States who had come along on afoot without a cent of money and scant clothing. The man had been employed on a ranch by one whom Clark knew to be a hard master, and had left because of ill-treatment, going away without taking his own clothes. Clark was indignant at the treatment the Yankee had received, and not only fitted him out comfortably, but gave him a good lift on his way towards the more settled region to the south. Very likely this Yankee wayfarer was a reputable man, but Clark admitted that vagabonds were becoming numerous—men who told stories of ill-treatment at some ranch afar off to gain the sympathy of the impulsive ranchman to whom he was talking.

In connection with the tramp of Patagonia must be mentioned the white men, who for more than fifty years have made their homes among the desert Indians for varying lengths of time. The Tehuelches learned a long time ago that white men, and especially white sailors, were skilful in a variety of arts useful to the Indians, and moreover that they almost invariably carried knives and other useful or ornamental things in their pockets. Whenever a ship came to anchor in the Strait of Magellan in former years the Indians came down to the beach to welcome the crew ashore. First of all, there was the trading of furs and feathers for rum, tobacco, and tools, and the last of all, was the coaxing of some of the crew to desert the ship. The Indians were wily. They told the sailorman that he was so skilful in his arts he should be made a chief, and so become entitled to a fine wigwam, many horses, and all the wives he wanted. Jack's bosom heaved with joy at the bare thought of such luxuries, and when opportunity offered he gathered as much plunder as possible from the vessel and fled to the Indians.

Then he found he had made the mistake of his life. He was not only robbed of all his plunder, but in every case was stripped of all his clothing except a shirt or a thin coat, a pair of trousers and possibly a pair of shoes. In many cases the shoes were taken also, leaving the poor devil to walk barefooted over the stony desert. Instead of becoming a chief he was made a slave, who had to gather fuel and to do other work beneath the dignity of the lordly Tehuelche. He had to walk when the camp was moved, and, what was worse than all else—it simply broke Jack's heart entirely — instead of having many pretty Indian girls for wives, he became "the white fool," the butt of the entire band down to the smallest youngster. Neither guile nor bravado nor real bravery ever availed to make Jack a chief, though cases are known where a man of good natural abilities did work out the condition of a slave to that of a warrior. The lives these men led were of the greatest hardship on account of the severity of the climate and their lack of clothing, so that many died from exposure. Others were killed in quarrels, and the happiest fate that could befall the runaway was to be carried back to his Captain and delivered up for a ransom, that he might receive the punishment he deserved when he stole from the ship and his comrades. The Rev. Titus Coan, the Yankee missionary who went to Patagonia, but concluded that the Arab-like life of the Tehuelches was unsuited to Yankee missionary tastes, found runaway sailors among the Tehuelches. That was in 1833. I did not see any of them when in Patagonia, but the gauchos told about them, and I have no doubt they are to be found there now.

It is common for people of New York who have accumulated enough money to enable them to retire from business to speak of themselves as "living in independent circumstances." They can live without work. These tramps are also in independent circumstances. They can live without work. It was written, that if a man will not work neither shall he eat. We now find ourselves obliged to modify the old-time interpretation of this scripture. I do not pretend to offer any suggestion in the matter of relieving the toilers from the incubus of the loafers but those who are engaged in solving the problem, ought to know and to consider the fact that in desert Patagonia the number of tramps is greater in proportion to the population than it is in the well-settled parts of the United States.

CHAPTER XIV.

THE JOURNEY ALONGSHORE.

IT was in the month of April—and that is to say in the fall of the year—that I started on my voyage in the wake of the old-time explorers Magellan, Wallis, Cook, Bougainville, and the others whose names are associated with the Cape Horn region. I had passed the previous summer in the fever-laden atmosphere of Rio Janeiro—had sweltered and fumed under torrid heats and breathed the odors from the streets that are too vile for description until the thoughts of ice floes and of the sweet breath of a gale from off the snow-capped ranges of the far south were like dreams of heaven. But just where I was to go—what points in the Patagonia coast and southward I was to visit—and how I was to make the journey, I did not know. Indeed, when I reached Buenos Ayres, I was half ashamed to make the inquiries which the lack of a guide book made necessary.

However, I made bold to confess my ignorance, and eventually learned that the Argentine Government kept three naval transports regularly employed in voyages along the coast to the south, and that one was loading for the voyage.

Four days later I piled my baggage into a carriage and drove to the ship. I found the deck thronged with people and littered with baggage. The officers were about in gold-laced uniforms. The people were in holiday attire. A gang of 'longshoremen gathered about the carriage to get at my baggage, but the ship's steward came to my rescue before I had ceased wondering how I could escape, and in a trice everything was on deck and under the eyes of policemen in sailor uniform who guard the docks there. Then I had leisure to look the steamer over in a cursory fashion. Here is what I learned :

The name of the ship was that of the capital of Argentine Tierra del Fuego—*Ushuaia*. She had been built in Stockholm as a River Platte lighter, but after some years of service in this humble capacity had been purchased by the Argentine Government and made over for use in carrying troops, supplies, passengers, and freight to and from the various settlements established on the southern coasts in 1884.

When the transformation was complete there was a saloon 14x7 feet large and 6 feet high between beams. On each side of the saloon were two state-rooms, of which the forward ones were fitted with four bunks and the others with two bunks. The larger state-rooms had the bunks lying athwartships and the floor space between the bunks was 20 inches wide. In the state-rooms aft the bunks lay fore and aft, and because of the curve in the side of the ship, were narrower at the after end than the forward. There was a little more spare space in these rooms than in the rooms designed for four passengers, however, and so they were to be preferred.

As said, the saloon was 7x14 feet large. In its centre was a table 3½x8 feet large, while the companionway came down just forward of the table. On the whole, the space left seemed scant, especially when I learned that we numbered ten passengers, of whom two were ladies, the wife and daughter of a Frenchman, bound to Santa Cruz to open a wholesale general store.

Pretty soon there was a call to breakfast, and then we began to realize just how scant the room was. Besides the ten passengers we had the purser, the ship's agent, and another man at the table, and the table was never intended to seat more than eight. There were six of us on each side of the table that was but eight feet long. The steward could not pass around the table to serve the food; he could only bring the platters and tureens down the ladder and place them at the head of the table, and then the purser had to do the rest without aid. However, the food was abundant, and, by the Italian standard, well cooked. People who don't like garlic might have objected to some of the dishes, but a traveller should learn to like garlic. We had cold beef tongue with onion salad, soup, a beef-stew called puchero that includes squashes among its vegetables, stewed tripe, beefsteak fried with onions and tomatoes, and we finished with fruit and black coffee. It was rather awkward sitting with one's shoulders edgewise to the table, but we got acquainted the easier for the discomfort and enjoyed the meal.

After breakfast we went on deck to smoke. We found the steward washing the dishes of the whole six courses in a single soup tureen full of water. The amount of water seemed rather small to me, but perhaps I was mistaken, because when I called the attention of my fellow-passengers to it they did not think it remarkable. They said he used a fresh tureen of water for each course. Perhaps he did, but I'm bound to say the dish water as I saw it was thicker than the soup we had eaten from the tureen an hour before.

At 12 o'clock sharp, the hour of sailing, the Captain mounted the bridge. He was a slender, swarthy little fellow with straight black hair and a thin moustache. His name was H. V. Chwaites, and I learned that he had reached a rank corresponding to the Yankee grade of commander in sixteen years. Lighting a cigarette he shoved his hands into his pockets and ordered the lines cast off. Nobody seemed to think it an unusual circumstance that a naval Captain on the bridge should smoke cigarettes or put his hands in his pockets.

As we rounded the turn in the bend of the channel below the docks the pilot (a member of the ship's staff) ordered the quartermaster to right the wheel immediately after the captain had ordered it hard over, and the result was that we had to anchor to avoid grounding. Later still in the long channel leading to the roadstead the pilot did the same thing again. We were steaming along with a stiff breeze over the starboard bow, while the steamer's nose was high out of water. In two minutes more we were skating along over Rio Plate mud outside the channel, and the upshot was that we had to call two tugs, which eventually towed us stern first into the channel once more. Having had some experience with ship captains, I was simply astounded when I found that this one did not swear at the pilot for running the ship out of the channel; why, he did not even remonstrate. He simply lighted a fresh cigarette and bowed his thanks to the tug captains.

That afternoon the stiff breeze became a gale, and some of the passengers looked with nervous apprehension at the spars of three different wrecked ships that we passed, but it appeared from the behavior of our steamer that she was a remarkable sea boat. Although but one hundred and sixty feet long and about thirty-five broad, she rolled so little in the sea that no racks were needed on the table when dinner was served. In fact, the few of us not seasick had a very pleasant time at the meal, for we had plenty of room.

Night brought new matters of interest. In spite of the storm it was a warm, oppressive night, and the air of the cabin would have been stifling even with the companionway wide open. The seasick ones wanted the doors closed, and so they were closed. Worse yet, I had chosen one of the after state-rooms because it had only two bunks. It had neither port-hole nor skylight nor window of any kind. The door was small, and it fitted the doorway, I thought, closer than any other two parts of the cabin fitted each other. When shut my room was hermetically sealed. My room-mate was very seasick and in a chill. Would I be so kind as to keep the door closed? There was but one answer. I had to say it would afford me great pleasure to do so. Reeking with perspiration I stripped, got into night clothes, and turned down the bedding, and found both sheets and blanket moister from the humidity of the air than the shirt I had discarded.

Although not wishing to anticipate my story, I may say I never saw the bedding a whit drier during the nine long weeks I was on board.

Morning came with surprises also. I was out early, but I had scarcely completed my toilet when one of the four gentlemen in the room forward of mine appeared and said:

"Will you make to me the favor of to permit me myself to wash in your room? The wash-bowl there in ours is broken."

I said, "With pleasure." He washed. Another and another one followed him. None of us thought about the slop pail under the bowl, and when it had been filled the slops ran over and flooded the floor, whereat my seasick room-mate groaned in anguish and swore feebly in French.

In the after state-room opposite mine was quartered an Argentine lieutenant bound to Ushuaia to take command of a small Government steamer. While the rest of us considered the slops we heard him calling for the steward, who had not yet appeared, and we asked him if we could be of assistance. He said we could. His door was shut and he could not open it. Would one of us open it for him? A glance at it showed us we could not. There was no knob to the lock.

My next door neighbor turned to look at his door, which had been open all night. It had no knob to the lock. Neither had the door to the state-room occupied by the French family. My door only of the four had a knob, but that was found to be removable. Thereafter, when a door was shut purposely or by the roll of the ship, the one imprisoned within would bang the panel with his knuckles and say:

"Señor, that you may wish to make me the favor to bring the door knob." Whereat every man present would skurry about to find the precious article, because each was sure to want such a favor done for him, sooner or later. We had a carpenter on board, too.

After washing ourselves a few of us gathered on deck near the head of the companionway to get a breath of fresh air before coffee was served. Among the rest was the French merchant, who was the best groomed man of the lot. We were inclined to be cheerful as we watched the tumble of waters, and hailed with delight the advent of the steward when he first appeared. When he got closer to us we were not so much delighted. He was carrying an open sugar-bowl and a platter of tiny sweet biscuit—the certain signs of coming coffee. But before reaching the companionway he had to pass a big chicken coop that occupied the centre of the quarter-deck, and, as he explained afterward, he never did like chickens. He had been seasick all night, and the sight and smell of that coop were too much for his stomach. Rushing to the rail he leaned far over, and, regardless of sugar-bowl and biscuit, paid a flowing tribute to Neptune.

At that the dapper Frenchman grew white, exclaimed "Oh, my God!" and, clasping his hands to his stomach, fled to the opposite rail.

However, the sea grew calm next day, and the warm sun came down on a sea rippled by a gentle breeze. Everybody came on deck then, perfectly willing and even anxious to be contented. But not all could succeed. There were some who did not think any better of chickens than the steward did.

The chicken coop, which stood on the quarter-deck, contained over thirty chickens, and it was provided with a slat bottom. People who object to having chickens roaming about over the lawn of a farmhouse will sympathize with the passengers on the *Ushuaia* who did not like to have a chicken coop in the centre of the quarter-deck. The roll of the ship was slight, but it swashed the refuse of that coop clear across the deck. Some of the passengers said such a condition was never before seen on the quarter-deck of a naval ship. However, we all knew that it would not do to brood over sorrows, and the livelier ones began to seek to amuse the rest. The Frenchman knew a dice game different from any the rest had ever heard of, but unfortunately had lost his dice. A German doctor bound to a Tierra del Fuego gold camp supplied the lack by whittling a set from a piece of Yankee pine.

Count Richard of Roedorn, Germany, a young man travelling for pleasure, and bound for the same camp, had several decks of cards, and had learned the Yankee game of poker. Several others knew enough of the game to make it interesting for a couple who knew it better yet. The rank of the Count, by the way, did not in any way interfere with his being a right good travelling companion. He was well educated, a traveller of experience, and he had a most cheerful disposition. So far as I observed, not even a finical critic could have found more than one habit about him to censure, though that, to be sure, would have excited the severest remarks among the knowing people of New York. Count though he was, he wore made-up ties.

However, to continue the story, Herr Ansorge, a miner, let us know that he was a member of a German singing club in Buenos Ayres, and two minutes later "Ta-ra-ra-boom-de-ay" was sung in four languages at once—Spanish, French, German, and English. A half dozen other songs followed in a way that demonstrated that if we were not trained musicians we formed a cosmopolitan crowd that could enjoy life under adverse circumstances off Patagonia.

Speaking of card playing reminds me that we saw much of it on that steamer, especially on the way home, but poker was not the game. They used the Spanish cards in which swords and cups take the place of spades and diamonds, and the game was like that known in the States as Banker in which the king was high. The lowest bet on this game was a dollar currency, and, of course, money changed hands rapidly, but the greatest win of any night's play was $150.

The prevailing winds of that region in April are found between west and south. The *Ushuaia* bunted and bobbed her way through a head sea for five days before the high alluvial cliffs that mark the entrance to New Gulf loomed through the chilled mist of a storming morning. Then the wind shifted and came on in scurrying squalls. We had theretofore travelled on with the utmost care for the safety of everything about the ship, but now the captain made sail to help the steam, until the masts groaned under the strain. She was a slow tub —good for eight or eight and a half knots in smooth water, but under the press of canvas she drove across New Gulf at more than ten. The passengers looked on in delight and wonder. Soon after noon we rounded to before a landscape that was made up of low, white alluvial cliffs, alternating with sloping brown stretches of sage brush and sand, behind which rose a range of hills to complete a picture for all the world like those to be seen in the deserts of southeastern California. Then, even before the sails were furled, the captain ordered a boat lowered into the water, and he was hastily rowed to the shore.

Later I got ashore myself. The captain met me at the landing. Would I like to meet the agent of the little railroad running down to Chubut? I would. He was a Welshman, who, of course, talked English, and had lived in the country twelve years. We walked over the desert sand to a long shanty of vertical boards roofed with galvanized iron. The captain walked in through an open door as one who felt at home might do. The room was a marvel of neatness, considering the surroundings, and there was a piano in the corner. While the captain enjoyed my admiring glance, a door to an adjoining room opened, and a most attractive girl of perhaps seventeen came in.

"Is this the agent of the railroad?" I asked, when we had been introduced.

"No, she is the telegraph operator," replied the captain; but she will tell you anything about the country you may wish to learn for the benefit of the North Americans."

"Will you do that?" said I to her.

"I shall be glad to, unless you would rather talk with father," she replied, turning her big blue eyes on me in a way that showed she knew very well no man would want to see, or hear, or think of anybody else while she was around.

Three or four days later the *Ushuaia* was steaming slowly down the coast, bound for the ancient resort of pirates called Port Desire. It was a dreamy, Indian summer day, and the passengers were idling about when a servant asked me to go to the captain's quarters. I found him picking a guitar, but he put it away as I entered, and took a slip cut from a newspaper out of his pocket and handed it to me. Would I be so kind as to translate the little poem printed on the slip from English into Spanish? I would try. It was the story of a girl who stood on a pier weeping for a sailor whom the sharks had eaten in a far-away port, and it had a refrain:

> "And the waves sigh low
> As they ebb and flow,
> For they know that the sea is fraught with woe."

"She gave it to me," said the captain. "It must be very beautiful," and he nodded his head to the point of the compass that was in a line to the anchorage we had left in New Gulf. "We will be back in thirty days," continued the captain, "and then I will ask her father."

It took us more than six weeks to get back. Then the captain once more hastened ashore. I watched him through a glass as he entered the door, but no one met him there. I do not know why this was so, but I guessed that this handsome little telegraph operator had some of the characteristics that make pretty girl operators in the States so tantalizingly charming. I guess she was a coquette who thought a naval ship captain legitimate prey.

At Port Desire the view of the settlement is disappointing. One hears in advance that sixty people live there. As the ship enters port one sees a long gray corrugated iron house that is two stories high in the middle, one story high at each end, and apparently one room deep. It stands on a little plateau on the left (south) just at the entrance of the harbor. Tower Rock, a Y-shaped natural column, rises a few hundred steps away behind it; and a tall-flagstaff, braced almost as well as a ship's mast, stands in front. Both tower and staff serve the mariner as landmarks in entering port. Then three

AMONG THE RUINS AT PORT DESIRE, PATAGONIA.

leagues away to the south of this building is seen another. It is of the sort found in American mine camps—a wood and iron structure. Next, the old ruins under the precipice at the north shore come into view, and among them are seen two more iron roofs, the bodies of the houses being very well concealed by the old stone walls. Last of all, one sees close down to the water on the south side, and not far from the first house noticed, another iron structure that is low, but wide and long, and has a pile of very crooked firewood on the beach before it. And that is all one sees of the settlement of Port Desire.

This settlement cannot be said to be growing. Desire River furnishes excellent pasturage. Vegetables in abundance can be grown, and even grain, to a fair extent, with a little irrigation, while the range for sheep is said to be much better than in many parts of the territory down near the strait; but people will not come here because it is so far from any base of supplies which they can visit on horseback. The calls the Argentine naval transports make are irregular. There was one stretch of nine months in the last two years when no steamer visited the port. Of course, nobody went hungry or suffered for lack of absolute necessaries during that time, because the cattle, the guanacos, the panthers, and the ostriches supplied all things needful. With plenty of meat, a little salt, and the guanaco fur robes, the frontier ranchman of the Argentina does very well— so well that he will not take the trouble to raise even his favorite vegetable, the squash. But what worries him, when the steamer fails to come, is the inevitable famine of *maté*, the wild tea of Paraguay. The consumption of this herb is a remarkable feature of Argentine life, north and south, but in Patagonia there is no citizen but would take *maté* rather than a good dinner if he had to choose between the two. Then, too, wine and the native rum become exhausted, and so does tobacco. The traveller who looks at the settlement dispassionately will say that so long as famines of drinks and tobacco impend, there is no great hope for its future.

For the last three or four years the post of sub-prefect at Port Desire has been filled by Don Juan Wilson. Don Juan when a boy was known as Johnnie Wilson at Alexandria, Va., but his people emigrated to the Argentine, and the lad entered the naval school, where he was graduated with honor. Something of his subsequent career is worth telling to illustrate the Argentine way of doing things. Lieutenant Wilson has been in all the wars but one of the Argentine for a quarter of a century. He has a dozen medals which were given to him for services rendered, and he can show more scars obtained in battle than he has medals, but he is a Lieutenant still, although men who entered the navy after and below him, rank as Commodores and Admirals. That looks as if he had been treated very unfairly, but the truth is he can thank his lucky stars, as he says, that he is no worse off. He has been in every revolution against the Government but one, and every time but once has been of the losing party. He might have been shot lawfully several times, but because he was a conspicuously good fighter, and therefore sure to be very useful in case of a war with a foreign nation, his life has not only been spared, but he has been retained in the service. But because he was always ripe for a revolt they sent him down to Patagonia. He could not revolt there or help anybody revolting in Buenos Ayres, and in case he were needed to fight Chili or Brazil he could be had very quickly. The reason he failed to take part in one revolution—the last—was that he was in Patagonia while the revolt was in the capital. When talking to me about it he seemed to be very sorry that he had not been able to join his comrades, and that, too, though every one of them was in prison under sentences of from twenty years up.

Of the life naval officers in Patagonia lead I had a glimpse at Port Desire, where I had dinner and remained over night with Lieutenant Wilson. The barracks were found to be comfortable and even cheerful within, though as bleak as the desert without. At the table the Lieutenant sat at the head, with a junior officer and his wife on the right, and the Lieutenant's son, a bright lad of seventeen, on the left. Two boys waited on the table with a military precision of motion that was very funny to a non-military spectator. We had excellent fare—Italian soup, fish from the river, roast beef, and two vegetables, with bread and coffee and cigarettes after.

One of the waiters had a history. He was a full-blooded Tehuelche Indian. The Lieutenant, while leading a squad of sailors up the Rio Negro in General Roca's war of extermination, heard a curious cry in the thick boughs of a tree. A sailor climbed up, expecting to find some strange beast or bird, but brought back a boy baby not over two years of age. He had been hidden there in a three-prong fork by his mother as the Indians fled because she was too much exhausted to carry him further. No doubt many Indians did the same, but all the babies starved save this one because the sailors held the territory. When old enough to serve as an apprentice, the lad was shipped in the navy with his adopted father, Mr. Wilson.

Certainly no other sergeant in the world has had such a history as this one.

When we reached Port Desire we all went ashore to inspect the old ruins of a Spanish fort, and then a desert cattle man invited us all to dine with him.

We found the home of our host standing among the old ruins. The contrast between the ancient Spanish and the modern Argentine architecture was very great. The old walls were of thick masonry carried up as high as a man could reach, and above these there had been wooden roofs thatched with grass. The modern structure, built by the Argentine Government to induce settlers to come, consisted of a light wooden frame entirely covered in with corrugated iron. One sees just such houses in the mine camps of the United States, where they are popular because cheaply and quickly built. But not till one has been in such a house built where the wind blows as it does on the Patagonia desert, can he fully appreciate its capabilities as a musical instrument. When we came to sit down to the long, bench-like table for dinner, after a walk over the hills that had sharpened our appetites, we paused to listen as if to the notes of a great organ played by the hands of a mad musician. Probably the corrugations of the iron, the sharp edges of the plates, the lengths of plates projecting unsupported beyond slender beams, and the differing degrees of rigidity with which the plates were secured to the beams, combined to vary the vibrations of the plates under the impulse of the whirling wind squalls.

There were soft and smooth murmurs, hoarse boomings, fair altos, and singing sopranos, alternately and combined in a way to interest and distract every unaccustomed listener.

The dinner was, in itself, a most interesting novelty. We had beef roasted in a fashion which the natives call "meat with skin." The ribs of a steer had been wrapped in the skin of the animal, and then impaled on a long iron rod, which was thrust into the ground so that the wrapped-up meat leaned directly above a small open fire. Here it had remained for about three hours, while a patient native fed the flames with brush, and occasionally turned the bundle of meat. It was then removed, the skin was stripped off, and it was brought, dripping with hot juice, in a big pan to the table, where the hungry passengers awaited it, knives in hand.

The knives were of a class novel to an American, and, in fact, so was everything about the table. Each knife blade was a triangle, an inch broad at the handle, and tapered to an acute point, four and a half inches away. This was a good shape for the usual purpose for which it was designed—the skinning of animals, but it was not a good table knife. Even at that the ranchman had not enough to go round, and three of us had to use the knives we had carried, in anticipation of such a lack. Shallow tins served as plates. And yet, in spite of so great poverty in table furniture, we had an abundance of very good claret, served in glasses of a proper shape.

The food, too, was as surprisingly good as the wine. No better roast was ever carved than that, and it was flanked with baked armadillos, the most toothsome morsel I had ever seen. Both kinds of meat were seasoned with salt and pepper only. With these we had hard biscuit of the Buenos Ayres sort—an oblong, globular little loaf, say two by three inches large in its longest and shortest diameters. The absence of garlic and Italian sauces completed our pleasure, and black coffee, served in tin cups, ended the meal.

The next port at which we called was Santa Cruz. The great profits made by the sheep owners who brought their stock from the Falklands to the Strait of Magellan, induced many of the young men of the Falklands to come over and try their luck in Patagonia. The Argentine Government encouraged them by giving ten-year leases on pasture land at the rate of $60 national money per year per league, and at the average one league would hold 1200 sheep. The traveller will hear all about the increase in the flocks on the Santa Cruz River before he gets there, and the stories of the wool shipments will prepare him to see a small but bustling community when he arrives. I really expected to see a large as well as a bustling place.

When the steamer had anchored in the stream about ten miles above the mouth there were seen in the distance at the south bank, under what is known as Weddell's Bluff, several new frame shanties which the ship's officers called the presidio. I went up there in a boat, and found enough of the little shanties to house at least 3000 soldiers, while an old hulk moored at the beach would have accommodated 200 sailors easily enough. There were a dozen sailors with two officers on board the hulk as shipkeepers, while the barracks were in charge of two officers and a score of soldiers, some of whom were keeping house with their families. The building of these barracks in that locality could have but one signification: The Argentine Government expects trouble, sooner or later, with Chili, and this is to be a base for operations against the Strait of Magellan possessions of the Western republic.

SANTA CRUZ, PATAGONIA.

The buildings were not all completed, and some of the soldiers were at work as carpenters and painters. This show of business activity only added to my mental picture of the town itself, and it was with considerable pleasure that I returned down stream to land near the ship, and make my first visit there.

Climbing to the low table land that borders the stream, I looked back into a wedge-shaped valley between the hills, the Valley of the Missionaries, and saw Santa Cruz —in all nine buildings, of which two were unoccupied, and not a human being in sight anywhere, nor any other evidences of life than a small flock of sheep and a thin red mare grazing idly. The buildings stood on three sides of a surveyed plaza—that is, there was one house on each of two sides, one stood back up the valley a few hundred yards, and the rest were on a third side of the plaza. Among them was the inevitable long low iron structure built for the home and office of the Sub-Prefect. There was also a one-story adobe-walled house that was a combined hotel and general store, having four rooms, while another was a pink wooden building, one story and a quarter high, having five rooms that served the same useful purpose.

Among the buildings was an old adobe-walled structure, about ten by twenty feet large, with two places for doors, and the remains of a couple of glazed windows. The earth served as a floor, and the usual iron for a roof. In one corner was a depression that looked like a dry hog wallow, and a porker grunted about outside the building. They said this had been the church that missionaries preached in long ago.

In the pink hotel I found a well-dressed young man who was glad to see all strangers, and particularly one who wrote for a newspaper. He accepted an invitation to take a cup of coffee, and when I asked him if he was acquainted with the region he said he had been just at the point of asking me if I would be interested in hearing something about it. Then the coffee came, and with it a Dutchess County, N. Y., brand of condensed milk, and a blue-print map. We combined the milk and coffee, and then spread out the map and weighted the corners with our cups, the coffee pot, and the milk can.

Being thus ready for business, the young man pointed at the map. It was the plan of a great city—a city with plazas connected by wide avenues and boulevards, with streets running at right angles between. Figures and letters scattered here and there on it showed sites for Government and other important buildings, while long broken lines showed the location of many street railways. The young man explained the peculiarities and advantages of the disposition of plazas and boulevards and street car lines, and eventually, from the lay of the land, I grasped the situation. This was the plan of the city of Santa Cruz, the great Patagonian metropolis that was to grow up right there in the valley, where now one could see nine houses all told, of which two were unoccupied. It would grow just as surely as the sun would set behind Weddell Bluff, to quote the words of the young man; and then he went on, in a way to make even a Kansas town-site boomer rub his eyes, to tell of the shipments of wool "aggregating 2,000,000 pounds last year," of the good pasture to be had "at £3 per square league annual rental," of the "traces of gold found on Lake Argentine, where good mineral developments will be made," of the "experiments in wheat culture to be made, which will doubtless succeed." All of this was said to show that I had arrived at just the right time to get in on the ground floor of a great real estate deal. I did not need to buy the lots. I could have all I would build on free of cost, save for the usual charges of making out and recording the papers.

I have frequently heard men who had done business with Spanish-American nations talk despairingly of the lack of enterprise to be found there. They speak of the depreciated currency there as "adobe money," and call the nations "the land of *poco tiempo*" and "the mañana country." As to many of these nations the terms are well applied, but the Argentine must be excepted. Neither in the suburbs of Brooklyn, nor on the plains of Oklahoma, nor among the orange groves of California have I seen a boomer who could tell his story in better form than the young man with a blue-print map of the future metropolis of Patagonia.

It is perhaps worth noting here that while the young man was talking I could see an ordinance on the wall above his head that prohibited the killing of either ostriches or guanacos "within the city limits," even with bolas, while the shooting of such game was prohibited in all the districts south of the river.

And yet I am not sure but a large town will grow there eventually, although Gallegos was made the capital town some time ago. The place certainly has some natural advantages. The Santa Cruz River is a wonder. Being absolutely unobstructed throughout its course, large, deep-draught river steamers could run easily to the source, Lake Argentine, and beyond. It is really likely that gold mines will be developed in the Andes there, and it is certain that a large lumber business will be done there sooner or later, for the forests produce cedars and other valuable saw timber of the best quality and great size. There are no trees immediately on Lake Argentine, but it is connected with other lakes by navigable channels where the timber is found. When I was in Santa Cruz a party of capitalists familiar with lumber had gone up to the lakes to look into the business. Driving the logs in rafts to the port of Santa Cruz would be so inexpensive that once a proper mill were established there the great markets of Buenos Ayres and Rio Janeiro, not to mention the smaller ports, would be supplied at prices to make serious inroads on the business of those who now supply them from the United States.

Of the value of the sheep and cattle ranches as a support for a town nothing need be said to readers in the United States, who have object lessons in the matter scattered over the prairie States, but the Patagonia ranches will scarcely make as good a support for a town as the Yankee ranches do, for the reason that the land system of the Argentine promotes great estates and discourages small owners. The capitalist in Argentine territory can buy all the land he wants. Gov. Mayer of Santa Cruz territory, for instance, owns thirty square leagues of land along the Santa Cruz and Chico rivers. In owning the water front, he controls all the range back of it, for no one will take up land that has no water. For all practical purposes, he controls say one hundred square leagues. The firm of Hamilton & Saunders of Gallegos, Scotchmen, own fifty-eight leagues, and so control three times as much. Of course, it would be much better for the country if fifty-eight families owned and lived on the land these two men have, nevertheless the country is filling up with shepherds, and a month after the two French merchants mentioned had landed in Santa Cruz with the wholesale stock of goods, they were doing a profitable business with their original packages.

There is but one drawback to the value of the valley in which Santa Cruz city is located that would operate against it seriously, and that is the lack of drinking water. The young boomer did not say a word about water. There is a scant supply from wells even for the seven occupied houses with their stock, and that is brackish. Of course, should the place become a great city, the supply would be drawn from the swift Santa Cruz, but while the settlement is growing to a village of a few thousand people the cost of twenty odd miles of pipe line would prohibit tapping the river. The tide rises over forty feet every day in the river mouth, so there is salt water a long way up stream.

It is worth noting that the Santa Cruz people draw water from their wells as the people in the cowboy parts of the United States often do. A pulley is suspended over the well. When water is wanted a horse is saddled, and one end of a lasso fastened to the saddle. The other end of the lasso is passed through the pulley and made fast to a pail, which is then lowered and filled. Then the water drawer mounts the horse, and rides away till the pail is up to the pulley. Next the rider dismounts, walks back to the well, takes the pail from the lasso and carries it to the house. Last of all he unsaddles the horse. I saw this done myself. I must admit that this description of the Patagonian way of drawing a pail of water reads like a traveller's untrue tale, but it is literally true.

Gallegos, the capital of Santa Cruz territory, the next port visited, stands on the south bank of the Gallegos River, several miles above the mouth. The Gallegos is a very interesting stream. Its head is in the Cordilleras, of course, and the head is made up of a number of small streams which unite in the foot hills to make a river never less than 180 feet wide and three feet deep in the dryest of seasons. The current is fair, and although there are three fording places along its route, large steamers drawing 2½ feet of water could navigate it to the forks the year round. But that steamers will ever be found there is a matter of doubt, although the country is rapidly filling up with settlers. There are several reasons for this. All branches of the stream rise within a few miles of the Pacific Ocean, the south heads being almost within sight of Skyring Water, just northwest from Punta Arenas, while between the north and the south forks there is a complete and a wide break in the Andes through which one may drive a wagon as easily as one can drive over the mesa of Patagonia anywhere. By cutting a road five miles long through a belt of timber a highway to the bays of Chili will be formed, and so the traffic of at least half the length of the Gallegos River will go to the west instead of down stream to the Argentine town of Gallegos. I say at least half, but it is not unlikely that more than half will go west, for the reason that the entire population of the territory south of the Gallegos, and about all between Rio Gallegos and Rio Santa Cruz have a strong feeling of friendship for Chili.

"In Chili, if you have right, you can get justice every time," said a Frenchman owning 100,000 sheep on the border line between Argentine and Chili. "In the Argentine you must have the judge for your friend or you will be beaten, right or wrong."

As to the Rio Gallegos lands, the traveller finds lava

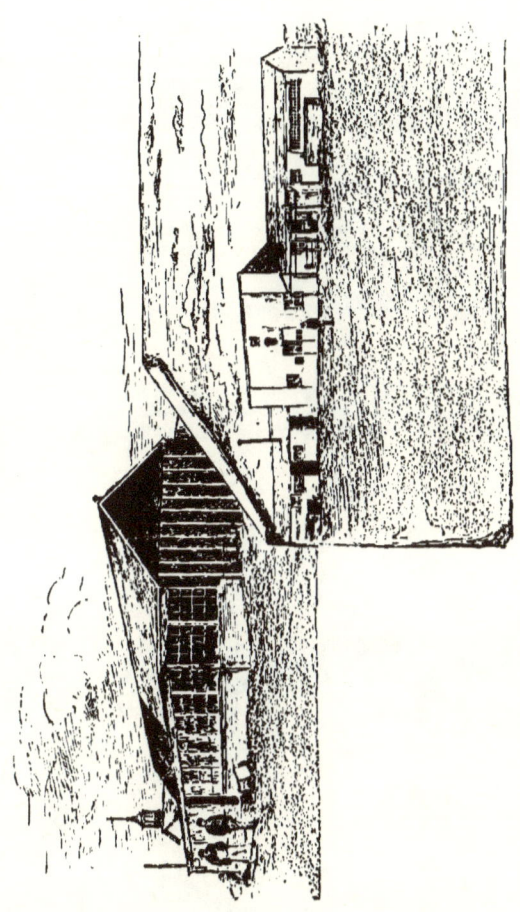

THE GOVERNOR'S HOME AND A BUSINESS BLOCK IN GALLEGOS, THE CAPITAL OF PATAGONIA.

beds and pasture lands alternating, but the pasture has the greater area, and it is simply perfect pasture. The low bottom lands are flooded in September and October when the Andes snow melts, but there is plenty of good upland pasture. Nearly all the land south of it is now taken up by shepherds, while the north side is being rapidly absorbed, the chief obstacle to rapid settlement being the lack of fuel. It is almost a bushless region.

On the whole, the town of Gallegos has a very good cattle country back of it. Along the sea-coast to the south it has some placer gold mines. The layer of black sand carrying gold crops out richer in some places than others, and there are places where the lack of drinking water makes mining impossible, but quite a number of men—perhaps fifty—can be found working the beach for gold between Gallegos and Cape Virgins.

What the traveller sees in the territorial capital now is a score or less of corrugated iron buildings, with half a dozen houses of wood and three of adobe. One of the adobe-walled houses is the territorial prison. Any smart rascal could burrow out in an hour. About one-third of the houses are hotels and stores, the outer appearance of these buildings being like that of a Yankee mining camp. Every store carries a considerable stock of liquors and tobacco, a moderate stock of hardware and cutlery likely to attract ranchmen, a small stock of wool and cotton fabrics, and a few samples of groceries. The stocks were not arranged to make anything like an attractive display, and, because sand storms were likely to come at any time to dust over the interior of every building, nobody thought it worth while to sweep or in any way clean house.

As hotels (every store was a hotel) the places were most unattractive; worse, for instance, than any I saw when *The Sun* sent me through the wilds of southern Mexico. In Mexico all of a party of travellers, men, women, children, and servants, would be lodged in a single room, with nothing but the tile floor or a bench to sleep on, but it was always a clean floor, while one could have a hammock under a veranda if he chose, and that was about the best kind of bed. Moreover, food was always abundant and good. At some Gallegos hotels one could not be certain of either quantity or quality of the food, while the blankets were neither washed nor aired nor changed.

However, there were exceptions to the rule, at least one exception. Doña Philomena, a rotund and jolly woman of middle age, with her son, a lad of about sixteen, kept a boarding-house in an adobe hut of one room, twelve by eighteen feet. She had a stove that smoked at every crevice on one side of the door, a rude table with benches at the other, a spare bed just beyond, and beyond this bed heaps and piles of boxes and bags and bundles, containing vegetables, groceries, clothing, Indian curios, saddles, and horse gear generally. There were three kinds of meat hanging from the rafters. There was but one tiny window, and that yielded light enough only for the table. In the extreme rear of the room all was concealed by impenetrable gloom. A Yankee wife would have said she never did see such a cluttered up place. Nevertheless, the mud walls had been whitewashed until they looked like the dried up bottom of a pool in an alkali desert. The mud floor was neatly swept. The spare bed had clean white sheets, and the blankets smelled sweet. The rude table was covered with a snowy cloth, and there was a stainless napkin at each plate. Doña Philomena wore a clean dress, with a bright-colored shawl over her shoulders. The picture of her as she worked over the stove in a thin halo of blue smoke, giving a stir to the potatoes frying in the pan or a peek at the mutton roasting in the oven, or cutting fresh bread, or opening Yankee condensed milk, while she smiled and joked and gossiped in a continuous flow of words, was something that the traveller would carry with him for a long time after. And when the meal was over and we all smoked and lingered over the coffee the boy got out an old guitar and played the tunes the Spanish lover plays to win a sweetheart—tunes that alternately swelled with importunate passion and faded into murmurs of hopeless longing, so that everybody stopped talking to stare into space and think of somebody else a long way off.

The Captain of the steamer introduced me to Gov. Edelmiro Mayer. The Governor lived in a large frame one-story building that had a glass-enclosed veranda overlooking the river. On the whole, this was a most remarkable home, considering the locality. Though like a mining-camp house, as the rest were in outward appearance, there were within Oriental rugs of great value on the floor; a grand piano of American make that cost $1500 in gold in New York stood in one corner of the parlor; a great organ such as professional musicians prefer was in another; a library of 5000 volumes, made up of standard works of science and literature, was in the glass-enclosed veranda, while the furniture and hangings and bric-à-brac were everything that a cultivated taste could ask for. So was the sideboard, with its old Kentucky whiskey. Having very little governing to do, the Governor devoted himself to literature and music, occupations in which he was ably assisted by his wife, a charming Argentina.

Gov. Mayer's name is not unknown to American history. Just for the love of adventure and free republican institutions he came to the United States to help during the war of the rebellion. He commanded a negro regiment with conspicuous success. Afterward, while down on the Rio Grande, he crossed over to help patriotic Mexicans overthrow Maximilian.

Although small in the number of its houses and its people, Gallegos is in full plumage as a territorial capital. A two-story frame building was in course of construction that will eventually be the White House of Santa Cruz territory. Besides the Governor, there was the usual list of other officials necessary for the dignity of such a place. As at Ushuaia, already described, no official had anything to do worth mention. Indeed, the Captain of Police, who in a United States territorial capital would need to be a man of nerve and muscle, was here a cripple who could neither sit on a horse nor walk unaided the length of the town's one street. Still, courts were held sometimes to decide conflicting claims of shepherds, and a gaucho who had slashed a comrade in a drunken brawl was arrested just before I arrived. Gallegos will be a favored stopping place for criminals when the country gets filled up, I guess, for it is very handy to the Chili line, and extradition treaties between two such countries as Chili and Argentine are of little value.

A peculiarity of the climate is the southwest wind of summer. It begins at 8 in the morning and increases in violence until after noon, when it occasionally blows hard enough to lift a man from the saddle. At 3 in the afternoon it moderates, and at 6 o'clock and thence on through the night there is usually a calm. This wind blows every day in spring and summer, and on many days it brings hail and sleet that no man can face. The winter season, though colder, is by far the most pleasant of the year. But in spite of wind and cold, Patagonia is pre-eminently a healthful region now. Every human being that I saw there carried the glow of health in his face and the spring of youth in his muscles. But there are zymotic diseases just as there are in Yankee villages, because of the juxtaposition of wells and cesspools, and these diseases will prevail wherever settlements are made, because of the utter indifference of Spanish-Americans to the rules of hygiene as applied in such matters.

To sum it all up, the settlements on the coast of Patagonia are small, the buildings are of the temporary or mine-camp class, and life in them is decidedly tranquil. The towns are new, and the bad name the country has borne in the matter of climate and sterility has kept foreigners away. "There has been no boom—just a slow, healthy growth," as the Kansas boomers' paper would put it, and in this case the statement is true. Santa Cruz territory now has 800,000 sheep. Its Governor expects to see 10,000,000 there in ten years more, besides some millions of horses and cattle. Settlements will very likely spring up in the interior, and the vast region over which the Tehuelche Indians held undisputed sway during the 350 years after the land was discovered by white men will become a peaceful, thinly populated pastoral land, whose people will grow comfortably rich supplying Europe and the United States with wool, hides, and tallow. But there are no indications worth mentioning that, as a whole, it will ever be anything else than this, and at present it is of interest to the Yankee nation chiefly as a region out of the way for tourists to visit.

After leaving Port Desire we had a variation in our meals on board ship. The sailors had gone fishing with a net, and with success. There were two kinds,—one rather like a Yankee smelt, only more slender, and the other somewhat like a Lake Erie pickerel. Both were excellent, but the little fellow boiled and made into a salad was particularly fine.

Then, too, a species of ducks had become very abundant. They were so dark above as to appear black, while the under parts were pure white. Their curiosity led them to hover about the ship in twos and threes, sometimes flying along, say fifty feet above the weather rail. On such occasions Captain Chwaites brought out a light shotgun. On the day we entered Santa Cruz he knocked so many down on deck that the passengers had roast duck for one course at dinner. In fact, for a citizen of South America, the captain was a remarkably fine sportsman. He never used a shotgun on a sitting bird. He could kill gulls at long range with a rifle when they were bobbing about on the waves. While we lay in Rio Gallegos he rode out on the table-land one day with a man living there and killed three guanacos, using the bolas Indian fashion to bring them down. The tourist who sails with Captain Chwaites can expect to have game at the table frequently during the voyage.

But it should not be inferred from what has been said so far that the table was beyond criticism during my voyage. For instance, the napkins were not changed at any time oftener than once a week, and at the last the interval increased to ten days. The table-cloth remained unchanged an equal period; this, too, during the home voyage, when the number of first-class passengers had increased to twenty-five and the table had to be set twice.

The captain was not unaware of the condition of affairs. He stood beside me one day while the steward shook the table-cloth over the rail. It looked as one could expect a cloth to look after ten days' use at sea.

"Look at that cloth," said the bold skipper. "Did you ever see such a dirty lot of passengers?"

I was eating in those days in the Captain's sitting-room, and his remark had no personal application. I replied:

"Looks vile, don't it? But why don't you order the steward to wash it?"

"I cannot. There is so little soap. Look at my hands. I have no soap to wash them with. The passengers know we have no soap. They ought to be careful, like gentlemen."

His hands certainly showed the lack of soap. So did those of the steward. We got a cup of coffee with a handful of sweet crackers in lieu of the meal called breakfast in the United States. One did not want even that many if he happened to see the steward serving them with his unwashed hands.

Then the vegetables, which were abundant on leaving Buenos Ayres, dwindled away before we entered the Straits of Magellan. At Punta Arenas cabbages, turnips, potatoes, and some other roots are grown and sold at low prices, but we got such a scant supply that for the last three weeks of the voyage our food consisted chiefly of meat, dried peas and beans, and hard bread.

Worse yet, the bed linen was not changed during the entire voyage of nine and a half weeks. Complaints were of no avail, so I was at last glad to leave my bunk and roll up in a fur robe of Indian manufacture that I bought when in the Rio Gallegos. With a lounge in place of a bunk, I was as dry and comfortable as I had been damp and miserable in the bunk. Should any reader of this try the voyage he will need to take a large supply of woollen under- and night-wear, including socks. The proper changes of these will serve in place of changes of bedding.

Nor is the list of discomforts complete. When leaving the River Plate the air in the saloon and state-rooms was insufferably close. There was no ventilation for the state-rooms save through the doors into the saloon. The saloon was ventilated through the doors at the head of the companionway and through the skylight, but there was no sort of wind sail or device to force the air down. In the summer time in the River Plate, where the thermometer sometimes marks 110° in the shade, that saloon is to be compared only with a Turkish bath. In winter, while coasting along Tierra del Fuego, that same saloon becomes like the vault of a cold storage company. The air is saturated with moisture, and the temperature barely above the freezing point. The moisture gathered like dew on the walls of the saloon as well as of the state-rooms, and sometimes trickled down to form little pools in the bunks and on the floor. There was no device for heating or drying the cabin, neither stove nor steam-coil. We were dressed continually in the heaviest flannels, and wore heavy overcoats, but the chill air penetrated everything, even to the marrow of the bones.

I once passed two weeks in Greenland in the month of October, and exactly two years later was digging away the snow in the Rocky Mountains nine thousand feet above the sea, that I might have bare ground for my blankets at night. My home is in the Adirondacks, where the snow lies four feet deep all winter long, but I have never suffered from the cold as I did during four weeks of this voyage.

And yet at times, when the conditions were such as to make us all most uncomfortable, we often enjoyed life rather better than at any others. Our greatest trouble when the weather first became cold was to pass the evenings. It was stupid turning into wet bunks at 7 P.M., and wretched work trying to play cards or spin stories in a raw, cold, reeking saloon.

But a happy inspiration struck one of us while standing by the hatch leading to the little store-room abaft the cabin. This store-room was in charge of the shortest and thickest man aboard ship—a person who looked as if he had once been a typical quartermaster on a Yankee man-o'-war—a great tall, broad-shouldered, impassive, full-whiskered man, but through some accident had been telescoped down to a stature of four feet nine. The first cold evening after leaving the River Plate a passenger, while walking the deck for exercise, stopped by the store-room hatch just as the captain's valet came there carrying a plate with a tumbler on it.

"Storekeeper?" said the lackey.

"Yes," replied the thick, short man.

"Cocktail."

"Yes, sir. Quickly."

A few minutes later the storekeeper came up the ladder carrying a glass tube about ten inches long and two wide. It was closed at the bottom and had a long-handled silver plunger in it. The tube had about two inches of a light brownish liquor in the bottom over a layer of sugar. Standing the tube on the deck the storekeeper pumped the plunger up and down vigorously. The aroma of gin, bitters, lemon, and something else greeted the nostrils of the passenger. The storekeeper poured the mixture into the glass until the glass was full. Then he looked at the tube. There was a quarter of an inch of the mixture left there. Backing carefully down into the store-room the storekeeper looked up at the passenger. He saw that the passenger was looking at the remnant in the tube. The storekeeper's face was absolutely impassive, as a whole, but when he caught the passenger's eye he looked down at the remnant, moistened his lips with his tongue, looked up slowly at the passenger again, and then his right eyelid trembled expressively as he said :

"It is a cold night, is it not, sir?"

The passenger went down into the saloon and gathered about the table the French merchant, the German count, the miner, the doctor, the Argentine lieutenant, and several others. Then the steward was called. Could he bring some things from the store-room? He would be pleased. What would the gentlemen have?

The order ran something like this : Brandy, sugar, lemons, claret, and a plenty of hot tea to be brought after the other articles were delivered. A hot soup tureen was also included in the order. Some sugar was placed in the tureen and a bottle of brandy poured over it. Then the brandy was fired, and the blazing mixture was stirred with a big spoon till the sugar was dissolved. After that a bottle of claret was stirred in, and then a pot of hot tea, equal in measure to the two bottles previously used, was stirred in also. Last of all a lemon was sliced in, peeling and all, while the stirring was continued.

Possibly this mixture would not be countenanced by the art drink mixers of New York. There may be something wrong with the process or something lacking in the alcoholic values, but for travellers on an Argentine naval transport, who are wearied through idleness and chilled by the mists and the blasts of the Patagonia coast, the drink is a blessing from Bacchus.

It was a temperate crowd, on the whole. The exceptional man was my best friend. I left him early one night on deck and turned in. We were then off Gu St. George. At 2 o'clock next morning came this man and dragged me from my fur robe and said hoarsely:

"On deck quickly. The ship sinks."

Then he fled on deck. Though but half awake, I could hear the ship's pump throbbing at lightning speed. I fled on deck as he had done. He had disappeared. The Captain tranquilly smoked a cigarette under the bridge.

"My friend So-and-so just told me the ship was sinking," said I. The Captain shrugged his shoulders.

"He has had six bottles to-night," said he. "It is he, not the ship, that is full." The engineer had been testing the pump, and the noise of it had made the fancies of my friend run on disaster at sea.

The curios which a traveller may gather on a voyage like this are not many in variety, but they are very interesting as far as they go. Most people would call the Patagonia guanaco skin robe or blanket the most valuable product of native industry. The pelage of the young guanaco is a soft and beautiful fur—red on the back, like that of a Virginia deer, and shading into pure white underneath. The skins of the young that are just about to be born or have just been born are preferred, because the fur is then exquisitely fine and the skin never gets hard and stiff. The Patagonia squaws cut the young skins into pieces, which they set together in the form of a great blanket in which the colors of the fur are shown to the greatest advantage. The sewing is done with sinews. These robes are everywhere used for beds in that region, while no desert man or sheep herder would think of living without one in lieu of any other kind of a blanket for his protection when sleeping in the open air. In Punta Arenas the price was $35 paper each, or not far from $9.50 gold. In Patagonia ports at the north they can be had for a little less. There is no difficulty in finding them on sale. They would probably bring from $60 to $75 gold each in the States.

The Patagonia squaw weaves as well as sews furs. The long hair is sheared from the guanaco skin and twisted into threads, which are woven much as the Pueblo Indians of New Mexico weave their threads of wool. The Patagonian makes small woven blankets called ponchos, which are used as neck and shoulder wraps and as saddle blankets, but would look very well as rugs on a Northern carpet. By the use of dyes, bought of the whites, a variety of bright colors are obtained, but these are intermingled only in plain stripes. When compared with the blankets produced by the Indians of Guatemala—blankets whose figures of fighting beasts and birds have a savage beauty that is marvellous to behold—the art of the Patagonia squaw makes but a sorry showing. Nevertheless, a special saddle blanket, woven with a long nap of twisted threads that is designed to fill in the hollow spaces on each side of the too-prominent backbone of the desert horses, is at once novel and pleasing to the eye.

Other things likely to please the tourist are ostrich

feathers and eggs; the bolas and lassos used by the plainsmen of all kinds when hunting; bows and arrows and spears of the Indians, and boots made of the skin of a colt's hind legs. The ostrich feathers are gray, with a little white mixed in, and are but little handsomer in their native state than a turkey's feathers. Of course, they may be dyed and dressed up by a competent worker.

Then there are shells of beautiful color and forms which the tourist can gather for himself, together with feathery white seaweed, and, if he have good luck, he may find in one of the perpendicular alluvial banks which the people there call barrancas, something more interesting still—the petrified remains of the kangaroo, the opossum, the monkey, and possibly other and stranger forms of life that once roamed under a tropical sky, where now the weather varies between that of a New York day early in March and another very late in November. I saw an Italian naturalist who had found the remains of two birds, which, he said, were different from any birds ever yet discovered, and belonged to that period of history when birds had teeth, and were just beginning to grow feathers on their bat-like wings.

In making a collection of shells, the tourist would probably wonder how it happened that a very pretty mussel shell found in New Gulf, Port Desire, and the Straits of Magellan should be almost entirely absent at Santa Cruz. And if he did not include an antediluvian oyster shell, say fifteen inches long, in this collection, it would be for lack of room and not because the bivalve was not interesting.

At Punta Arenas and at Ushuaia a new class of curios appears. Most prominent are rugs of mingled otter skins, of seal fur, and swan's down. The snow-white down beside the dark fur is so beautiful that few, indeed, can resist the desire to buy in spite of the high prices asked. A lovelier present for a dainty sweetheart could scarcely be imagined.

Though less beautiful, the basket woven from rushes by the Yahgan Indians—a pearl-shaped affair to hold from two to four gallons—would be more interesting to the tourist who is a naturalist. The arrow-heads made by the Ona Indians of Tierra del Fuego from pieces of glass bottles that have been cast over from Cape Horn ships are equally interesting. The bows and arrows are not of a form to attract special attention, except that the arrows are very light. One wonders how such a weapon could pierce a guanaco or a lone prospector, as they are said to do. That the arrow points are usually a genuine Indian product I presume there is no doubt, though not necessarily Ona made, for the Tehuelches of Patagonia can make a glass arrow-head. But one finds so many new bows on sale at Punta Arenas, bows that show the mark of a jack-knife, too, that a doubt is thrown over the whole collection.

The Onas, too, are continually at war with the whites. The two races go hunting each other with considerable success on both sides. The whites, of course, capture some bows and arrows, but they do not usually bring them in as trophies. The whites of Tierra del Fuego are sheep herders or gold diggers, who do not want to be bothered with such stuff. Besides, bows from the battlefields are never new and clean, nor do they show marks of a jack-knife.

Like the Eskimos of the west coast of Greenland, the Yahgans of the Cape Horn region have learned that the whites will buy curios, and they supply the market by making models of their canoes and weapons. At first thought a model of either is an abomination to one who has a proper love of specimens of aboriginal handicraft, but these models, if genuine, are really good exhibits of what the Indians can do, and they are usually of such perfect form as to portray, in a convenient form for handling, the articles used by the natives in their daily lives. The weapons of full size may readily be had—I saw offered for sale one spear reeking with the blood of a bird the Indian had just slain, but in place of a canoe the tourist may very well be content with a model.

Gold dust can be had at both Punta Arenas and Ushuaia, where Storekeeper Figue of Ushuaia commonly has nuggets as well as dust. The Tierra del Fuego gold is very pure, and the usual way of buying is to exchange a British sovereign for its weight in dust—a very good trade for the buyer.

The scenery along the Patagonia coast, and until one has passed the first narrows in Magellan Strait, is not likely to please the ordinary tourist. At every point one finds steep alluvial bluffs or rounded hills and ridges, with wide arid mesas above and beyond that are of dull colors and without variety. Nevertheless, there is something about the desert that fascinates the lover of nature unmarred by human hands. What it may be I cannot tell, but that it is always powerful and sometimes irresistible I do not doubt. I saw men there who had travelled the world over, had had the best of education, had enjoyed the luxuries of life in civilized countries, and had the means of returning to them at any time, but, nevertheless, could not shake off the spell. They were content to live in a floorless mud hut, even in no shelter at all save that of a clump of the thorny brush in some wild gulch, where their only companions were the horses and dogs, with an occasional visit from one like themselves or a family of ill-smelling Indians.

South from Punta Arenas, through Cockburn Channel and east through the channels below Tierra del Fuego, the scenery is wholly different. Snow-capped mountains rise out of the sea, barren and gray just below the snow, and green with perpetual verdure for a thousand feet above the water. There are black gulfs and inlets, and narrow channels that seem to end abruptly, crags where the sea birds build their nests, gulches and cañons where torrents come roaring and sprawling down. Elsewhere, as told in the story of the Yahgans, there are rolling foot-hills with green meadows among groves of trees that wave and flash in the sunlight on a pleasant day.

There are glaciers that lie in hollows on the mountain side, and here and there push little moraines before them in their heavy course down the valleys to the water. A couple reach to the water's edge and throw off tiny icebergs that go drifting about with the tide and wind. Better yet, if one really loves nature, are the storms. Seen from a sailing-vessel in danger of drifting on the rocks that are a hundred leagues from help, the storms are fearsome; but when seen from the deck of a well-found steamer, when wrapped in water-proofs and furs, they are magnificent. The gale goes roaring up the mountain, carrying the snow in fluffy masses to the very crest and hurls it thence in smoky, quivering tongues, 1200 feet into the air. The same phenomenon may be seen on the coast of Greenland, but in the Beagle Channel the mountains are nearer at hand, their sides more precipitous, and the winds fiercer. And then there are the "williwaws" the whalers tell about, the whirling squalls that pick up the water, as the sand is picked up on the plains of New Mexico to form writhing columns a thousand feet high. There is something in the whizz and swish of wind and water, as one of these passes the ship, that stirs the blood as nothing else in nature, short of a tornado or live volcano, can do.

American art students go to Europe to complete their education by copying old-time paintings of apostles—apostles standing erect in a boat not large enough to accommodate their feet without pinching—and then come home to gabble about the beauties of nature. The picture of a saint, regardless of surroundings, may inspire the soul with religious fervor and teach the struggling youth to put that fervor on the canvas, but if one would paint a landscape that will at once thrill the soul with terror and awake it to an appreciation of the wildest scene in nature, let him make studies of the williwaws in the Cape Horn region, with frozen volcanoes vomiting flames of snow for a background.

The *Ushuaia* sailed out of Buenos Ayres on Wednesday, April 18th. She arrived back on Saturday, June 23d. I should say there is probably no other voyage in the world that a tourist could make in which he would suffer more physical discomforts. The most of these as I saw them were due to the wretched design of the remodelled lighter, but some were inseparable from such a voyage because due to the climate and the distance one goes from civilized communities.

Nevertheless, the liking for North Americans which the Argentines everywhere professed, their hearty efforts to make me comfortable because I was a North American, the delights of visiting the old-time ports and waters of which one reads in the thrilling tales of early exploration, these, with many other things that come to mind, combine to crowd from the memory everything disagreeable, and I can think of the voyage, as a whole, only with the greatest pleasure.

INDEX.

A

Aborigines of Cape Horn, story of, 47 *et seq.*
"Adobe Money" depreciated, currency of Spanish-American nations, 279
Adventures in Patagonia, by Titus Coan, 154
Aguirre Bay (*see* Spaniard Harbour).
Akers, Mr. C. E., author of *Argentine, Patagonian, and Chilian Sketches*, 249
Alaculoof Indians, called Fuegians, 100; seen by early navigators, 128; home of, 134; described by early navigators, 134; story of agressiveness of, 134 *et seq.*; R. C. Mission to, 136
Alaska, reference to colony of outlaws in, 67
Albatross, white, seen off Staten Island, 141; enormous specimens of, in Patagonia, 209; eaten by early navigators, 209; superstition of sailors concerning, 209
Allen Gardiner (*see* Mission schooner).
Alluvial banks of Cape Horn region, 7-21, 295; beds of Patagonia and Tierra del Fuego, 64, 125; cliffs of New Gulf, 171, 268
American lion (*see* Panther).
Andes, break in the, in Patagonia, at Gallegos River, 125, 282; in Tierra del Fuego, from San Sebastian to Useless Bay, 125
Animals, found in Patagonia, 184 *et seq.*, 194-200; of the desert, able to live without water, 200
Anson, Admiral, description of land of the Yahgans by, 49
Ansorge, Herr Bruno, gold miner at Paramo, 14; found bit of gold ore, 22; member of singing club, 267
Antarctic Highlanders (*see* Yahgans).
Archipelago of Cape Horn, 47
Arctic, S. S., wrecked on Cape Virgin, 6
Arenas, Punta (*see* under Punta).
Argentine, Capital (*see* Ushuaia).
Argentine, Government sends engineer to gold region of Patagonia, 7; establishes settlement at Ushuaia, fearing Chilian en-

croachment, 101 *et seq.*, 108; grants land to Mr. Bridges, 121; transport *Ushuaia* sails for Staten Island, 138 (*see Ushuaia*); generous to Welsh colonists, 174 *et seq.;* depressed condition of currency of, 221; hospitality shown on pampas of, 256; naval transports of, 260; great consumption of *maté* in, 271; prepares Santa Cruz as base of operations, 276; Lake, traces of gold at, 278; land system discourages small owners, 280; connected with other lakes by navigable channels, 280; population on border line of, friendly to Chili, 282; difficulty of obtaining justice in, 282

Argentine, Patagonian, and Chilian Sketches, by Mr. C. E. Akers, 249

Armadillo, prey of panther, 195; two varieties of, 198; interesting habits of, 198 *et seq.;* methods of killing snakes, 199; delicious article of food, 199; not found south of Santa Cruz River, 199; grubs for worms, 199; methods of catching mice, 199; robs nests, 199; suggestion as to importation of, into United States, 200

Arms, Mr., sent to Patagonia with Rev. Mr. Coan, 154

Asado, or beef roasting, by gauchos, 229

Asses' Ears, point of New Island, 16, 17

Axes, of Yahgans, shell, 57–59 (*see* Yahgans).

B

Baccarat, favorite game in Punta Arenas, 44

Backhausen, Herr Carlos, gold miner at Paramo, 14
Bala College, 169
Banner Cove (*see* Picton Island).
Baptists at Frondrey, 177
Barrancas, vertical earth banks, 21; perpendicular alluvial banks, 295
Bars, number of licensed, in Punta Arenas, 40
Beagle Channel, *Ushuaia* in, 15; ranch of Mr. Bridges on, 62; milder climate of, 117; charming scenery, 117; profits of ranching on, 119, 122; market for products, 120, 138
Beech, Antarctic, trees of Fuegian Islands, 50
Beer made at Quilmes, 244
Bell snake, gaucho term for rattlesnake, 246
Benfield, Mr. Theo., story of wonderful find by, 21 *et seq.*
Berberis, berry of thorn bush, 76; medicinal decoction of, 134
Big Feet, name given to Tehuelches, 173
Birds, of Patagonia, 201–214; interesting to sportsmen, 206; interesting to naturalists, 208; in North Patagonia migrate farther south, 210; thirteen Arctic varieties of, migrate to Patagonia, 210; and insects, 173
Bolas, weapons used by Ona Indians, 59; "the lost," used by Tehuelche Indians, 164; used in hunting panthers, 194; how to make them, 235; how to use them, 235; effective weapons, 235
Bongos, canoes of Bay of Panama, 55
Bougainville, M., 150; French explorer, 260
Bows and arrows, weapons of Onas, 129, 296; weapons of Tehuelches, 164, 296

INDEX. 303

Brecknock Pass, 15
Bridges, Rev. Thomas, describes Yahgan canoes, 55; compiles grammar of Yahgan language, 62; descriptions of Yahgan character, 66; descriptions of Yahgan cooking, 76; first arrival at Keppel Island, 85; learns Yahgan language, 87; becomes a missionary, 90; labors among Yahgans, 91; reports condition of Ushuaia, 93 *et seq.*; method of solving Hidugalahgoon's matrimonial troubles, 94; picture of life at the station, 97; turns ranchman, 118; home of, on Beagle Channel, 118; family of, 119; profits of ranching, 119; how ranch was obtained, 120; extract of lecture in Buenos Ayres, 121; charges against, 122; land of, belonged to Yahgans, 124; safe journey of, through Ona country, 133
Buenos Ayres, excitement in, over gold discoveries, 8; Mr. Bridges lectures in, 120; Mentions of, "the Athens of South America," 248, 252; *Ushuaia* starts from, 261; hard biscuit of, 275; *Ushuaia* returns to, 299
Bunch Grass, 178; seed, 157; eaten by Indians and gauchos, 238
Burleigh, Rev. Mr., at mission station, Tekenika Bay, 104
Button, Jemmy, a Yahgan, taken to England by Darwin, 62; goes to Keppel Island, 85; conduct towards his fellows, 99

C

Cabbages, size of, at Ushuaia, 115; grown at Punta Arenas, 289
Cape Horn (*see* Horn).

Cape Virgin (*see* Virgin).
Canoes of Yahgans, 54–57
Caramba, use of the word, 231
Caranchos, species of vulture, 162; abundant, 212; aid panther hunters, 213
Carmen de Patagones, Spanish colony on Rio Negro, 152; paid tribute to natives, 152
Cattle and sheep raising conducive to over-hospitality, 254 *et seq.*
Celery, wild, found in Fuego, a delicate vegetable, 49
Centenera, Del Barco, Spanish writer, 192
Channels, labyrinthian, of Cape Horn, 25
Cheenah, Indian squaw, 147 *et seq.*
Chico River, 280
Chili, takes possession of Port Famine and the Straits of Magallanes, 27; renames Port Famine, 28; depressed condition of currency of, 221; justice to be had in, 282
Chiloé, island of, 4
Chisels, wooden, 59 (*see* Yahgans).
Chubut, Welsh colony settled at, 168; hardships of colony at, 171 *et seq.*; foes of the desert, 173; area and population of, 177; railroad constructed from, to New Gulf, 179, 269; Welsh colony of, 252; tramp element in Welsh colony of, 256
Chubut River, 33, 168, 173
Chwaites, H. V., Captain of the *Ushuaia*, 263, 285; a fine sportsman, 288; hunting guanacos with bolas, 288
Clark, Mr. William, ranchman at Gallegos, 225, 256 *et seq.*
Climate of Cape Horn region, 23; of Punta Arenas, 46, 91; of land of Yahgans, 49, 53; 12° below zero the coldest, 52; of Gallegos, peculiarity of, 286

INDEX.

Coan, Rev. Mr. Titus, theological student, 154; sent to Patagonia, 154; experiences in, 154; author of *Adventures in Patagonia*, 154; found runaway sailors among Tehuelches, 258
Cockburn Channel, 15, 47; scenery of, 298
Colonia de Magallanes, La, or Port Famine, 27; nicknamed Sandy Point, 28 *et seq.*; penal colony established at, 28; prison burned, 33
Colony, Welsh (*see* under Welsh).
Condors, size of, 212; aids to panther hunters, 213
Cook, Captain, describes land of the Yahgans, 49; wild celery, 49; sailors of, find albatross good eating, 209; early navigator, 260
Coots found on Chubut River, 173
Cordilleras, wild cattle hunting in, 31; snow-capped peaks of, 34, 224; Gallegos River rises in, 282
Cormorants found in Patagonia, 208
Coypu, hunted for fur, good eating, 197; aquatic 'possum, or species of beaver, 197; peculiar formation of, 197
Cripple Creek, 140
Cruz, Santa, River (*see* under Santa).
Cuerpo de Bomberos, gambling club in Punta Arenas, 44
Curios to be found in Patagonia, 43, 293–297
Currency of Argentina and Chili, depressed condition of, 221; value of gold and paper, 222

D

Darwin, Sound, 15; Mt., peak of coast range on Tierra del Fuego, 47
Darwin, Charles, the naturalist, describes Yahgans, 62; takes Jemmy Button to England, 62; explores Santa Cruz River, 169; opinion of Patagonia, 183; misstatements concerning guanacos, 185; mentions black-faced Ibises, 211
Dandelions thrive in the desert, 157
Deer, found in forests of Andes, 198; destroy desert snakes, 198
Denominational churches in Welsh colony, 177
Deserts of Patagonia, 157; inhospitable region, 157; springs far apart, 157; well adapted to guanacos and ostriches, 157; foes of the, 173; bushes of the, 183, 232; snakes of, destroyed by deer, 198; similar to desert regions of United States, 199; armadilloes thrive in, 199; animals of, able to live without water, 200; ostrich hunting in, 204 *et seq.*; silence of the, 212, 232; fascination of, 227, 232; sparrow of the, 232
Desire, Port (*see* under Port).
Desolation Bay, 15
Diaz, Don Rui, Spanish Captain, 192
Dido, S. S., sent to Spaniard Harbour, 84
Dragon fly, called "the son of the southwest gale," 246
Ducks, uncounted hosts at Cape Horn, 75; enormous quantities at Staten Island, 140; near Chubut, 173; prey of panther, 195; curiosity of wild, 206 shooting too easy, 206; quantities of, in interior, 207; favorite breeding places, 208; curious air dance of, 212; color and curiosity of, off Santa Cruz, 288
Dugouts, canoes used in Caribbean Sea, 55

INDEX. 305

E

Eggs, methods of gathering, 68; methods of cooking, 76, 238; panthers eat, 195; ostrich, 202; size of ostrich, 238
Elephants formerly existed in Patagonia, 157
Elizabeth Island, sheep thrive on, 31
El Paramo (*see* Paramo).
Endeavor, Captain Cook's ship, 209
Eskimos, Yahgans compared with, 49
Extradition treaty between Chili and Argentine of little value, 286

F

Fables of Tehuelches, 159 (*see* Tehuelches).
Falkland Islands, 27, 150, 222
Famine, Port (*see* under Port Famine).
Farina, a ground root, 222
Fauna of Patagonia, 68, 75, 76, 83, 140, 157, 173, 183, 184 *et seq.*, 194 *et seq.*, 198-200, 206 *et seq.*, 212, 288
Felis Concolor (*see* Panther).
Ferns, 45
Figue, Adolph and Louis, merchants at Ushuaia, 22, 115, 297
Fish, native methods of catching, 59, 60; sea filled with, 75, 83
Fitzroy, Captain, 67, 73, 81
Flints and agates abound in the Ona country, 132
Flora of Patagonia, 11, 43, 45, 49, 50, 68, 75, 76, 83, 115, 157, 178, 183, 200, 222, 238, 289
Flores Island, quarantine station of Uruguay, 228
Flowers in great profusion in Punta Arenas, 45
Fossil, mastodon's jaw, 21; of opossum, kangaroo, and monkey, 64; in Tierra del Fuego, 125; of glyptodon, 201, 295
Fox, gray, flourishes in Patagonia, 198
"Friend of Man," gaucho term for panther, 246
Frondrey, village of, 177
Fruits, small, 76
Fuegians (*see* Alaculoof).
Fuegian Islands, mountains of, 50
Fuego, Tierra del, 7; placer gold found on, 1, 7, 22; explored by Popper, 9; Bay of Port Pantaloons in, 17; peaks of coast range on, 47; magnificent vegetation of, 49; prairies of, 124; climate and fertility of, 124; size and shape of island, 125; contrast to Patagonia, 125; bones of animals found in, 125; rainfall and frosts of, 125; sheep raising introduced into, 126; the industry spreads, 127; three Argentine stations in, 127; origin of name, 128; ships wrecked on, 254; Ona Indians of, 296; scenery through channels of, 298
Fungus, yellow, vegetable food, 75, 157; eaten by Indians and gauchos, 238
Fuschias, 45
Future Bay, near Punta Arenas, 10

G

Gable Island, in Beagle Channel, 62; sheep ranch of Mr. Bridges on, 118
Gallegos, successful sheep raising in, 216; ranchmen at, 224 *et seq.*; description of ranchmen, 225; game of cards, corn kernels for chips, 225; ordinance against tramps in, 255; the capital of Santa Cruz territory, 281; location of, 281; build-

ings of, like a Yankee mining camp 283 ; good cattle country back of, 283 ; placer gold mines along coast south of, 283 ; size of the capital city, 283 ; unattractive appearance of, 283 ; every store a hotel, 284 ; hotels compared with those of Mexico, 284 ; queer boarding-house in, 284 *et seq.*; Doña Philomela, the hostess, 284 ; occasional arrests and trials in, 286 ; government officials of, 286 ; Captain of Police in, a cripple, 286 ; peculiar climate of, 286 ; high winds in, 286 ; winter the pleasantest season, 287

Gallegos River, 14, 16 ; probably a strait in former ages, 125 ; volcanic mountain peak south of, 157 ; parrots found at the heads of, 213 ; population between Santa Cruz River and, friendly to Chili, 282 ; rises in Cordilleras near Pacific Ocean, 282 ; size of, 282; navigable, 282 ; lava beds, 282 *et seq.* ; perfect pasture land along, 283 ; lands south, filled with shepherds, 283 ; lack of fuel on north side of, 283 ; Captain Chwaites hunts the guanaco with bolas, 288

Galletas, bullet-like loaves of bread, 241

Gardiner, Captain Allen Francis, R. N., first missionary to Fuegian Indians, 80 ; attempt to live among Yahgans fails, 81 ; fits out launches in England and returns to Tierra del Fuego, 82

Gauchos, or cowboys, 33; methods of fox hunting, 198 ; methods of ostrich hunting, 205 ; methods of hunting prairie chickens, 208 ; definition of the word, 228 ; resemble Nantucket whalers, 229 ; peculiar dress of, 230 ; in the wilderness, 231 ; reasons for becoming, 233 ; wild life fascinating to all men, 233 *et seq.*; blankets and fur robes used by, 233, 235 ; the ways and manners of, 234 ; dress of, 234 ; outfit of, inexpensive, 234 ; weapons of, 235 ; methods of fighting, 236 ; wild life of, 236 *et seq.* ; usual breakfast of, 236 *et seq.*; superb riders, 237 ; method of cooking ostrich eggs, 238 ; fat of panther most satisfying food, 238 ; appetite of, 238 *et seq.*; meat diet alone not satisfying, 238 ; as seen by travellers, 239 ; ways of spending money, 239 ; enjoyment of " jags," 239 ; pride of, 240; dangerous to insult, 240 ; etiquette of smoking, 240 ; branding cattle, 241 ; powers of endurance, 241 ; description of house of, 242 ; manner of eating, 242 *et seq.* ; home life of, 243 ; amusements of, 243 ; cheating at cards counted a mark of superior skill by, 243 ; description of saloons, 244; native drinks, 244 *et seq.*; liquor glasses, 244 ; etiquette of drinking, 245 : *maté* tea making, 245 ; character of, 246 *et seq.* ; terms and sayings of, 246 *et seq.* ; religion of, 247 ; compared with North American cowboys, 247 *et seq.* ; enjoyment of life, 248

Geese, myriads of, 75 ; prey of panther, 195 ; beautiful colors of wild, 207 ; two varieties of wild, 207 ; good sport, 207 ; favorite breeding places of, 208

Gente Grande Bay, rich pastures of, 126 ; introduction and spread of sheep raising in, 126 *et seq.*

INDEX. 307

Glyptodons, fossil remains of, 201
Gold, first discoveries of, on Patagonian coast, 1-5; sailors wrecked at Cape Virgin, 4; story of, 5; bearing banks of Cape Horn region, 7; rich finds of, at New Island, 16 *et seq.*; at Port Pantaloons, 17; marvellous quality of, at Sloggett Bay, 20; peculiar difficulties of mining in Sloggett Bay, 21; on New Year's Island, 150; found in Welsh colony, 178; traces of, at Lake Argentine, 278
Gold diggings, story of, 2-4, 7; at Cape Virgin worked out, 10; further explorations, 10; at Paramo, richness of, 12 *et seq.*; supply renewed after storms and spring tides, 13; ore found in a bit of drift rock, 22; no quartz veins in Cape Horn region, 22; miners at work between Gallegos and Cape Virgin, 283; dust obtained at Punta Arenas and Ushuaia, 297
Gnats (*see* Punkies).
Grand Chaco forests of the Argentine, 228
Greenwood, Mr. W. H., 193
Grey, Mr. H., Yankee merchant, 30
Grubb, Mr. W. Balbrooke, school teacher at Keppel Island, 88
Guanaco, hunted, 31; red-haired, 51; modified camel, 64. 75; how hunted by Onas, 129; first view of, 184; habits of, 184; description of, 184 *et seq.*; Darwin's observations of, 185, 186; curious habits of, 185, 186, 189; wallowing places of, 187; methods of self-defence, 187; vast herds of, 188; sense of smell and curiosity of, 188, 195; sure footed, 189; pleasing pets when young, 189; flesh good eating, 190; mainstay of Indian, 190; hides valuable, 190; price of skins of, 190; medicinal quality of ball in stomach of, 190; the staple food of panther, 195; beautiful fur of, 293; skins used for beds, 294; price of skins of, 294
Gulf of St. George, 293
Gulls of Cape Horn, 75; tiny species off Staten Island, 141; called Cape Horn pigeon, 208
Guy Mannering wrecked off Staten Island, 144

H

Hamilton, James, D.D., *Memoir of Richard Williams*, by, 84; John, 215; sheap raiser in Patagonia, 280
Hansen, Harry, gold prospector, 15
Hermit Island, gold-bearing banks on, 7; a few Yahgans left on, 72, 78
Hidugalahgoon, matrimonial difficulties of, 94
Hope, Point, in Alaska, 77
Horn, Cape, gold-bearing banks on, 7; first view of mine camp at, 9; miners of, 24; labyrinthian channels of region of, 25; metropolis of, 27; archipelago, 47; story of aborigines of, 47 *et seq.*; mission, 79; region, snow storms every month in the year, 91, 125; pigeons, species of gull, 208; beauty of pigeons, 209; Indians of, eat penguins, 209
Horse meat, great delicacy to Onas and Tehuelches, 129
Hospitality, unbounded, in the Argentine pampas and Patagonia ranches, 256
Hudson, Mr. W. H., author of *Naturalist in La Plata*, 186
Humming birds, 214

INDEX.

I

Ibañez (Gregorio), Don, Argentine sailor, wrecked on Cape Virgin, 4 ; finds gold, 5
Ibises, black-faced, song and dance of, 211 *et seq.*
Indians, attack explorers at San Sebastian Bay, 11 ; trade with, 43 ; squaw in tailor-made gown, 44 ; three tribes of, in Cape Horn Archipelago, 74 *et seq. ;* nomads of Patagonia (*see* Tehuelche), 151 *et seq. ;* make use of all parts of guanacos, 190 ; of Patagonia eat skunks, 198 ; make pets of skunks, 198 ; of Cape Horn region eat penguins, 209 ; vegetable food of, 238
Insects, varieties of, 173, 183
Iron ore found on one island only, 76

J

Jones, Mr. Lewis, 169
Jones, Dr. Michael, founder of Welsh colony at Chubut, 169 ; wishes to perpetuate Welsh language, 181 ; Spanish the language of the Argentine, 182
Journey, alongshore in Cape Horn region, 15 ; begun, 260 *et seq. ;* departure from Buenos Ayres, 261 ; life on board *Ushuaia*, 261-268 ; prevailing winds, 268 ; arrival at New Gulf, 268 ; attractive telegraph operator, 269 ; *en route* for Port Desire, 269 ; captain's confidence, 270 ; view of Port Desire disappointing, 270 ; description of Port Desire, 271 ; visit to the Sub-Prefect, 273 ; dinner with a ranchman, 275 ; arrival at Santa Cruz, 276 ; town consists of nine buildings, 277 ; plan of city, 278 ; arrival at Gallegos, 281 ; unattractiveness of Gallegos, 283 *et seq. ;* one clean hotel, 284 ; introduced to Gov. Mayer, 285 ; discomforts on the *Ushuaia*, 288-291 ; interesting curios to be collected, 293-297 ; return to Buenos Ayres, 299 ; pleasant memories of, 300 ; (*see* also under Staten Island).

K

Kangaroo, petrified remains of, 64, 157
Kayaks, canoes of Eskimos, 55
Keppel Island, mission station established on, 85 ; preparatory school of the mission, 87
Kevalinyes, the, of Point Hope, 67
King, Mr., describes magnificent vegetation in land of Yahgans, 49
Knives, weapons of Tehuelches, 164 ; price of, used by gauchos, 235 ; useful at meal times, 242 ; murderous weapons, 248 ; size of, 275

L

Lagoons of Rio Gallegos, 211
Lake Nehuel-Huapi, 164
Land of Yahgans, 49-52
Lapwings, spurwinged, dance quadrilles, 210 ; description of the dancing, 210 *et seq.*
Lassoes, used by Tehuelches and gauchos, 164 ; description of, horsehair rope, 235
Lava beds at Santa Cruz, 217
Lawrence, Rev. John, Yahgan canoes described by, 55, 78 ; children of, continue mission work, 104 *et seq.*
Le Maire, Straits of, 15 ; *Ushuaia* in, 138 ; strong currents, and tide rips in, 139

INDEX. 309

Lennox Island, gold-bearing banks on, 7; same formation of bank and beach as at Cape Virgin, 16; harbour, 85
Lezama, Don Gregorio, organizes expedition to gold diggings, 8
Lichens, 45
Lignite, found in Punta Arenas, 42; found in Welsh colony, 178
Lista, Don Ramon, Argentine explorer and writer, 4, 120; collects Tehuelche tales, 159
Literati of Yahgan tribe, 65
Locusts, pests of the desert, 173
Lucia, Stephen, 94

M

Madryn, Welsh town in Patagonia, 180; on New Gulf, 251; captain of the port of, 251
Magellan's search for shorter route to Spice Islands, 2; visited St. Julian Harbor in Patagonia, 151, 260
Magellan, Straits of, placer gold in streams flowing into, 22; bleak pictures of, given by early navigators, 34; Cape Horn Archipelago south of, 47; Chilian possessions in, 276; narrows in, 297
Magnolia trees, size of, in Fuegian Islands, 50
Maidment, Mr., catechist, 82
Maldonada, Senorita, story of, and panther, 192
Mammals, 83
"Mañana country," Spanish American nations so called, 279
Manufacturing industries of Punta Arenas, 42
Maria, Santa (*see* under Santa).
Marriages of Yahgans (*see* Yahgans).

Marshall, storekeeper at Chubut, 178
Maté, wild tea of Paraguay, 237; drinking, 245 *et seq.* (*see* Gaucho); great consumption of, in Argentine, 271; meat and drink to Patagonians, 272
Mayer, Edelmiro, Governor of Patagonian territory of Santa Cruz, 215; large land owners along Santa Cruz and Chico rivers, 280; Governor of Gallegos, 285; description of home of, 285; devoted to music and literature, 285; wife of, 286; commanded a negro regiment in War of the Rebellion, 286; helped Mexicans overthrow Maximilian, 286
Mesa, plains of Patagonia, 183, 187
Meteorological condition of islands, 51
Methodists at Rawson, 177
Minas, Las, creek near Punta Arenas, 4; gold found in large quantity, 5; enormous nuggets, 6
Mine camps at Paramo and Ushuaia small affairs, 23, 24
Miners of Cape Horn, headquarters of, at Punta Arenas, 24; cost of outfit of, 24.
Misery, Mount, on Navarin Island, 51
Mission school at Keppel Island, 89; first station of Cape Horn, 79; on Beagle Channel, 89, 100; growth of, 100 *et seq.*
Mission, schooner, *Allen Gardiner*, 89; built in England, 85; commanded by Capt. W. P. Snow, 85; steamship to replace schooner, 100; Roman Catholic, established near San Sebastian Bay, 133; in country of the Alaculoofs, 136
Missionaries, to Yahgans, spiritual teachings of, 66, 71, 99;

land at Picton Island, 82;
miserable death of, 85; second
party of, arrive at Keppel
Island, 85; some murdered by
Yahgans, 86; are reinforced,
87 *et seq.*; station at Ushuaia
founded, 89; Mr. Bridges in
charge, 90 *et seq.*; material
teachings of, 90–98; extracts
from records of, 93–100, 102,
103; natives receive scant pay
from, 95 *et seq.*; unhappy
transformation of tribe into
laborers, 101 *et seq.*; tribe dies
out, 105; Mr. Bridges turns
ranchman, 118 *et seq.*; sell
clothing sent to be given to
Indians, 122; opportunities
for trade, 123; reasons for so
doing, 123; salaries of, 123
Missiones, 229
Mojave, desert of, 23
Monkeys, fossil remains of, 64
Morrell, Captain Benjamin, tales
of aborigines by, 153 *et seq.*
Mosquitoes numerous in Patagonia, 173, 183
Mount Misery (*see* Misery).
Mount Sarmiento (*see* Sarmiento).
Mountains, snow-capped, 23;
possible gold veins in, 23;
difficulties of ascent of, 23;
precipitous, of Fuegian Islands,
50; covered with forests of
beech and magnolias, 50; sea
mosses above tree line, 51;
eternal snows, 51
Mouse, prey of panther, 195
Mouse-bird (*see* desert sparrow).
Musters, George Chaworth, Commander, 4

N

Naturalist in La Plata, by Mr.
W. H. Hudson, 186
Navarin Island, gold-bearing
banks on, 7; rolling hills,

meadows and groves on, 51;
murder of some of the missionaries on, 86; climate near, 117
Negro, Rio, Spanish colony, 152
(*see* Carmen de Patagones);
parrots found in region of, 213;
valley and ranches of, 250,
254, 256
Nehuel-Huapi, Lake, apple
orchards on, 164
New Gulf, in Patagonia, Welsh
land at, 170; plenty of gypsum
at, 172; first view of Patagonian tramp at Madryn on,
251; *Ushuaia* arrives at, 268;
first view of, 268; attractive
telegraph operator in, 269
New Island, gold-bearing banks
on, 7; extraordinary finds at,
16 *et seq.*
New Year's Island, north of
Staten Island, 18, 140; gold
on, 148, 150
Nomads of Patagonia, the Tehuelches, 151 *et seq.*
Nugget weighing 300 grammes
found at Las Minas, 6

O

Ocean Queen, S. S., 82
Ona Indians, of Tierra del
Fuego, 59; weapons and implements of, 59, 60; efforts to
civilize and teach them sheep
raising, 126; flock to ranch,
but steal sheep at night, 126;
a distinct race, 127; children
used as servants in Argentine
Government families, 127;
cause of name Tierra del Fuego, 128; land tribe, 128; slight
mention of, by early explorers,
128; same origin as Tehuelches,
129; fine runners, 129; have
no boats, but are found in
Patagonia, 129; have no horses,
129; weapons of, 129; language
of, harsh, 129, 132; food of,

INDEX. 311

129 ; methods of hunting, 129; homes of, 130 ; no lack of intelligence, 130 ; migratory habits, 130 ; beard plucking, 131 ; personal appearance of, 131 ; habits of, 131 ; capacity for food, 131 *et seq.;* methods of lighting fires, 132 ; making of weapons, 132 ; religious beliefs of, unknown, 132; cruelty of, towards whites, 132; cannibals, 133; medicinal remedy discovered by, 134 ; glass arrow-heads of, 296 ; frequent fights with shepherds and gold diggers of Tierra del Fuego, 296

Oomiaks, canoes of Eskimos, 55

Opossum, fossil remains of, 64 ; thrives in treeless Patagonia, 196 ; does not lose climbing instinct, 196; family of, transported to a plantation with trees, 196 ; different species of, 197

Ostriches, fossil remains of, 64, 201 ; desert peculiarly adapted to, 157 ; prey of panther, 195 ; foes of, 201; two kinds of, in Patagonia, 201 ; angular gait of, 201 ; not such fools as reported, 202: hiding their heads in the sand a real safeguard, 202 ; color of sand and desert bushes, 203 ; reasons for survival of, 202 ; flies and grasshoppers the food of, 202 ; nest built by male, 202 ; brood cared for by male, 202 ; danger signal of male, 202 ; learn habits of their hunters, 203 ; easily domesticated, 204 ; will flock to a place of safety from great distances, 204 ; hunting, glorious sport, 204 ; appearance of different varieties when pursued, 204 *et seq.;* will run from a gun two miles away, 204; savage traits of the cocks,

204; Indian method of capturing, 205 ; appearance of white one at Carmen de Patagones, 206 ; taken with the bolas, 205 ; eggs and flesh of, good eating, 206 ; value of feathers of, 239

Otten, Fred, 6

Otters found at Cape Horn, 75

Outlaws, colony of, on Siberian coast, 67

P

Panther, also called American lion, 173 ; description of, 190 *et seq.;* characteristics of, 191 *et seq.;* story of a, 191 *et seq.;* hunting, 193; war of extermination against, 193 ; habits of, when pursued, 193; *et seq.;* how eaten in Patagonia, 194 ; hunting habits of the, 194; food of, 195; wiliness of, 195 ; wanton destructiveness of, 195 ; instinctive dislike to dogs, 196 ; charming household pet, 196; fat most satisfying food of the desert, 238

Paramo, El, meaning of name, 9; founded by Popper, 9 ; first mine camp established at, 9 ; arrival of supplies for camp at, 11 ; description of camp, 12 ; grassy plains and treeless hills, 12 ; richness of gold bed on beach at, 12 *et seq.;* gold bed renewed by storms, 13 ; methods of washing gold, 14 ; land in, controlled by German-Argentine corporation, 14 ; Argentine military station, 127

Parrots, fossil remains of, 157 ; found in forests of Andes, 213

Partridge, prey of panther, 190

Patagonia, 2 ; description of, 5 ; engineer sent to, by Argentine Government, 7; thousand miles of gold vein on coast of, 15 ;

nomads of, 151 *et seq.*; desert east of Andes, 152; Jesuits plant apples in, 152; Spanish colonies attempted, 152; Mr. Coan and Mr. Arms in, 154; condition of, in 1865, 169; grant of land in, to Welsh, 169; Welsh pilgrims land at New Gulf, 169 *et seq.*; winter season in, 170; dreary surroundings of Welsh colonists in, 170 *et seq.*; gypsum and alkali, 171; Welsh colonists make homes, 172; "Big Feet," 173 (*see* Tehuelches); transportation difficult, 179; railway constructed, 179; new towns, 179; railway prospered, 180; railway building not expensive, 181; zoölogy of, 183; natives of, consume fat like Eskimos, 194; panther an esteemed article of diet in, 194; home of panthers and 'possums, 196; interesting characteristics of zoölogy of, 200; resembles desert regions of United States, 200; varieties of animals found in, 194-200; desert animals of, able to live without water, 200; birds of, 201 *et seq.*; birds interesting to sportsmen, 206 *et seq.*; birds interesting to naturalists, 208 *et seq.*; thirteen Arctic varieties of birds migrate to, 210; birds of north, migrate farther south, 210; silence of desert, 212; sheep raising successful in, 216; stories of successful ranchmen in, 216; well watered, 219; description of a ranch in, 222; ranchmen of, 226; extent of prairie and desert region in, 228; description of prairies and deserts, 232; wild horses of the plains of, 236; tramps in, 250; trackless deserts of, 250; hospitality in ranches of, 256; astonishing number of tramps in, 259; natives of, prefer *maté* to all else, 272; Santa Cruz the planned metropolis of, 278; Gallegos the capital of, 279; settlements small, but slow healthy growth, in, 287; healthful region, 287; most valuable product of native industry, 293; squaws make guanaco skin robes, 294; weave guanaco hair into blankets, 294; scenery along coast of, 297; fascination of the desert, 297

Penguins, numerous, 75; rapid movements of, 141; fly through water, 209; not eaten by Patagonians, 209; eagerly pursued by Cape Horn Indians, 209

Phillips, Mr. Garland, catechist, 85, 86

Philomena, Doña, boardinghouse keeper in Gallegos, 284

Picton Island, missionaries landed at Banner Cove in, 82; story of failure to establish mission on, 82 *et seq.*; death of missionaries, 84; relief ship arrives at, 84

Pigeons, Cape Horn, species of gull, 141; description of, 208 *et seq.*

Placer gold diggings on Patagonian coast, 3; gold found in all the streams of Tierra del Fuego, 22; gold mines along coast south of Gallegos, 283

Plate River, 228, 261, 290

Poco Tiempo, land of Spanish-American nations, 279

Point Hope, in Alaska, 67

Poncho, Indian blanket worn by gauchos, 234; woven by Indian squaws, 294; not equal in beauty to work of Indians of Guatemala, 294; used for wraps and saddle blankets, 294

Popper, Herr Julius, founder of El Paramo, 9; murder of, 10;

INDEX. 313

describes Punta Arenas, 46;
finds gold in San Sebastian
Bay, 120
Port Desire, on Patagonian coast,
27; Spanish colony, 152; volcanic bluffs at, 157; discovered
by Cavendish, 169; ibises of,
211; condors of, 212; ancient
resort of pirates, 269; view of,
disappointing, 270; Tower
Rock, 270; description of, 271;
life in, 271 *et seq.;* no lack of
food in, 271; luxuries depend
upon visits of transports, 271 *et
seq.;* story of sub-prefect of,
272; story of Lieut. Wilson's
servant, 273; life of naval
officers in, 273; ruins of Spanish fort in, 274; visit to home
of a ranchman, 274; interesting dinner, 275
Port Famine, ancient port, 27;
Chili took possession of, 27;
penal colony of Chili, 28;
buildings of, destroyed by
convicts, 28; colony re-established farther north, 28
Port Pantaloons, Bay of, on
Tierra del Fuego, 17; description of scenery at, 17; gold
found at, 17
Port St. Julian, Spanish colony,
152
Potatoes, at Ushuaia, 115; at
Punta Arenas, 289
Potro boots, worn by gauchos, 234
Prairie chickens, easily unnerved
by noise, 208; simulate death,
208; often frightened to death,
208; two varieties of, 208;
good shooting and eating, 208;
home of, 208
Prairie dog, prey of panther, 196
Prospectors, gold, difficulties of,
15, 23; model of sloop of, 24;
food supply of, 25; long absences of, 25
Puchero, beef stew, on the
Ushuaia, 262

Puerta San Juan del Salvamiento
(*see* St. John Bay), 143
Puma, foe of the ostrich, 201
Punkies, gnats, 183
Punta Arenas, or Sandy Point,
2; Commander Musters stops
at, 4; Don Ramon Lista visits,
4; inhabitants excited by gold
discoveries, 6; supply station
for sealing schooners, 7; headquarters of gold miners, 24;
story of foundation of, 27 *et
seq.;* development of colony
of, 29 *et seq.;* elements of
growth, 30; industry of sheep
raising begun, 31; mutiny in,
32 *et seq.;* miserable end of
mutineers, 33; latitude of, 33;
arrival of *Ushuaia* at, 33; appearance of, in May, 33, 34;
description of town, 34 *et seq.;*
gambling and dance houses, 36
et seq.; government of Chili
nominally republican, but ruled
by army, 39, 40; bars in, 40;
description of women in, 40;
sidewalks in, 40; Governor's
residence, 41; scenery about,
41; coal discovered in, 42;
brick making in, 42; possibilities of, 43; region rich in
tan bark, 43; trade with Indians, 43; goods delivered by
sailboats, 43; Indian squaws
make rugs, baskets, etc., in,
44; Cuerpo de Bomberos
gambling club in, 44; profusion of flowers in, 45; population of, 45; future prosperity
of, 46; profits of sheep raising
in, 219; fate of escaped convicts from, 213; tramps from,
254; vegetables grown in, 282,
289; price of guanaco-skin
robes in, 293; curios to be
found at, 295 *et seq.;* gold
dust obtained at, 297; scenery
south of, 298

Q

Quillango, fur robe, 233; worn by gauchos, 235
Quilmes, near Buenos Ayres, 244

R

Railroad from New Gulf to Chubut, 179, 180, 269
Rails, song and dance of the long-legged, 211
Ranch, on Beagle Channel, 117; dinner at, at Santa Cruz, 223
Ranchman, marriage of, to Tehuelche girl, 224; divorce, 224; income of, 226; restraints of civilization unbearable to, after wild life of the deserts, 226
Rawson, capital, 172, 177
Records of missionary life and training at Keppel, 87 *et seq.*
Religion of Yahgans, 70 *et seq.*
Reynard, Mr. H. L., introduces sheep raising into Punta Arenas, 31
Rio Gallegos (*see* Gallegos).
Rio Grande do Sul, in Brazil, 228
Rio Negro, Spanish colony (*see* Carmen de Patagones).
Rio Santa Cruz (*see* Santa Cruz).
Roca's expeditions against Tehuelches, 156, 276
Roedorn, Count Richard of, passenger on *Ushuaia*, 267
Rufous (*see* Prairie chicken).
Rugs of otter, seal, and swan's down, 296
Rum cheap in the Argentine, 244

S

Sagebrush and swamps found at San Sebastian Bay, 11
St. George, Gulf of, 293
St. John Bay, 15; Harbor, 138; Cape of, 139; description of tide rip at entrance of, 142; Government post established in 1884, 143; Government post of Staten Island to support lighthouse, 143; governor's residence, 144 *et seq.,;* description of lighthouse, 146; story of runaway sailor boy, 146-148
St. Julian harbor, 151
St. Lawrence Bay, 67
Salt fields on Rio Negro, 152, 157
Sandy Point (*see* Punta Arenas)
San Sebastian Bay, placer gold found at, 10; gold seekers attacked by Indians, 11; no running water near gold layers, 11; gold found by Popper, 120; break in Andes at, 125
Santa Cruz, guanaco cemetery at, 186; Gallegos, capital of territory of, 215; amount of profitable land in, 217; amount of worthless land in, 217; price of sheep in, 218; 800,000 sheep in, 287; future prosperity of, 287; fine sheep ranch near city of, 222; description of house on sheep ranch near, 223; passengers to, 262; *Ushuaia* arrives at, 276; Weddell's Bluff, 276; presidio, or barracks, 276; to be used as base of operations in case of trouble with Chili, 276; profitable sheep raising in, 276; town consisted of nine buildings, 277; deserted missionary church in, 277; plan of prospective city, 278; price of land at, 278; enormous shipments of wool from, 278; good pasture land in, 278; traces of gold at Lake Argentine, 278; enterprising land "boomer" of, 279; natural advantages of, 279; probable gold mines in Andes, 279; fine timber land near, 279 *et seq.;* lack of good drinking water, 281; method

INDEX. 315

of drawing water from wells with horse and lasso, 281
Santa Cruz River, 32 ; explored by Darwin, 169 ; impassable barrier to armadilloes, 199 ; tramp at, 253 ; navigable throughout its course, 279 ; owners of water front control all the range back, 280 ; Gov. Mayer large land owner on, 280 ; tide rises over forty feet at mouth of, 281
Santa Maria River, gold found at, 10
Sarmiento, reference to, 3 ; starving colony, 34, 80 ; Pedro, 169
Samiento Mount, 25 ; snow capped peaks of, 41 ; peak of coast range on Tierra del Fuego, 47
Saunders, James, 215 ; sheep raiser in Patagonia, 280
Scenery, of Punta Arenas like Adirondacks, 34, 41 ; along Patagonia coast, 297, 299
Sea fowl, methods of gathering eggs of, 68
Sea mosses above tree line on mountains of Fuegian islands, 51
Seals, fur and hair, in Cape Horn region, 75
Seaweed, uses of, 68 ; varieties of, 295
Serpents easily destroyed by panther, 196
Sheep, long-wooled variety in favor, 219 ; diseases of, 220 ; 800,000 in Santa Cruz territory, 287.
Sheep raising, a productive industry in Patagonia, 215 ; profits for one year, 216 ; success in, at Gallegos, 216 ; profitable to the individual, 217 ; amount of capital needed for, 218, expenses of, 218, 220 ; care of lambs, 219 ; profits of, in Punta Arenas, 219 ; average pounds of wool per sheep, 220 ; as compared with Argentine and United States, 220 ; havoc made by foxes and wildcats, 220 ; conservative estimate of profits of, 221 ; compared with cattle business in the United States, 221 ; wool sold for gold, 222 ; ranchmen paid in paper, 222
Sheep ranch, established on Keppel Island, 85 ; description of, at Santa Cruz, 222
Shells, curious, 295 ; antediluvian oyster, 295 ; mussel, 295
Shell fish, 59, 76, 83, 295
Skees, Norwegian, 149
Skunks, made pets by Indians, 198 ; eaten by Indians, 198
Skyring Water near Punta Arenas, 282
Slings, Yahgans expert in use of, 59, 60
Sloggett Bay, rich in nugget gold, 18 ; story of one expedition to, 19 ; peculiar difficulties of mining in, 20 *et seq.*
Sloop of prospectors, 24
Snakes of desert destroyed by deer, 193
Snow, Captain W. Parker, commander of mission ship, 85 ; establishes mission on Keppel Island, 85
Snow storms every month in Cape Horn region, 91
"Son of the southwest gale," gaucho term for dragon fly, 246
Spaniard Harbour, or Aguirre Bay, 84
Spanish-American nations, lack of enterprise among, 279 ; Argentine an exception, 279 ; "adobe money" of, 279
Sparrow, desert, 232 ; description of, 232
Spears used by Yahgans, 58 ; by Tehuelches, 164

Spider of the hot pampas attacks man, 246
Springs one hundred miles apart in Patagonian desert, 157
Squash the favorite vegetable of Argentine ranchmen, 271
Squirrel, prairie, food of Onas, 129
Staten Island of Cape Horn, 15, 137; similarity of ridges of, to Rocky Mountains, 139; end of backbone of Western Hemisphere, 139; *Ushuaia* bound for Antarctic, 138; view of, 139, 140; mountain ridge 2,000 to 3,000 feet high, 140; vegetation of mountains, 140; varied and interesting forms of bird-life off, 141; terrific seas and tide rips in, 142; Goverment post at St. John Harbor, 142; St. John Bay, 143; lighthouse of St. John's Cape, 143-146; story of runaway sailor boy, 146 *et seq.*; peculiar formation of the island, 148; bays of, filling with sand, 148; interior of, almost impassable, 149; supply of wood, 150; climate, 150; gold on New Year's Island, 150
Steubenrach, Mr., British Consular agent, 126; introduces sheep raising on Fuegian prairies, 126; places missionary in charge of ranch, 126
Stirling, Rev. W. H., missionary to Keppel, 87; Bishop of South America, takes up residence on mainland, 89; ordained Bishop of Falkland Islands, 90; safe journey through Ona country, 133
Story-tellers, skilful, among Yahgan tribe, 65
Straits of Magellan (*see* Magellan).
Straits of Le Maire (*see* Le Maire).

Swans, myriads of in Cape Horn region, 75; black and white, 207; good eating, 208; favorite breeding places, 208

T

Tan bark in Punta Arenas, 43
Tea, Paraguay (*see Maté*).
Tehuelches, half-breed squaw in tailor-made gown, 44; Indian tribe of Patagonia, 128; same origin as Onas, 129; have no boats, 129; consider horse meat a delicacy, 129; liquid language of, 132; make tents of skins, 130, 165; are nomads, 151; a noble race, 151; visited by Magellan, 151; exact tribute from Spanish colony, 152 *et seq.*; obtain horses, 152; character of, 152; chief demanding tribute in Carmen de Patagones, 153; story of efforts to convert, 153 *et seq.*; receive missionaries kindly, 154; maintain independence for 360 years, 155; war of extermination against, 155; prisoners tortured by whites, 156; home region of, 156; alluvial soil, 157; salt lakes and beds, 157; volcanic rocks, 157; physical proportions of, 157 *et seq.*; prodigious strength, 158; personal appearance, 158; attractive women, 158; habit of gum chewing, 159; population before and after war of extermination, 159; mental qualities of, 159; literature of, 159; fables of, 159 *et seq.*; religious beliefs of, 160 *et seq.*; religious rites of, 161; medicine men and women, 161; superstitions of, 161 *et seq.*; musical instruments of, 162; division of time, 162; astron-

omy of, 162; government,
162; ceremonies of marriage
and divorce, 163; happy home
life of, 163; cider festivals
164; love of liquor chief vice,
164; apple orchards of, 164;
weapons of, 164; use of guns
and pistols, 164; methods of
hunting game, 164 *et seq.*;
modesty of, 165; morality of,
165; corrupted by whites, 165
et seq.; methods of cooking,
166; habits of cleanliness
among, 166; food of, 166,
167; characteristics of, 167;
meaning of name, 173; help
Welsh colonists, 173; chief's
dying remark, 175; blankets
made by squaws, 234 *et seq.*;
beguiled sailors to desert, 257
et seq.; made slaves of them,
258; story of baby found
by Lieut. Wilson, 273; glass
arrowheads made by, 296
Tekenika Bay, 104
Teresina B., story of dismantled
sloop named, 134 *et seq.*
Thetis Bay, Argentine military
station, 127
Tierra del Fuego (*see* under
Fuego).
Tinamon, spotted (*see* Prairie
chicken).
Tower Rock (*see* Port Desire).
Tramps, of Patagonia, 250; first
view of, at Madryn, 251;
story of mysterious, at Madryn, 251 *et seq.*; from Sandy
Point, 253 *et seq.*; causes of
development of, 254, 256; ordinance against, at Gallegos,
255; in Chubut, 256; sailors
beguiled by Indians to desert,
257; hardships of, among Indians, 258; number of, compared with those in the United
States, 259
Transport, trip on Argentine (*see
Ushuaia*).

Tropical luxuriance of growth
in Tierra del Fuego, 23
Turner, L. M., on Eskimo language, 63
Turnips, size of, at Tierra del
Fuego, 115; grown at Punta
Arenas, 289

U

Uruguay, quarantine station of,
228 (*see* Flores Island).
Useless Bay, on Tierra del
Fuego, 10, 125
Ushuaia, capital of Argentine
Tierra del Fuego, 15, 79, 261;
mining camp, 24; coldest spot
of the region, 52; location of,
on Tierra del Fuego, 79; first
missionary station at, 89; near
Chili line, 101; military post
established at, 102; a remarkable capital, 107; sub-prefectura, 108; good harbor, 109;
first view of, 109; description
of the capital, 110; latitude of,
111; lack of sunshine in, 111;
inhabitants of, 112; life in,
113 *et seq.*; size of vegetables
in, 115; good pasturage in,
115; Figue, storekeeper at,
115, 297; work done by Yahgans, 116; severe climate, 116;
life dull in, 117; curios to be
found at, 295 *et seq.*; gold
dust obtained at, 297
Ushuaia, Argentine naval transport, voyage on, 9; in dangerous waters, 15; arrives at
Punta Arenas, 33; voyage
continued, 117; bound for
Antarctic Staten Island, able
sea boat, 139, 264; view of
Staten Island from, 140; anchors in St. John Bay, 143;
sails from Buenos Ayres, 261;
description of, 261 *et seq.*; life
on board, 261–268; first meal
on board, 262; dish-washing

on board, 262; captain of, 263;
amusing discomforts on board,
265 *et seq.;* " Ta-ra-ra-boom-
de-ay " in four languages, 267;
encounters head winds and
seas, 268; arrives at New Gulf,
268; a slow tub, 268; card
playing on board of, 268; bet-
ting, 268; arrives at Port Desire, 270; arrives at Santa
Cruz, 276; arrives at Gallegos, 281; captain a fine sportsman, 288; ducks thick off
Santa Cruz, 288; table not
beyond criticism, 288; variety
of fish and game courses, 288;
lack of fresh vegetables, 289;
serious discomforts on board
of, 288-291; a novel mixed
drink, 292; returns to Buenos
Ayres, 299

Ushuaia Bay, description of, 90

V

Valley of the Missionaries, near Santa Cruz, 277
Vegetable food native to Cape Horn region, 49, 75, 115, 157, 178, 238, 289
Vendettas among Yahgan tribe, 67 *et seq.*
Vincent, Mr. Frank, remarks upon Punta Arenas, 46
Virgin, Cape, wreck of Argentine sailors on, 4; wreck of S. S. *Arctic* on, 6, 10; gold supply renewed after storms at, 13, 283
Vizcacha Lagostomus Trichodactylus (*see* Prairie dog).
Vocabulary of Yahgans, 63
Volcanic bluffs at Port Desire, 157; volcanic peaks, range of, south of Rio Gallegos, 157

W

Wallis, Capt. Samuel, early navigator, 43, 260

Weasels, malignant faces of, 197; larger than United States variety, 197; travel in packs, 197
Weddell's Bluff (*see* Santa Cruz).
Wells, Ensign Roger, U. S. N., 62; prepared Eskimo-English vocabulary, 63
Welsh settlement at Chubut, 33, 168; cause of founding colony, 168 *et seq.;* pilgrims, landing of, 169; obtains grant of land in Patagonia, 169; great sufferings of, 171; alkali water, 171; gypsum, 171; lay out capital city, named Rawson, 172; make friends with Tehuelches, 173; foes of the desert, 173; provisions supplied by Argentine Government, 173; hardships of, 173 *et seq.;* succeeds at last, 175 *et seq.;* wheat and barley crops, 176; denominational churches of, 177; no physicians in, 178; prospectors for gold, 178; lignite and quartz workings, 178; import sheep, 178; profit in sheep raising, 179; colony sixty miles long, 252
Whaits, Mr. R., mission carpenter, 88
Whale Sound, 15
Whales abounded in Cape Horn waters, 75
Wheelright, Mr. William, founder of Pacific Steam Navigation Co., 29
" Wild mirth of the desert," gaucho term for ostrich hunting, 246
Williams, Mr. Richard, catechist and surgeon, 82
Willis, Captain, of mission schooner, 123
" Williwaws," whirling squalls, 299
Wilson, Don Juan, sub-prefect of Port Desire, 272; story of, 272 *et seq.;* story of his servant, 273

INDEX.

Winds, high, in Tierra del Fuego, 15, 23, 51, 138, 235, 298
Wollaston Island, gold-bearing banks on, 7, 48, 87

Y

Yahgans, or Antarctic Highlanders, Indian tribe described by Darwin, 48 *et seq.*; compared with Eskimos, 49; without clothing or shelter, 49; description of, 50; homes of, 52; dress of, 53; habits of, 54; canoes of, 54; dimensions of canoes, 55; method of building canoes, 56; weapons of, 57; implements of, 57 *et seq.*; methods of fishing and extracting oil, 59–61; utensils of, 61; language of, 62; vocabulary, 63; remarkable mental development, 63; origin of, 64; country of, explored, 64; language of, melodious, 64, 132; government of, 66; treatment of squaws, 64; native politeness of, 65; skilful storytellers, 65; poets, novelists, and historians, 65; clever talkers, 66; abundance of food, 66, 75; songs and dances of, 66; abundant leisure, 66; lax notions about property, 67; vendettas of, 67 *et seq.*; crimes of, 69; favorite modes of revenge, 68; marriages of, 69; religion of, 70; ideas of death, 71; treatment of the sick, 71; customs of mourning, 71; folk lore, 71; personal appearance of, 73 *et seq.*; women of tribe, 74; ferocity towards whites, 75; methods of cooking, 76; traditions of, 76; not cannibals, 77; characteristics of, 77 *et seq.*; civilization the ruin of, 77, 78; first missionary to, 81; missionaries' plan for civilizing, 91; become farm laborers, 92; report of Mr. Bridges, 93 *et seq.*; work required by missionaries of, 95; scanty pay, 95, 98; change of dress and habits of, 101; epidemics among, 102 *et seq.*; civilization an evil to, 104–106; physical deterioration and diminution of, 103–105; work done by, in Argentine capital, 116; work on Mr. Bridge's ranch, 119; described by early navigators, 52, 128; rush baskets of, 296; make models of their canoes and weapons for sale, 297

Z

Zanibelli, Luis, dealer in Indian relics, 44

www.ingramcontent.com/pod-product-compliance
Lightning Source LLC
Chambersburg PA
CBHW030252240426
43673CB00040B/948